a feast of astonish ments

a feast
of
astonish
ments

Charlotte Moorman
and the Avant-Garde,
1960s–1980s

Edited by Lisa Graziose Corrin and Corinne Granof

Mary and Leigh Block Museum of Art

Northwestern University Press / Evanston, Illinois

Northwestern University Press
www.nupress.northwestern.edu

Northwestern

MARY AND LEIGH
BLOCK MUSEUM OF ART

Mary and Leigh Block Museum of Art
www.blockmuseum.northwestern.edu

All possible care has been taken to secure
permission from copyright holders and to provide
attributions for artists and artworks in this catalog
and in the exhibition. Given the ephemeral nature
of performance art and sometimes limited documentation, several artworks are known by various titles
and some photographers are unidentified.

Published in conjunction with the
exhibition *A Feast of Astonishments: Charlotte
Moorman and the Avant-Garde, 1960s–1980s*.

Block Museum of Art, Northwestern University
January 16–July 17, 2016

Grey Art Gallery, New York University
September 8–December 10, 2016

Museum der Moderne Salzburg
March 4–June 18, 2017

The exhibition is supported by major grants from the
Terra Foundation for American Art, the Andy Warhol
Foundation for the Visual Arts, and the National
Endowment for the Arts. Additional generous support
is provided by the Elizabeth F. Cheney Foundation;
the Alumnae of Northwestern University; the Colonel
Eugene E. Myers Foundations; the Illinois Arts Coun-
cil Agency; Dean of Libraries Discretionary Fund; the
Charles Deering McCormick Fund for Special Collec-
tions; the Florence Walton Taylor Fund; and the Block
Museum Science and Technology Endowment.

Andy Warhol Foundation for the Visual Arts

Design and composition by Hal Kugeler.

Printed in Canada.

10 9 8 7 6 5 4 3 2 1

ISBN 978-0-8101-3327-3 (paper)

Library of Congress Cataloging-in-Publication
data are available from the Library
of Congress.

FRONTISPIECE
Charlotte Moorman performs Nam
June Paik's *Concerto for TV Cello
and Videotapes* wearing *TV Glasses*,
New York City, 1971. © Takahiko
iimura.

Contents

vii   Foreword by Lisa G. Corrin, Block Museum of Art,
Northwestern University

xiv   Acknowledgments

xix   Foreword by Lynn Gumpert, Grey Art Gallery, New York University

xx   Foreword by Sabine Breitwieser, Museum der Moderne Salzburg

3   Introduction
"In times like this . . ." Moorman's Art in Context
Corinne Granof

19   **Charlotte Moorman's Experimental Performance Practice**
Ryan Dohoney

29   **Beyond the Score:
Charlotte Moorman and John Cage's *26'1.1499" for a String Player***
Jason Rosenholtz-Witt

41   **Messy Bodies and Frilly Valentines: Charlotte Moorman's *Opera Sextronique***
Laura Wertheim Joseph

61   **Live Art in the Eternal Network: The Annual New York Avant Garde Festivals**
Hannah B Higgins

92   **Festival Posters**
Introduction by Joan Rothfuss

109   *Noise Bodies* **and Noisy Women: A Conversation with Carolee Schneemann**
Lisa G. Corrin

123   *Sky Kiss*
Joan Rothfuss

135   **I Love Germany and Germany Loves Me:
Charlotte Moorman and the Transatlantic Avant-Garde**
Rachel Jans

153   **Bomb-Paper-Ice: Charlotte Moorman and the Metaphysics of Extension**
Kathy O'Dell

169   **"Necessity's Other": Charlotte Moorman and the Plasticity of Denial and Consent**
Kristine Stiles

185   **"Don't Throw Anything Out": Charlotte Moorman's Archive**
Scott Krafft

197   Index

Foreword

Lisa G. Corrin
Block Museum of Art
Northwestern University

In 2012 I arrived at Northwestern University, where I had been appointed the new director of the Mary and Leigh Block Museum of Art. My first question was, "What is the DNA of Northwestern? What makes it unique?" I soon discovered one of the answers — Northwestern University Library's extraordinary Charles Deering McCormick Library of Special Collections. I was astounded to discover that among its greatest treasures is the Charlotte Moorman Archive. Acquired by a librarian with great foresight in 2001, it complements related archives of composer John Cage and Fluxus artist Dick Higgins also housed at Northwestern. Moorman's archive documents her career as a musician and performance artist and as the producer of fifteen annual avant-garde festivals. Most significantly, it also documents Moorman's collaborations with and her championing of experimental composers, artists, choreographers, and writers — many boundary-crossing pioneers who transformed the cultural landscape of the time: Joseph Beuys, Earle Brown, John Cage, Giuseppe Chiari, Shirley Clarke, Philip Corner, Morton Feldman, Simone Forti, Geoffrey Hendricks, Dick Higgins, Toshi Ichiyanagi, Allan Kaprow, Alison Knowles, Takehisa Kosugi, Jim McWilliams, Max Neuhaus, Yoko Ono, Nam June Paik, Otto Piene, Carolee Schneemann, James Tenney, Edgard Varèse, Ben Vautier, Wolf Vostell, La Monte Young — and these are just a handful of names on an extraordinary roster of regulars. Through correspondence, scores, artist proposals, photographs, videos and films, audio recordings, posters, artwork, and even answering machine tapes, the Charlotte Moorman Archive provides an exceptionally complete documentation of Moorman's activities, her personal life, and the transatlantic connections she forged in the 1960s through the 1980s between the New York art scenes and those of Europe, also reaching as far as Australia, South America, and Japan.

Upon discovering that this remarkable collection is at Northwestern, I asked my colleague, Scott Krafft, curator of the Charles Deering McCormick Library of Special Collections, whether it would be possible to organize an exhibition about Moorman to spotlight these holdings. The moment was auspicious. Northwestern was soon to open a new building for the Bienen School of Music and its School of Communications across from the Block. It is now the centerpiece of the Arts Circle, in which music, theater, dance, film, performance studies, and visual arts are all united

Peter Moore. Ay-O's *Rainbow Streamer II* on the deck of the *Alexander Hamilton* riverboat, 9th Annual New York Avant Garde Festival, South Street Seaport, October 28, 1972. Photograph © Barbara Moore / Licensed by VAGA, NY.

My own awareness of Moorman was limited to a photograph by Peter Moore owned by a friend in which Moorman is performing *Concerto for TV Cello*. I had slept in a room with this arresting and beguiling image many times, but I had thought of it only as Moorman performing a work by Nam June Paik, as this is primarily the way in which she is known. I had yet to understand the nature of their collaborations or of her partnerships with so many better-known artistic figures.

The archive told a different story. Moorman's performance repertoire, which made her sought after across the globe, featured many works written specifically for her, as well as others she performed so frequently she made them her own. She was anything but a vessel for the creativity of the male-dominated artist community. Moorman had conceived of herself not merely as a performer but as an artist in her own right. I have often wondered whether the words that were applied to her—"performer" or "musician"—might have contributed to our limited understanding of the range of her endeavors. Moorman's activities are as complex and difficult to categorize as the emerging new hybrid art forms she championed through the fifteen avant-garde festivals she organized between 1963 and 1980. These art forms also resisted easy definition. They arose at a time when conventions—social and artistic—were being questioned and reinvented. Moorman's life was a process of constant invention, and, as in music, it involved much improvisation.

In his book *Experimentalism Otherwise: The New York Avant-Garde and Its Limits* (University of California Press, 2011), musicologist Ben Piekut offers a meticulous analysis of Moorman's performance of John Cage's *26'1.1499" for a String Player* that demonstrates the originality and artistry Moorman brought to her performances of Cage's work. It would become her magnum opus. Moorman took Cage's openness to how such works could be performed to the outer limits of what he might have ever imagined, taking liberties with the score that turned it into a Mount Everest of her own making; Moorman never succeeded in performing the work within the time limit Cage had so clearly designated in his title. It is a

in one neighborhood. An exhibition focusing on a major cultural figure in whose life and work so many diverse art forms played a role seemed the ideal way to mark this watershed event at Northwestern. Moorman's activities, with their strong emphasis on collaboration and cross-media creativity, seemed an exemplary model for the Block to consider as a future artistic direction within the context of the Arts Circle.

sign of her devotion and her tenacity that she often traveled with her personally annotated copy of his score. Moorman's copy of the Cage score—or, to put it more accurately, her copy of what became a wholly new work inspired by Cage's composition—is one of the stars of the Moorman Archive. An aide-mémoire, a road map, and a diary, it is a window onto how Moorman viewed her role in relation to a score: while she deeply admired Cage, his score was just the starting point for her own creativity.

Like so many objects in the exhibition, this remarkable document demonstrates that Moorman continued to operate like the classical musician she was trained to be, performing the works in her repertoire over and over for decades to master and to find within them a continuous wellspring of artistic inspiration. The "repertoire" became an organizing principle for this exhibition. This section of the exhibition dives deeply into works Moorman repeatedly performed for decades, when possible with documentation of multiple performances demonstrating how they changed over time, including the John Cage piece, *Cut Piece* by Yoko Ono, *TV Cello* and *TV Bra* by Nam June Paik, *Chamber Music* by Takehisa Kosugi, *Infiltration Homogen for Cello* by Joseph Beuys, and *Sky Kiss* by Jim McWilliams.

Discussions leading to identifying "the repertoire" as an anchor for the exhibition narrative were an opportunity to think critically about why Moorman has been one of the most overlooked artists of her generation. Our ambition has been to build upon *Topless Cellist: The Improbable Life of Charlotte Moorman,* the authoritative biography by Joan Rothfuss (MIT Press, 2014). With Scott Krafft and the staff of Special Collections, Rothfuss spent a decade immersed in the vast Charlotte Moorman Archive. Having her on board as the project's consulting curator was critical to rewriting Charlotte Moorman's story and to conveying to a broad public Moorman's multifaceted identity, including how she fostered the production and dissemination of experimental art forms from the 1960s through the 1980s.

We were heartened to discover a number of emerging scholars focusing on Moorman, and we invited them to participate in our

Peter Moore. Al Hansen's *Pigeons Eating Art,* 4th Annual New York Avant Garde Festival, Central Park, September 9, 1966. Photograph © Barbara Moore / Licensed by VAGA, NY.

discussions and also invited several to contribute to this publication. They, too, were searching for a nuanced language by which to understand Moorman's activities and her complex identity.

How did this energetic and energizing woman, part artist, part creative collaborator, and part impresario, at once muse and talent magnet, the Joan of Arc of New Music, as Edgard Varèse described her—how could she have wound up so marginalized in art and cultural history? Moorman's use of her femininity seems to have evoked ambivalence in spite of the ways in which she challenged so many conventions and turned them on their heads. Her reputation may have suffered as she came to be seen by feminists as someone who allowed her body to be exploited. According to her close friend, artist Carolee Schneemann, many of her contemporaries also viewed her as a narcissist. Friends report that she played up her femininity in ways that seemed counterproductive to feminist principles. Yet, Moorman seems to have been very much in control. In fact, like Schneemann, herself an icon of feminist art, Moorman was the master of her own body, both as a raw material and as a vehicle for her creativity. To Schneemann, Moorman's avant-garde festivals were also

"a powerful feminist statement." Moorman was, in Schneemann's words, quoted in the interview published here, "a pioneer of feminist principles by making this free and radical community, by being central to it, imagining it, constructing it, sustaining it, and extending it into a larger public."

Moorman exemplifies some of the very qualities that helped define art and performance in the latter part of the twentieth century, not least of which is how she opened up art to a broader public in truly revolutionary ways. Her work transcends the comfortable boundaries of art history and becomes a messy and imaginative concoction. She was as difficult to categorize as the art she supported.

Besides her own performances, which range from the understated to the spectacular, more often to the latter, Moorman

Peter Moore. Publicity photograph for 11th Annual New York Avant Garde Festival, Shea Stadium, November 16, 1974. Front: Charlotte Moorman and Marilyn Wood. Middle: Ay-O, Juan Crovetto, Lil Picard, Si Fried. Back: Marty Reisman, Bob Wood, Jim McWilliams, Shridhar Bapat. Photograph © Barbara Moore/ Licensed by VAGA, NY.

fostered communities of artists that were especially open and inclusive. Primarily through the organizing of her festivals, she brought together musicians and artists under the umbrella of the avant-garde. We have endeavored to present the festivals in all of their diversity, exuberant chaos and as the *feasts of astonishments* they truly were even when they involved glorious failures. They are a significant chapter in the history of curating and are as important to assessing Moorman's contributions as her performances. The festivals included many artists who were little known when they participated but whose work is widely recognized today, such as Bill Viola and Dara Birnbaum. The exhibition will also feature work included

in the festivals by Ay-O, John Cage, Alison Knowles, Max Neuhaus, and Yoko Ono, and the monumental inflatable red sculpture by Otto Piene, *Grand Rapids Carousel*.

Photographer Peter Moore was a regular at each of the festivals. The exhibition includes nearly a hundred of his photographs of Moorman and the festivals. A witness and an artist in his own right, Moore's personal relationship with the artists and his insights into their work communicate the audacity, the spontaneity, and the inventiveness of these events.

Moorman brought an entirely fresh ethos to her activities. She maintained unwavering faith that new art should be made accessible to all. A fearless risk taker

Peter Moore. Publicity photograph for 4th Annual New York Avant Garde Festival, Central Park, August 13, 1966. Photograph © Barbara Moore/Licensed by VAGA, NY.

Peter Moore. Publicity photograph for 9th Annual New York Avant Garde Festival, *Alexander Hamilton* riverboat, South Street Seaport, October 28, 1972. Photograph © Barbara Moore / Licensed by VAGA, NY.

as a performer and as a curator, she also refused to acknowledge rigid separations between creative forms. Through this connection and collision among the arts, she was a significant member of a generation of artists working internationally who were redefining art and renegotiating the roles between artist and audience, giving agency to both in the creation of meaning. Taking art to the streets—or, more specifically, to Central Park, Shea Stadium, and Grand Central Terminal, to cite just three locations of her festivals—Moorman believed that museums, galleries, and concert halls were not the only, nor indeed necessarily the ideal, venues for making and experiencing evolving hybrid art forms. In that way, she was a precursor for so much of current art and curatorial practice. What could be more relevant than to connect the dots between the past and the present by telling Moorman's story?

Moorman was also the consummate networker and a powerful convener. Many were willingly ensnared in "Charlotte's web."

A tight-knit community of festival regulars gradually developed; their friends and others they drew in expanded the circle with newcomers for each festival. Images by Peter Moore used as press photographs for the festivals show members of Moorman's inner circle posing in New York City, on the deck of the *Alexander Hamilton* riverboat, and at Floyd Bennett Field in Brooklyn, with props, costumes, and banners, clustered around Moorman's centripetal force. The camaraderie led to collaborations, and the sense of community was essential to artists taking significant creative risks.

As the Charlotte Moorman exhibition and associated programming tie into the year-long celebration of Northwestern's new Arts Circle in 2016, they will explore the work of a woman who fostered avant-garde and experimental art through her own performances and created opportunities for artists of her generation across media. We are thrilled that the exhibition will then travel to New York, the primary site of Moorman's activities and influence. Although she was originally from Little Rock, Arkansas, Moorman was most active in her role as promoter of avant-garde and experimental music in the fertile environment of the music and art scenes in New York.

We are especially pleased that the exhibition will subsequently be seen in Salzburg, a European capital of music and performance. Moorman performed her fabulous *Sky Kiss* in nearby Linz, Austria, a city long open to artistic experimentation. It is thrilling to bring her work to the Museum der Moderne Salzburg, which features cutting-edge performance and questions some of the traditional roles of the performer in a city steeped in tradition.

As a university art museum, the Block serves as a teaching and learning resource across fields of study and in which art is a springboard for discussions about ideas and issues that are relevant to our time. This project—comprising an exhibition, a publication, and extensive programming—could not be a more fitting realization of the mission. A core value for us is to raise critical questions and offer fresh perspectives on the history and writing about culture. Charlotte Moorman

and, indeed, her relative invisibility within cultural history, provide a catalyst for such questioning. The exhibition and this publication serve as a prelude to Moorman's feast of astonishments, and we very much hope they will be a catalyst for others to engage with the Charlotte Moorman Archive and continue to fill historical gaps in our understanding of experimental art.

Peter Moore. Publicity photograph for 12th Annual New York Avant Garde Festival, Gateway National Recreation Area / Floyd Bennett Field, Brooklyn, September 27, 1975. Photograph © Barbara Moore / Licensed by VAGA, NY.

Acknowledgments

A Feast of Astonishments is the first exhibition to explore in depth the life, work, and activities of Charlotte Moorman. This exhibition—four years in the planning—brings together little-known facets of Moorman's work and her world to create a fuller picture of the richness and extraordinary range of her contributions. The tremendous commitment and generosity of funders, lenders, cultural organizations, and many individuals has been a source of inspiration to all of us involved with the project. Given its ambition, this exhibition would not have been possible without their support.

Weaving together the complexity of Moorman's story and bringing recognition to her many roles—as performer, collaborator, impresario, and curator at a time when the art world was undergoing radical transformation—required significant expertise, as well as familiarity with the Charlotte Moorman Archive housed in the Northwestern University Libraries. We built a collaborative curatorial team for the exhibition with Joan Rothfuss, author of *Topless Cellist: The Improbable Life of Charlotte Moorman,* and Scott Krafft, curator of the Charles Deering McCormick Library of Special Collections. Their perspectives on Moorman and her cohort had a shaping impact on the checklist and the exhibition narrative, laying the critical foundation for our work. They both frequently delved into the archive, surfacing with a new bit of information or an object, document, or photograph that shifted our understanding of Moorman. Without their important groundwork, built over more than a cumulative decade, such a project would not have been possible for many years to come. Laura Wertheim Joseph, a recent Ph.D. from the University of Minnesota, joined the team as a consulting curatorial associate in 2014, contributing to all facets of the exhibition and publication. A talented curator with an expansive intellect, she contributed immensely to the project.

The Terra Foundation for American Art provided leadership funding for the exhibition and this publication, and made possible their presentation in New York and Salzburg. We thank the Terra Board of Directors, as well as Elizabeth Glassman, president and chief executive officer, and Carrie Haslett, program director, Exhibition and Academic Grants, for enabling the Block to realize the project that has raised our sights and standards and transformed our capacity to contribute to the field of American art. For this exhibition, the Block received its first grant from the Andy Warhol Foundation for the Visual Arts. We also received a grant from the National Endowment for the Arts. We are grateful to these organizations for their meaningful support and confidence in the Block's capacity to realize a landmark project. The Block also thanks the Elizabeth F. Cheney Foundation; the Alumnae of Northwestern University; the Colonel Eugene E. Myers Foundations; and the Illinois Arts Council Agency. Further support has come from the Dean of Libraries Discretionary Fund; the Charles Deering McCormick Fund for Special Collections; the Florence Walton Taylor Fund; and the Block Museum Science and Technology Endowment.

The Graham Foundation for Advanced Studies in the Fine Arts made an in-kind donation of display cases. We thank director Sarah Herda for ensuring that our visitors had the best possible viewing experience.

The confluence of several factors contributed to the origins of the project. The purchase of the Charlotte Moorman Archive by former curator R. Russell Maylone of the Charles Deering McCormick Library of Special Collections at Northwestern University Library was a singular catalyst. Not only did it bring Joan Rothfuss to Evanston to work on the project over a number of years, but it made the Block Museum at Northwestern University the logical organizer of the project. We would like to thank the library for agreeing to be our partner and primary lender in this project. We thank the library personnel for the energy and enthusiasm they brought to supporting the project in ways too numerous to list. Foremost we wish to acknowledge Sarah Pritchard, Dean of Libraries and a friend to the Block who embraces partnership and enthusiastically shares ideas to make the treasures in her care accessible to all. D.J. Hoek, Associate University Librarian for Collections Strategies, as well as a Cage scholar in his own right, saw the opportunities afforded by our collaboration early. We also heartily thank the dedicated and diligent Sigrid Pohl Perry, whose tremendous organizational skills and memory served the project many times. In Special Collections, we also thank Susan Lewis and Nick Munagian. In the Preservation Department we wish to thank Ann Duncan-Gibbs, Scott Devine, and Susan Russick. In the Music Library, we thank Gregory MacAyeal, and in Digital Collections, Stefan Elnabli, Dan Zellner, and the staff, who were critical to preparing objects and digital files for the exhibition and publication. Clare Roccaforte and Drew Scott have been enthusiastic promoters of this story and the events surrounding it.

It was important to connect with members of Moorman's inner circle of friends and collaborators. Barbara Moore, who administered Moorman's estate and who is responsible for the Peter Moore Estate, was incredibly helpful, especially in helping to fill in valuable information about Moorman's avant-garde festivals. Barbara generously opened Peter Moore's archive to us for research and agreed to lend to the exhibition a significant number of photographs by Peter Moore, many never before seen. She fact-checked details about the festivals against her own annotated festival programs. Our meals with Barbara and filmmaker Andrew Gurian were full of anecdotes that only close friends of Moorman could share. We thank Barbara for being instrumental to the evolution of our thinking, for her tireless commitment to getting historic details right, and for championing the exhibition from the first time we met. From our New York circle, we are especially grateful to Christian Xatrec of the Emily Harvey Foundation, who has been especially generous in many ways.

We thank artist and graphic designer Jim McWilliams, one of Moorman's closest friends and artistic collaborators, for offering to create a limited-edition poster for the exhibition. In addition to creating many performance works for Moorman, including Sky Kiss, Jim designed all the posters for the avant-garde festivals beginning in 1966. With this exuberant graphic art, Jim pays tribute to an artist who inspired and supported him.

In May 2014 several of us spent a wonderful afternoon with Elizabeth Goldring and Otto Piene. Their hospitality and warmth will not be forgotten, and we learned so much about Moorman from our talk. We will never forget the sight of the impressive Grand Rapids Carousel inflated against the bright blue sky. During our research, we spent a few days in upstate New York visiting Carolee Schneemann's studio. Here, too, we learned so much from speaking with a close friend of Moorman's and learning firsthand about Noise Bodies, the avant-garde festivals, and the times.

We are grateful to the exhibition's many lenders, who include individuals, galleries, museums, and artists. In addition to the Charles Deering McCormick Library of Special Collections, Northwestern University Library, lenders include Sandra Binion; Andrew Gurian; the Hakuta family; the Emily Harvey Foundation; Geoffrey Hendricks; Deborah Hoyt; Alison Knowles; the Museum of Contemporary Art Chicago; the Museum of Modern Art, New York; Yoko Ono; the Estate of Otto Piene; Sammlung Hoffmann, Berlin; Estate of Frank Pileggi; Barbara Moore; Paula Cooper Gallery; Rose Art Museum at Brandeis University; C. Schneemann and P·P·O·W Gallery; the Walker Art Center, Minneapolis; Peter Wenzel; Barbara Wilks; and a private collection.

Many individuals facilitated our work by providing assistance in organizing the loans or photography or by giving approval to include their works in the exhibition and catalog. We especially thank the Archiv künstlerischer Fotografie der rheinischen Kunstszene (AFORK), Robert Burridge,

Rene Casteran, Christo, Vin Grabill, Jonathan Henery at the Christo and Jeanne-Claude Studio, Takahiko iimura, the Ray Johnson Estate, Northwestern University Music Library, Silvia Neuhaus and the Max Neuhaus Estate; and Virginia Mokslaveskas, Getty Research Institute. At the Museum of Contemporary Art Chicago, Mary Richardson and Bonnie Rosenberg were very helpful. All have been responsive to our requests, helped us with our sleuthing to find works, and trusted us with fragile works of art.

In addition, we thank Allora McCullough and Andy Archer; Frank Connet; Jon Hendricks; Ellinor Kuhn; Sur Rodney (Sur); Catherine Skopic; Deborah Walker; Marilyn Wood. Many thanks to Paul Shambroom for his expertise in the preparation of image files for many photographs in this publication. We also thank Chris Protopapas, the extraordinary film technician at ColorEdge in New York, and in Chicago Tom Van Eynde.

The organizers of the exhibition benefitted immeasurably from the insights and discussions that took place among historians, critics, and curators at the Block Museum on April 17 and 18, 2014. The two-day event explored many themes, including the broader context in which Charlotte Moorman's work developed, questions of presentation and the challenges of display of relics and documentation, and Moorman's extensive networking. The participants in this event included Elise Archais, Kathleen Edwards, Faye Gleisser, Saisha Grayson, Hannah Higgins, D.J. Hoek, Rachel Jans, Laura Wertheim Joseph, Scott Krafft, Jacob Proctor, Ramón Rivera-Servera, Joan Rothfuss, Abigail Sebaly, Kristine Stiles, Krista Thompson, and Kirsten L. Speyer Carithers.

The authors of this book willingly took on the challenge of piecing together and interpreting complicated and multifaceted histories. They have provided lucid interpretations of Charlotte Moorman's many-tiered life and career and of the time in which she lived and worked, including its blending of visual art, music, and performance. Their work offers important additions to our understanding of Moorman's milieu—its music, its creative protagonists, its politics, its ideals, and its failures. From them we also learned much about an intrepid and single-minded woman from Little Rock, Arkansas, who charged and changed the art scenes in New York and beyond in an artistically transformative era. Through their writing they have played a critical role in shaping a history that has been amorphous and diffuse. We are thankful for meaningful and provocative contributions from Ryan Dohoney, Hannah Higgins, Rachel Jans, Laura Wertheim Joseph, Scott Krafft, Kathy O'Dell, Joan Rothfuss, Jason Rosenholtz-Witt, and Kristine Stiles.

Many generous colleagues have helped us by providing contact information and graciously sharing their expertise, including curators John Hanhardt and Michael Mansfield. Kim Conaty, formerly at MoMA, now at the Rose Art Museum, was especially helpful. We are fortunate to have a remarkable community of scholars invested in this period living in and near Chicago. We recognize Simon Anderson and Bruce Jenkins, School of the Art Institute; Hannah Higgins, University of Illinois at Chicago; and Jacob Proctor, University of Chicago. The Block Museum has also formed significant partnerships with individuals and institutions throughout the city, including Peter Margasak, Mark Jeffery at IN>TIME, and Caroline Picard and Devon King of Sector 2337. We learned much from several visits to the MCA Chicago, where we met with colleagues including Lynne Warren, who was fortunate to have worked with Moorman during the Nam June Paik retrospective in 1982, and Dennis O'Shea, who met Moorman and filmed the interview with her that is included in the exhibition.

Faculty and campus partners at Northwestern University brought important dimensions to the project from diverse fields of study. We are grateful to many faculty who have contributed ideas, organized programs, and developed courses to enrich the exhibition, including Josh Takano Chambers-Letson, John Alba Cutler, Huey Copeland, Ryan Dohoney, Harris Feinsod, Amanda Jane Graham, James J. Hodge, Iñigo Manglano-Ovalle, Susan Manning, Ramón Rivera-Servera, Krista Thompson,

Joel Valentín-Martínez, and Wendy Wall, Tom Burke, and Jill Mannor at the Alice Kaplan Institute for the Humanities.

A Feast of Astonishments is as much a project about the history of music as it is about art, and the Bienen School of Music has been one of our key partners. We express our gratitude to the faculty and students; in particular we recognize Toni-Marie Montgomery, dean of the Bienen School of Music, as well as Hans Jensen, Hans Thomalla, and Ben Bolter. Ryan Dohoney has integrated the Charlotte Moorman Archive into his classes in inspiring ways and has been a consistent supporter of the project.

Students are the heart of a university. Among the many students who have provided time, expertise, and enthusiasm for the project and have made valuable contributions are Faye Gleisser, Elliot Mercer, Didier Morelli, Ira Murfin, Jason Rosenholtz-Witt, and Block Museum undergraduate intern Cathaleen Chen. Jesse Itskowitz, a recent graduate of Northwestern, has become a vital team member.

Northwestern University Press has been a committed partner, and we are grateful for the many conversations and exchanges with Jane Bunker, director; Anne Gendler, managing editor; Mike Levine, acquisitions editor; Marianne Jankowski, creative director; Parneisha Jones, sales and subsidiary rights manager; Dino Robinson, production manager; and freelance editor Lori Meek Schuldt. The book's stunning look has been developed by visionary designer Hal Kugeler.

We are thrilled that the exhibition will be seen in New York and Salzburg. We feel a special connection with the staff of the Grey Art Gallery, who share a sensibility and interest in presenting exhibitions that look at underexplored topics with a commitment to meaningful scholarship. We also are delighted to be working with the Museum der Moderne Salzburg. We will never forget the glorious days we spent in Salzburg, and we feel fortunate to be working with such an outstanding group of people.

The staff of the Block Museum is a talented and collaborative group, and everyone on staff contributes in significant ways. Michelle Puetz, the Block's curator of Media Arts, hit the ground running when she arrived at the Block in July 2015. An expert in experimental films of the period, she helped refine the presentation of moving pictures in the exhibition, including a special section devoted to film and video, and developed a complementary film program for Block Cinema.

Special mention of the exhibition team must be made, as the work and vision of Dan Silverstein, associate director of Collections and Exhibition Management, has been critical to the realization of the project. He is joined by Kristina Bottomley, senior registrar; Liz Wolf, Collections and Exhibitions assistant, who created the graphic design within the exhibition; Emily Moorhead, registrar assistant; and Mark Leonhart, lead preparator.

The engagement team, led by Susy Bielak, with Cynthia Noble and Nicole Mauser, has created a true "feast of astonishments" through its imaginative programming, combining scholarship, performance, and the voices of artists. Its members also fostered meaningful partnerships, including encouraging development of a number of courses at Northwestern as well as at other area universities that will study Moorman and her times.

The Block staff is unified in its commitment to collaboration, innovation, and excellence. Each and every one of our colleagues contributed to ensuring that this exhibition and its programs would serve the Block's mission and values and be an unforgettable experience for our visitors. In addition to the exhibition and engagement staff, these people include Kathleen Bickford Berzock, who provides inspired leadership in the Curatorial Department. Special recognition must also go to Samantha Topol and Holly Lee Warren for their tremendous support. We also thank Maggie Borowitz, Aaron Chatman, Janet Dees, James Foster, Joanna Gueller, Helen Hilken, Justin Lintelman, Rebecca Lyon, Allen McClendon, Marina Miliou-Theocharaki, Elliot Reichert, Rita Shorts, and Jeffery Smith. In addition, members of the Visitors Services team provide a secure environment for works of art, not to mention putting out the welcome mat for every visitor.

In supporting this project, Northwestern University's administration continues in its extraordinary commitment to the arts and to the Block. Mary Baglivo, vice president for global marketing, and her team have contributed their creativity and strategic thinking to helping Northwestern tell its arts story. With this exhibition as one focal point, they have worked their magic to share our programming for this exhibition with our community through their new arts marketing initiative. Their support enabled us to bring Anne Edgar Associates on board to assist with marketing. Anne has been a cheerleader for Charlotte Moorman and the Block Museum. She helped bring Moorman's story to a broader public through national coverage of this exhibition. We thank her and her colleague, Cindy Bokser, a Northwestern graduate, for their advocacy.

The Office of the Provost has encouraged the Block to be bold in realizing its goals as a university museum dedicated to teaching and learning across academic disciplines. Provost Dan Linzer and Associate Provost Jean Shedd have helped deepen the Block's relationship to the university and to our field by investing in the museum's growth. They have also wholeheartedly supported its efforts as a convener through programs in which art is a springboard for discussions about ideas and issues that are relevant to our faculty, to our students, and to the communities surrounding our campus. We are appreciative beyond words for their belief in the important role of an art museum to the life of a great research university.

Finally, we must acknowledge Charlotte Moorman herself, a tireless and intrepid woman who changed the art scene in New York and beyond during a fertile and transformative era. We have learned much from her—her courage, her vision, and her belief in the audience's ability to respond authentically to challenging new art forms. Whatever obstacles she faced, she never lost her idealism or faith in the power of art. The irony has not been lost on us that much of her work as a maker, advocate, and organizer in the art world challenged the institutions of art and their conventions. She recognized that to stay relevant to one's time meant asking questions, breaking the rules or pushing them to their limits, even if it resulted in glorious failures. For Moorman, this was as true for artists as it was for museums or concert halls. She has been an inspiration on many levels, and the Block hopes to live up to her example by embracing her courage, creativity, vision, and tremendous productivity.

Lisa G. Corrin
Ellen Philips Katz Director

Corinne Granof
Curator of Academic Programs

Block Museum of Art
Northwestern University

Foreword

Lynn Gumpert
Grey Art Gallery
New York University

Some artists manage to uncannily embody in their work key concerns of their times. Charlotte Moorman numbers among them. The Grey Art Gallery at New York University is delighted to partner with the Block Museum of Art at Northwestern University, which has bravely undertaken the daunting task of organizing the first monographic exhibition of this extraordinary musician and prescient performance artist. That this important show not come to New York would be unthinkable, as much of Moorman's groundbreaking work took place here.

Located in the heart of Greenwich Village, the Grey Art Gallery provides an ideal setting for examining avant-garde activities of the 1960s through the 1980s in cultural and social perspective. As university museums, the Grey and the Block share a commitment to experimenting with how notions about art exhibitions can be expanded, especially apropos in this case given the unconventionality of Moorman's work. Furthermore, along with our colleagues at NYU's Fales Library—which houses the exceptional Downtown Collection—we at the Grey strive to highlight the significant contributions of visual artists, musicians, writers, theater people, and other creative spirits who, from the 1960s to today, continue the merging of disciplines begun by their predecessors. While many of Moorman's endeavors were not situated in Lower Manhattan, she herself personifies the very notion of "downtown."

A Feast of Astonishments would not have been possible without the foresight and creativity of like-minded colleagues at the Block. At the Grey, I am extremely fortunate to work alongside remarkable individuals: Laurie Duke, Jodi Hanel, Noah Landfield, Amber Lynn, Ally Mintz, Lucy Oakley, Richard Wager, and Michèle Wong—each of whom wears at least two hats—who heartily embraced and realized both the installation at NYU and its accompanying public programs. Everyone who visits the show, I'm convinced, will truly be both sated and amazed.

Foreword

Sabine Breitwieser
Museum der Moderne Salzburg

Since I started as the director of the Museum der Moderne Salzburg in fall 2013, the museum has emphasized a multidisciplinary conception of art in accordance with Max Reinhardt's vision of the city as a stage, referring to the integral role of the Salzburg Festival. The museum is open to art that crosses disciplines, genres, and media, thereby realizing new alliances with local and international institutions. In 2014 and 2015 our exhibitions have also put an emphasis on women artists organizing first large-scale exhibitions in Austria or even in the international context, for instance with Ana Mendieta, Simone Forti, Etel Adnan, Andrea Fraser, and Carolee Schneemann.

I am extremely proud to be able to introduce the work and legacy of Charlotte Moorman at the only venue in Europe for this exhibition organized by the Block Museum of Art in the United States. Moorman and her exceptional role within the New York avant-garde of the 1960s and 1970s perfectly fit with the focus of the museum's program. Past exhibitions, such as *Sound of Art* (2008), have already highlighted the connections between music and visual art since 1900, including selected works by Moorman. I still remember watching Moorman performing in the sky during the Ars Electronica Festival 1982 in Linz, Austria. In a number of earlier projects I came across her legendary New York Avant Garde Festival. Her very open approach to all kinds of art genres made her an important advocate for the art and artists of her time, and she eventually also changed the perception of the musician's body. While we already agree that the body of the musician is an integral part of the performance, Moorman turned it to something indistinguishable from the musical instrument itself.

I would like to express my gratitude to Lisa Graziose Corrin and Corinne Granof from the Block Museum of Art for putting this important exhibition and publication together and for their efforts to bring this project to Salzburg. I would also like to thank Tina Teufel, curator overseeing the installation at the Museum der Moderne Salzburg.

a feast of astonish ments

"In times like this . . . " Moorman's Art in Context

Corinne Granof

"Dear Charlotte: We've got your bomb. . . ." On November 18, 1969, Karin Rosenberg, director of public relations at the Museum of Contemporary Art (MCA) in Chicago, wrote to cellist Charlotte Moorman with the good news that her "bomb" had been found.[1] Moorman had recently performed at the MCA with Nam June Paik as part of the exhibition *Art by Telephone*. The program for an evening of performances titled "Mixed Media" lists several works from Moorman's repertoire, including John Cage's *26'1.1499" for a String Player*. Cage's score allows for sounds and actions to be determined by the performer within a time frame of 26 minutes and 1.1499 seconds. A note on Moorman's interpretative score indicates "to bomb," at which point she plays a few bars on a military surplus practice bomb transformed into a cello with strings and a contact microphone attached. After the performance, the bomb cello went missing and was only discovered a few weeks later after a few attempts of looking at the hotel where Moorman had stayed.[2] This anecdote gives a sense of the unusual logistical circumstances surrounding the staging of Moorman's performances. It also brings focus to a work that not only was closely identified with Moorman and her sometimes outrageous style but also

resonated within the framework of a larger cultural critique. We will return to how Moorman incorporated the bomb cellos into her public appearances later in this introduction.

Although trained within the traditions and conventions of classical cello, Moorman made her mark in the world of experimental music. She was called the Joan of Arc of New Music by Edgard Varèse for her commitment to the innovative work of her own time.[3] In the press release for the Chicago performance, Moorman affirmed her dedication to contemporary music: "I would give anything to have been the first to perform Brahm's [*sic*] Double Concerto. Since I couldn't do that, I am satisfied and thrilled to play the newest and most exciting music of our time. It's what I live for."[4] However, her involvement with new expressive and conceptual forms was not limited to the realm of music. She played a major role in nurturing experimental art forms and artists and bringing their work to broad audiences. Her work was fundamental to expanding the very definition of visual arts, music, poetry, and performance in the 1960s and '70s, and (as one reporter put it) she had "unbounded energy" and a passion for promoting and propelling the avant-garde into the public sphere.[5]

OPPOSITE
Charlotte Moorman. *Two Bomb Cellos,* ca. 1965 and 1990. Painted metal, 47 in. each. Sammlung Hoffmann, Berlin.

3

Charlotte Moorman with TV Cello and TV Glasses
Photo Thomas Haar

Announcement for
Nam June Paik exhibition, 1982.
Courtesy of Museum of
Contemporary Art Chicago
Library and Archives.

has been acknowledged among the loose network of Fluxus artists or considered a muse or partner of Nam June Paik, whose position as the "father of video art" has long been established. Moorman is associated specifically with two works by Paik, *TV Bra for Living Sculpture* (1969) and the iconic *TV Cello* (1971), both of which were created for, worn by, or played exclusively by her. Moorman herself was an essential part of the *TV Cello*, a work that was also conceived of as a "living sculpture." When the 1982 Paik retrospective opened at the MCA in Chicago, the announcement card included only one image of an artwork by Paik: Thomas Haar's majestic photograph of Charlotte Moorman playing the *TV Cello*, with the name NAM JUNE PAIK running alongside. Although the artwork is attributed to Paik, Moorman is irrevocably linked with it.

In her 1991 obituary in the *New York Times*, Moorman is identified as "cellist, avant-gardist, and performance artist who won notoriety for her arrest by the New York City police in 1967 for playing the cello nude from the waist up."[6] This reference to Nam June Paik's *Opera Sextronique* cites perhaps her most notable performance, which resulted in the nickname the "topless cellist." The name stuck and became both a blessing and a curse throughout and beyond her lifetime. On one hand, the notoriety brought her a fair amount of recognition, which Moorman used strategically. On the other, it reduced her to a novelty performer, prevented her from being taken seriously in some circles, and overshadowed her many genuine contributions.

Moorman's personal story is fascinating and indeed improbable in many ways. Born in 1933 in Little Rock, Arkansas, she studied cello performance at a small liberal arts institution, Centenary College of Louisiana, and later in a master's program at the University of Texas in Austin. In 1957 Moorman went to New York to study at the Juilliard School, but soon after underwent a fundamental transformation, almost a conversion.[7] She became increasingly drawn to experimental art and music, immersing herself in a world of new expression. Although she continued to play in classical groups

Although Moorman has helped shape how we experience art today, her own work has not received serious critical attention, evaluation, or analysis until recently. The thorough and compelling biography *Topless Cellist: The Improbable Life of Charlotte Moorman* by Joan Rothfuss has brought Moorman's life and work into focus. She has, however, generally been missing from narratives of twentieth-century art. At most she and ensembles—primarily as a way of earning money—in her first few years there, she eventually abandoned the classical canon in favor of a repertoire of radical new and experimental music. The scores Moorman followed faithfully had her submerging herself in a tank of water, performing in various states of undress, being carried aloft by helium balloons, or allowing audience members to cut fabric from her dress.

She performed many of these daring feats repeatedly, and—in line with her training as a classical musician—developed a repertoire that consisted of rotations of sound-based and non-sound-based performance pieces, including *26'1.1499" for a String Player* by Cage, *Cut Piece* by Yoko Ono, *Per Arco* by Giuseppe Chiari, and *Chamber Music* by Takehisa Kosugi. Moorman's life was sadly cut short by cancer, and in her

Peter Moore. Charlotte Moorman performs Aria 2 of Nam June Paik's *Opera Sextronique*, New York City, February 9, 1967. Photograph © Barbara Moore/Licensed by VAGA, NY.

Alice Neel. *Woman Playing Cello,*
ca. 1959. © The Estate of Alice Neel.
Courtesy David Zwirner, New York/
London.

Charlotte Moorman and Philip
Corner perform *Complements 1* at
Moorman's debut recital, New York
City, 1963. Photographer unknown.
Courtesy of Charlotte Moorman
Archive, Charles Deering McCormick
Library of Special Collections,
Northwestern University Library.

last decade she struggled with her health and suffered tremendous pain, even as she continued to travel and perform, before she died in 1991 at age fifty-eight.

Moorman's complicated background, life, and work do not easily conform to established standards of the music or art worlds. She worked in a time of cultural transition marked by changing approaches to art making, evolving ideas about artists, artwork, and display, and increasing skepticism about rigid conventions of the art world. As traditional artworks became increasingly regarded as precious collector and consumer-driven objects, their centrality in spheres of experimental artistic practice diminished as various performative and non-object-centered art became more prominent. In the 1960s, many artists were working in alternative art forms, such as performance, happenings, sound, and movement-based works, and experimenting in new media, such as film. Moorman's performance-based work embraced these shifts and innovative practices. Established categories—painting, sculpture, drawing, photography, printmaking—were generally irrelevant to much of the work she produced or organized. Although photographic or textual documentation of time-based works exists, there are often no artworks, objects, or even relics that remain from the performances or events.

Moorman's work has historically been connected to Fluxus, through both Nam June Paik and other artists she worked with, including John Cage, Ay-O, Geoffrey Hendricks, Yoko Ono, Dick Higgins, and Alison Knowles. However, she was never fully embraced or truly part of Fluxus. She was boycotted and denounced by the founder and leading voice of Fluxus, George Maciunas, who put her on a "Flux-blacklist" and refused to work with "any exhibit, gallery, concert hall or individual that ever included her in any program or show, past and future."[8] As an example, a work that Geoffrey Hendricks performed as part of the 8th Annual Avant Garde Festival included a box assembled by Maciunas that was supposed to be buried in a mound of dirt. Acknowledging Maciunas's hardline nonparticipation

policy, Hendricks did not ultimately use the box in the festival performance, but he added a label to the work that read, "This was not buried for twelve hours at the 8th Annual New York Avant Garde Festival, 69th Regiment Armory," and signed "Geoff Hendricks, 19 November, 1971."[9]

Peter Moore. Charlotte Moorman performs Nam June Paik's *Concerto for TV Cello and Videotapes* wearing *TV Glasses,* Galeria Bonino, New York City, November 23, 1971. Photograph © Barbara Moore / Licensed by VAGA, NY.

While Moorman's name is identified loosely with Fluxus or closely with Nam June Paik, her reputation was never fully cemented with either. *A Feast of Astonishments* aims to bring attention to and establish Moorman's extensive connections and contributions to the art world during the 1960s, '70s, and '80s. The title, taken from a review of the 1964 festival that Moorman organized, appeared in *The Nation* and aptly describes the arc of Moorman's career.[10] The exhibition focuses on Moorman's most dynamic and active period and brings together sculpture, sound pieces, film, documentation, ephemera, and photographs to provide insight into her significance, her roles as performer, organizer, and collaborator, and her extraordinary impact on the creation, display, and reception of art. Although centered on Moorman's work and life, the exhibition is not monographic. Because Moorman worked extensively with other artists and musicians, the exhibition includes works by many contemporaries—some well known and others less so—including Paik, Cage, Knowles, Higgins, Ono, Joseph Beuys, Jim McWilliams, Peter Moore, Otto Piene, Carolee Schneemann, and many others.

The exhibition is divided into thematic sections, such as Moorman's repertoire, which considers a number of works Moorman performed repeatedly throughout her career. She used the framework of a classical musician, who perfects a series of works to be played at various times and in different places as signature pieces throughout her career. The repertoire enabled Moorman to perform artwork in diverse venues and allowed for mobility. Moorman performed all over the world—Iceland, Sweden, Venezuela, Australia, Israel, France, and West Germany—to name a few countries.

The thematic sections in *A Feast of Astonishments* are punctuated with in-depth focal points. Over twenty years and in myriad venues, from the concert hall to popular television, Moorman performed variations on John Cage's *26'1.1499" for a String Player*. Venues included daytime television talk shows and *The Tonight Show* with Johnny Carson. The watershed performance of Nam June Paik's *Opera Sextronique*, which led to her arrest in 1967 and her renown, or notoriety, as the topless cellist, will also be thoroughly explored. The 1964 American premiere of Karlheinz Stockhausen's *Originale* was a key moment

Peter Moore. Charlotte Moorman performs Yoko Ono's *Cut Piece*, New York University, December 16, 1967. Photograph © Barbara Moore/Licensed by VAGA, NY.

in Moorman's career, which led to her meeting Nam June Paik and their decades-long collaborations. Her multiple realizations of works on which she collaborated and for which she became known will be given extensive treatment. *Sky Kiss*, for example, involved her playing cello as she is lifted off the ground by helium balloons. Moorman also often performed *Cut Piece*, the audience-participation piece by Yoko Ono. Having typically included this work at the end of a program, Moorman claimed to have performed it more than seven hundred times.[11] Although that is likely an exaggeration, in 1989 Moorman said, "I have performed that piece for 25 years. . . . Far more than Yoko ever performed it. Every town that I perform in I do 'Cut Piece' because it is so beautiful. What I do is, I wear the gown for the first half of the performance. At the end of the first half, I invite the audience to come up and cut. They are allowed one cut, and it is so beautiful. The gown is an expensive gown. It's real."[12]

•

A section on Moorman abroad will consider specifically her relationships with an international cohort of artists and her participation in arts festivals beginning in the mid-1960s especially in West Germany, such as the *24 Hours* (*24 Stunden*) happening in Wuppertal (1965) and the groundbreaking *Happening & Fluxus* exhibition in Cologne (1970). Her work with artists at the Düsseldorf Art Academy, for example, encouraged an international cultural dialogue and mutual exchange. She continued to work with such artists as Joseph Beuys, Jörg Immendorff, and especially Wolf Vostell, even after she returned to the United States. The section aims to show how Moorman made important connections through her performances at a time when the reinvention of art was critical to the cultural renewal in postwar Europe.

An unprecedented exploration of the fifteen Annual New York Avant Garde Festivals, as they came to be known, will present new research and bring together documents, artworks, films, and photographs that help mine the history of these kaleidoscopic public extravaganzas organized between

1963 and 1980. One of Moorman's greatest contributions was to replace the insulated and rarefied spaces of the gallery, museum, stage, or concert hall with sites in the city that would be visited by a cross section of the urban population. Moorman brought new art to the widest possible audience, creating a truly democratic arena for experimentation. The festivals took place in a different location in the city (and beyond) each year and grew to involve hundreds of artists. They were important vehicles for showcasing new work, and, as one critic put it, "a no-holds-barred, free-for-all break with the past [or] . . . a plunge into the future."[13] New art was made accessible by bringing it to the public's shared spaces and weaving it into everyday experience in fresh and surprising ways. Venues included Central Park, the Staten Island Ferry, Grand Central Terminal, Shea Stadium, and the World Trade Center. At the 1967 Staten Island Ferry festival, performances, music, events, and dances took place over a twenty-four-hour period, from 11:30 P.M. September 29 until 11:30 P.M. September 30, and were integrated into the normal ferry route and schedule.[14] Through these encounters Moorman also provided a nonhierarchical model of inclusiveness and acceptance as diverse artists and media were welcomed and encouraged. They included a range of participatory activities, such as Allan Kaprow's *Towers* in Central Park, Yoko Ono's *Shadow Painting* at the 69th Regiment Armory, and Alison Knowles's *Identical Lunch* at Shea Stadium.

Charlotte Moorman performs Nam June Paik's *TV Bed,* Bochum Art Week, Bochum, West Germany, August 28–September 3, 1973. Photograph © Hartmut Beifuss.

Writing about the eighth festival in the *Village Voice*, Fred McDarrah described the atmosphere in the armory as "a combination trade show, circus, and high school Christmas fair."[15] While it would be impossible to re-create the sometimes carnivalesque atmosphere of these events, *A Feast of Astonishments* aims to give a sense of what it was like to participate in and experience the festivals, as well as to consider their impact and legacies.

Jim McWilliams performs his *American Picnic*, 4th Annual New York Avant Garde Festival, Central Park, September 9, 1966. Photograph © Robert Burridge.

On one hand, it is nearly impossible to understand Moorman's mode of working in the days before email and the Internet. She used correspondence, telephone, telegraph, and personal visits to arrange enormously complicated events involving many, many people. On the other hand, Moorman's do-it-yourself feats were only possible in an era that was less litigious and allowed for more risks. The contracts and agreements that Moorman would have to resolve today to make the festivals happen would make it impossible for one person to undertake the organizing, and the unpredictable nature of the events would likely not gain approval from city officials. The festivals took formidable energy, coordinating, and planning.

They facilitated encounters between hundreds of artists and the public in ways that would actually be difficult to realize today. To obtain permits for festival sites, Moorman utilized her connections, perseverance, and charm, and sometimes she even flirted, using her Southern accent and making bargains with city officials. She would then invite artists, musicians, poets, dancers, filmmakers, many of them friends, to participate. According to Carolee Schneemann, who worked with Moorman often and over many years and premiered such works as *Noise Bodies* (1965) and *Trackings* (the original title for *Up to and Including Her Limits*, 1973) at festivals, "everyone ended each festival saying they wouldn't do it again, but most came back the following year."[16]

Some of the complexity of Moorman's transactions will be explored in the companion exhibition *Don't Throw Anything Out*, organized by Scott Krafft, curator of the Charles Deering McCormick Library of Special Collections at Northwestern University Library, which oversees the Charlotte Moorman Archive. It will give a glimpse into the volume of stuff in the Moorman Archive and the artifacts of her life as preserved through the things—documents, letters, receipts, photographs, relics—that she saved over the years.

In addition to exploring Moorman, her life, her art, and the creativity she fostered, *A Feast of Astonishments* presents an opportunity to appreciate the incredible contributions and achievements of photographer Peter Moore. It is largely through Moore's work that we have come to know Moorman's performances—both her own and ones she organized. Moore photographed many of Moorman's performances and events and may have been the only photographer to have attended each of the fifteen festivals. In addition, he often took publicity photographs with Moorman and several participants on location in advance of the event. His work and his eye have brought much to our understanding of the festivals and our ability to envision them as they happened. Many of his photographs not only tell the story of a particular moment but also stand as iconic and independent artworks.

The exhibition and publication bring to light many unknown works by Moore, his artistic eye, and the vision he brought to our understanding of performance in the mid-twentieth century through his presence and through his camera lens.

•

In a time of fracture and social disjuncture, and in a society divided by social issues—war, civil rights, feminism, the sexual revolution, and the generation gap—Moorman sought to bring people together, to shape meaningful encounters around art that did not always clearly fit into conventional categories.[17]

As groundbreaking as Moorman's festivals and performances were, they were resonant with and reflected the sensibilities of their times. Although Moorman was not consistently or overtly political, her work has undercurrents of a larger critique taking place in the 1960s. Explaining the mission and vision of the Avant Garde Festivals to a *New York Post* reporter in 1967, she said, "We're just trying to express ourselves. And show our new work. Our generation, with the assassination of Kennedy, the war, the bomb—well, in times like this you just can't expect the kind of art you had before."[18]

It was Moorman's bomb cello, included in many performances of *26'1.1499"*, that registered most deeply on emotional and visceral levels.[19] It referred to the past and the legacies of World War II but also to the present with its immediate allusions to the Cold War, the Vietnam War, and sites of political unrest—international and domestic. There was a sentiment among many Americans and Europeans that an end must be put to all war, and the rhetoric was particularly pronounced among the youth and as a rejection of the establishment. At a time when the younger generation especially grappled with the threat of "the bomb," Moorman symbolically neutralized one by adding strings and playing it. By transforming the bomb from an object of destruction into a musical instrument, a vehicle for human culture and expression, Moorman subverted and repurposed it, transforming it into something powerfully constructive.[20]

The theme of war and antiwar demonstration is similarly seen in such works as *Guadalcanal Requiem* (1977, reedited 1979), a video by Paik on which Moorman collaborated extensively. Shot in the Solomon Islands, a site of a military campaign on the Pacific front during World War II, it includes scenes of Moorman crawling military-style on her belly with her cello strapped to her

Introduction   13

Peter Moore. Charlotte Moorman performs Giuseppe Chiari's *Per Arco*, New York Women's Improv Festival, New York City, October 26, 1986. Photograph © Barbara Moore/Licensed by VAGA, NY.

back in a work by Paik titled *Guadalcanal*, also known as *Peace Sonata*. Moorman and Paik also performed *Infiltration Homogen for Cello*, by Joseph Beuys, with its implicit gesture of healing in the use of felt and the symbol of the red cross. The film is considered one of Paik's strongest antiwar statements.

Similarly, Moorman performed *Per Arco*, by Giuseppe Chiari, a cello piece with an audio recording of German bombing in Italy during World War II. Moorman played the piece many times throughout her career. Shortly after including it on the program at the *24 Hours* festival in Wuppertal in 1965, she described the emotional power of playing the work in West Germany, closer to the site of the bombing.[21] In the catalog for the happening, an excerpt from Moorman's contribution read:

> i have played chiari's "Per Arco"
> in many countries but this time
> i have quite a strange feeling because
> i am in the german country
> that is bombing italy on the tape
> do you recognize your sound
> vietnam dominican republic
> mississippi!!
> i can not keep from crying[22]

Connecting the tragedies of World War II with current events, such as the violence of the civil rights movement in the South, the Vietnam War, and unrest in the Caribbean, Moorman speaks to the profound relevance of Chiari's composition. Linking past and present, foreign and domestic violence, and evoking civil rights protests associated with her Southern background, Moorman claims to make a universal statement about tragedy and violence. Photographs of Moorman playing *Per Arco* often show her with "her head lowered as if prayerfully committed to the horror of war and in memoriam to the dead" and deeply moved to the point of weeping.[23]

All these works must be considered against the backdrop of a vigorous antiwar movement that was escalating in cities and college campuses in opposition to the Vietnam War. Moorman's leitmotif of subtle and not-so-subtle antiwar performances, in the playing of the bomb cello, the restorative gesture of the felt-wrapped cello, the mourning of war in *Per Arco*, and her participation in *Guadalcanal Requiem*, deeply reminiscent of the footage familiar from the nightly news, can be seen in consideration of the prevalent antiwar protests.[24] Although couched within the broader theater of her performance, Moorman's antiwar statements are woven throughout her work. Given her reputation as the "topless cellist," she often had to agree to a "no politics" policy to obtain the public venues for her festivals. For example, to secure the 69th Regiment Armory for the eighth festival in 1971, she promised the military colonel "no nudes, no sex, no politics, no dope, no nothing."[25] Still, she often vocalized dissent and identified with the hippies, pacifists, and college students who wanted to change the world. This identification comes across eloquently during her appearance on *The Mike Douglas Show* on November 12, 1969. After Moorman performed a short excerpt from *26'1.1499" for a String Player*, Douglas asked about the meaning of the props. Moorman replied, "The bomb . . . I think it is very obvious what I mean about that." And when Douglas sympathized, saying it "has a bad tone," Moorman rhetorically replied, "War generally has a bad tone, doesn't it?"[26]

That same year, when *Source* magazine surveyed artists on whether their work has "ever been used for political or social ends," Moorman's response was general but unequivocal. She listed several works in her repertoire that she identified as having political or social implications, including *Per Arco*, *26'1.1499" for a String Player*, *Opera Sextronique, Cut Piece*, and *TV Bra for Living Sculpture*. Moorman described *Per Arco* as an emotional outlet: "The sounds of war are played for about five or six minutes, then I react with the cello, I hit the cello, I touch the cello, I go through very painful experiences, and then the piece is over. It touches the audience, it moves them, it's relative to what's going on now, and it makes them think. . . ." While she generally only alluded to these works, her claims for political or social meanings in them gave her work currency at the time.[27]

Moorman's broad and seemingly inexhaustible activities are truly a "feast of astonishments." Because of the sheer number of her endeavors, the exhibition is not, and cannot be, comprehensive; instead it brings key performances and artworks to light, rediscovers forgotten or unknown works, and suggests the texture and reception of Moorman's work through a variety of objects and documents. The publication serves as a companion to the exhibition, with essays exploring such facets of Moorman's work and issues surrounding her as her relation to experimental music and feminism, her travel and performances in West Germany, the cellos as extensions of herself, and key pieces by Moorman and her collaborators. These endeavors—the exhibition and publication, along with Rothfuss's groundbreaking biography—will help us situate Moorman's place more firmly in a history that has left her on the sidelines and encourage further research and scholarship on Moorman and her circle. Exploring Moorman's work and world, we are drawn into a vast web of well-known and lesser-known artists of the late twentieth century, as well as their transitory artworks that both speak of the times in which they were created and performed and help reshape the way we experience art today.

Notes

1. Karin Rosenberg to Charlotte Moorman, November 18, 1969, Museum of Contemporary Art Archive, Chicago.

2. The bomb cello created obvious inconveniences for shipping and transportation. The 1965 version has a sticker from the Museum of Contemporary Art performance that reads: "This is a stage prop, not a bomb. Don't worry." Noted in *The Estate of Charlotte Moorman: Personal Property Estate Appraisal* (New York: Abigail Hartmann Associates, 1993), 17.

3. Cited in Joan Rothfuss, *Topless Cellist: The Improbable Life of Charlotte Moorman* (Cambridge, Mass.: MIT Press, 2014).

4. Museum of Contemporary Art, "Charlotte Moorman and Nam June Paik to Present 'Mixed Media,'" press release, October 24, 1969.

5. J.P., "Charlotte's Festival: Why Do They Do It?" *Village Voice,* November 25, 1971, 31.

6. Glenn Collins, "Charlotte Moorman, 58, Is Dead; A Cellist in Avant-Garde Works," *New York Times*, November 9, 1991.

7. Rothfuss, *Topless Cellist*, 26.

8. Quoted in Kathy O'Dell, "Fluxus Feminus," *Drama Review* 41 (Spring 1997): 44.

9. Geoffrey Hendricks, conversation with author, February 25, 2015.

10. Faubion Bowers, "A Feast of Astonishments," *The Nation*, September 28, 1964,172–75. Bowers's descriptive review concludes with the sentence, "A jolly good time was had by some."

11. Paul Taylor, "Charlotte Moorman," *Yoko Only* 25 (Summer 1989): 10–11. It is not known how she documented the performances, but it is likely she may have performed it closer to fifty to one hundred times.

12. Ibid., 10.

13. Bowers, "Feast of Astonishments," 172.

14. Elenore Lester, "The Night the Hippies Invaded the Staten Island Ferry," *New York Times*, October 8, 1967, 7. See also Appendix Avant-Garde Festivals, in Rothfuss, *Topless Cellist*, 363–77.

15. Fred McDarrah, "Avant Garde Festival: Down to His Last Mouse," *Village Voice*, November 25, 1971, 90.

16. Letter from Carolee Schneemann to Jean-Jacques Lebel, February 7, 1966, in Kristine Stiles, ed., *Correspondence Course: An Epistolary History of Carolee Schneemann and Her Circle* (Durham, N.C.: Duke University Press, 2010): 99–100.

17. Moorman's festivals laid the groundwork for many of the objectives and concerns so prominent in the practices of contemporary artists.

18. Jay Levin, "Where It's Happening—On the Hippiest Ferry," *New York Post*, September 30, 1967.

19. The idea of the bomb cello may have originated with Nam June Paik, who used a candy-filled bomb in John Cage's *Theater Piece* during the Avant Garde Festival in 1965. See Rothfuss, *Topless Cellist*, 401n12.

20. Her approach is comparable to the emblematic 1967 photograph *Flower Power*, by Bernie Boston for the *Washington Evening Star,* in which a young man puts carnations in gun barrels during an antiwar demonstration at the Pentagon. She sometimes played the cello with plastic flower bouquets.

21. *24 Stunden* (Wuppertal: Itzehoe-Vosskate, Hansen und Hansen, 1965).

22. Ibid.

23. Ibid.

24. For Moorman's friends and colleagues Yoko Ono and John Lennon, antiwar protest was often at the center of their work, as in the famous Bed-Ins for Peace in Amsterdam and in Montreal in 1969.

25. McDarrah, "Avant Garde Festival," 90.

26. *The Mike Douglas Show*, November 12, 1969, courtesy of the Emily Harvey Foundation Archives, New York.

27. Published in *Source: Music of the Avant Garde* 3 (1969): 90.

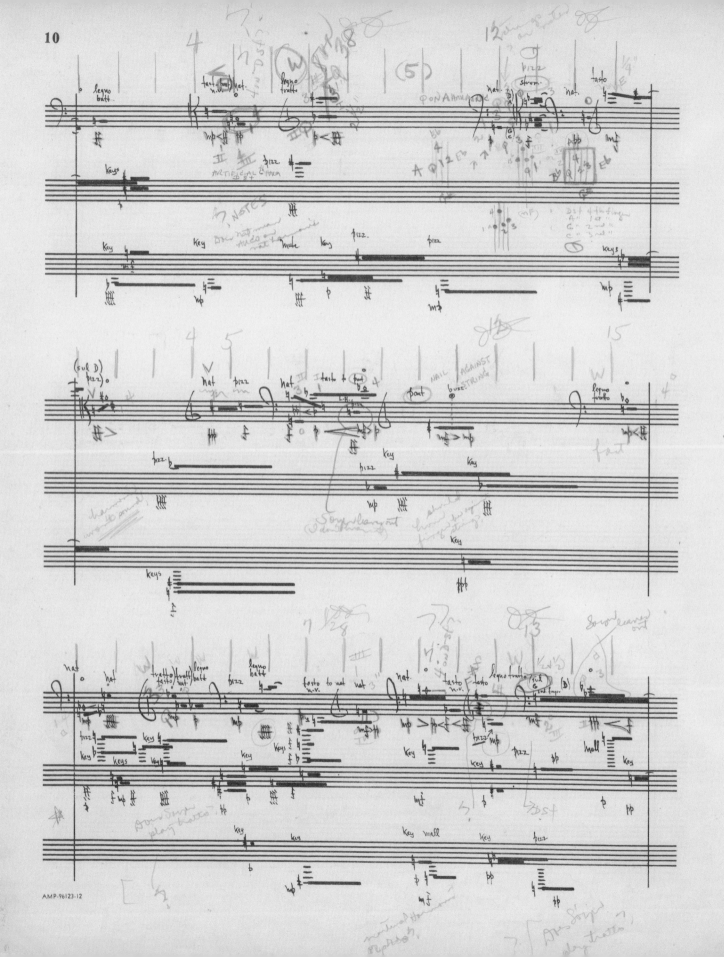

Charlotte Moorman's Experimental Performance Practice

Ryan Dohoney

> All revolutions are misunderstood. Donatello misunderstood
> Greek sculpture. And if it wasn't for the misunderstanding
> maybe we wouldn't have anything new.
>
> —Morton Feldman

In an interview conducted in the spring prior to the 1963 festival of six concerts that was to become the first of Charlotte Moorman's annual avant-garde festivals, Robert Ashley asked fellow composer Morton Feldman to assess the contemporary landscape of experimental performance:

ROBERT ASHLEY: You will agree that a certain "revolution" happened in music in the early '50s in America. You were a main part of it. If we may skip over for the moment all of the precedents for that revolution, I would like to talk about its consequences. For instance, you might say, "We wanted to emancipate the sound—which is an end in itself." But in fact you may have emancipated something else.

MORTON FELDMAN: Of course, more than sound. For example we emancipated the musician, the performer. That certainly wasn't part of the deal; I mean the sounds were to be free, but not the performer. But it happened; it happened with David Tudor, and it happened with other very good people; so it more or less "came to pass," I would say.[1]

Feldman's comments point to the early 1960s as a moment of crisis within the avant-garde. What was the meaning of the "revolution" begun in the 1950s? What were the ends of liberation? Feldman is unequivocal here as he is elsewhere: "I was not only allowing the sounds to be free—I was also liberating the performer. I had never thought of the graph [score] as an art of improvisation, but more as a totally abstract sonic adventure."[2] Feldman's concern here is with the shift in the idea of "freedom" from the "originators"—the New York school musicians of Feldman, John Cage, Christian Wolff, Earle Brown, Edgard Varèse, Stefan Wolpe, and David Tudor—and those who extended their work into the 1960s. Moorman is certainly to be counted as essential to the New York school's second generation along with Robert Ashley, Gordon Mumma, Yoko Ono, Jackson Mac Low, Allan Kaprow, and the numerous other artists who moved the avant-garde toward performance, theatricality, and the further exploration of new technologies. Yet Moorman's work as an impresario and performer of this music affords us a unique vantage point on this controversy—on what Benjamin Piekut has called the "actually existing experimentalism" as it was practiced and proliferated beyond any single intention.[3]

OPPOSITE
Earle Brown. Score for *Music for Cello and Piano,* p. 10, with annotations by Charlotte Moorman. © 1961 by Associated Music Publishers. Used by permission of The Earle Brown Foundation. Courtesy of Charlotte Moorman Archive, Charles Deering McCormick Library of Special Collections, Northwestern University Library.

The previous generation of avant-gardists described their work in ascetic, almost religious terms. As Christian Wolff wrote in 1958, "Roughly, since 1950, . . . one finds a concern for a kind of objectivity, almost anonymity—sound comes into its own."[4] Objectivity was not aspirational for Moorman and her generation, nor was fidelity to the intentions of Feldman, Cage, or Wolff.

Respect was, though, and one can hear in Moorman's programming for the early avant-garde festivals an honoring of those who came before as well as an extension of their so-called revolution. The generational tension enacted through the festivals' programs had been noted by Feldman in the months prior to their inauguration. His interview with Ashley continued:

ASHLEY: Last time we talked you did, offhandedly, somewhat reject the composers of this kind of music as being the inheritors of your revolution, you know, you said that they weren't part of your revolution.

FELDMAN: I'm ambivalent about the whole question myself. I know that in performance I have occasions within my works where I would designate a certain amount of notes to play in the graph things, and I would hear "Yankee Doodle" coming out of the horn section. The players decide together, before the concert, actually to sabotage it—and they decided in this particular section they were going to play "Yankee Doodle," with the amount of notes called for and in the register in

the score—there was nothing I could say about it that wasn't inherent in the instructions of the piece. But of course I said, "Manslaughter is one thing, but not homicide; I have not given you license to murder the piece." So for the younger generation the implication is a moral question that has to be decided ultimately. For example, that Korean fellow in Germany, [Nam June] Paik, does he have that? Whether or not he brings to music an element of violence that was never wholly inherited from John [Cage], but you could say the implication was there?[5]

It is doubtful that Moorman also understood the stakes of the new music in such moralizing terms, and Feldman himself seems ambivalent about how he has framed the issue (though he does not seem hopeful that Paik, with his implicit violence, will answer the question in an ethical manner).

By raising the question of tensions within the 1960s avant-garde, I do not mean to side with Feldman, who seems to have valued musicians inasmuch as their performances re-created the scene of composition, handling sound with "love or interest."[6] Moorman certainly approached her music making with love and interest and took full advantage of the new freedoms that had "come to pass." By the early 1960s, Euro-American modernists and avant-gardists recognized that since Feldman and Cage, composers and performers had transformed the hierarchy of musical roles.[7] Practices usually associated with composition—the fixing of sonic parameters of pitch, duration, instrumentation, articulation—were transferred to performers. Creativity, already distributed and relational, as is the case with all musical performance, became more so as performers including Moorman and David Tudor began to "realize" the open works of Cage, Feldman, Earle Brown, Sylvano Bussotti, and others.

"Realization" is a strange description of this practice. "Cocomposition" might be a better word that more honestly recognizes the myriad mediations at play in the performance of indeterminate, graphic, event, or instruction-based scores.[8] Feldman describes the practice of realization in uncertain terms:

> I think, for example, that while David [Tudor] now will "realize" a [Sylvano] Bussotti score, or a John Cage score (say the imperfections on the paper), in the early days I never really felt that there was any realization involved. I'm not clear myself what is meant by "realization" now. Does it mean that the situation is ambiguous and has to be "realized?" I think that as the music of the scores became, in a sense, much more ambiguous, the sophistication of the performers and the realization also increased certainly in tightening the gradual gradations of ambiguity that make a part in these graphic scores.[9]

Within Western musical performance, "realization" was first used in 1911 to describe a performer's role in harmonizing a bass line in seventeenth- and eighteenth-century compositions. This work was originally done through improvisation on the part of a keyboardist but was gradually abandoned as composers did the work of realization themselves and improvisation fell out of much Euro-American musical practice. During the early music revival in the early twentieth century, "realization" became the composing-out of a bass line by editors, musicologists, and musicians no longer skilled in the improvisatory practices that would have been expected of the musicians of Claudio Monteverdi's or Johann Sebastian Bach's day.[10] Composer Benjamin Britten (1913–1976) used the term "realizations" in the 1940s when he developed new accompaniments to songs by Henry Purcell (1659–1695) based on the extant bass lines. Britten's connection to the U.S. avant-garde is tenuous at best, but his adoption of the term for his practice of finishing the composition of another gives a sense of its currency. Yet, the exact moment that it leapt from early music performance practice to experimental music is unclear. By 1963,

Feldman places "realization" in scare quotes. This indicates perhaps its newness and its fraught adoption as a term that is at best an approximation for what is really going on in the performance practice of Moorman, Tudor, Ashley, Mumma, and others.

Though it may seem perverse to invite such a comparison, Moorman's realization of Feldman's *Projection 1* is conceptually similar to working out a figured-bass notation. Instead of harmonizing a given bass line, however, Feldman asks his performers to choose a specific pitch within a given set of parameters, and Moorman follows suit. Moorman described the piece in the WBAI broadcast of her performance:

> Projection 1 that you are about to hear is an unaccompanied cello piece written in graphic notation. It is the first graphic piece ever written. It is simply soft, pure sounds projected into space. The composer projects rhythm, register, quality, and duration, allowing the performer freedom of specific choice of notes.[11]

Moorman here understands Feldman as offering freedom of choice within an otherwise determined situation (indicating that Moorman "misunderstood" Feldman's goal of freeing sound). With her detailed realization of the score for *Projection 1*, Moorman offers us an important document of experimental performance practice as it had developed over the previous twelve years. In their earliest performances, Feldman did envision his *Projections* as a form of real-time music making arising from interaction with the graphic notation, even though he later eschewed improvisation as a descriptive term. In a program note for the 1952 premiere of *Projection 2*, Feldman states, "What particular sounds these are is left to the choice of the musicians at the moment of playing. . . . Since each performance of this composition is different, yet essentially the same, it will be played twice in succession."[12] The tension between these ideas of difference and sameness hinged on the ways performers such as Moorman negotiated this freedom of choice.

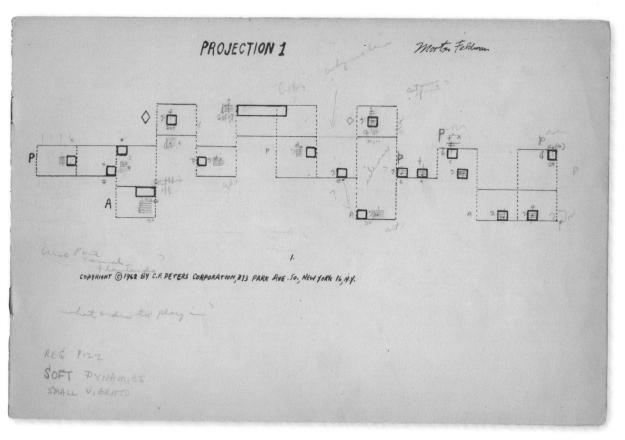

Morton Feldman. Score for *Projection 1*, with annotations by Charlotte Moorman. Used by permission of the C. F. Peters Corporation. Courtesy of Charlotte Moorman Archive, Charles Deering McCormick Library of Special Collections, Northwestern University Library.

In 1951 Feldman offered the grid as a spur to spontaneous music making, but by 1963 Moorman's realization demonstrates that the performance practice had become something quite different. The first page of her copy of *Projection 1* shows Moorman meticulously working out the pitch content of her performances. She transforms each specific box (indicating a sounding pitch) into staff notation, essentially making the grid into a conventional performing score.[13] She further fixes each box with clef designations (save the first three boxes) that correspond to the shifts in range (high, middle, low). Beyond that, Moorman indicates other mnemonic markings—reminders about what type of articulation is to be produced—natural bowed sound (marked *A* for *arco*), plucked string sound (marked *P* for *pizzicato*), or a harmonic effect (marked by a lozenge).[14] Moorman's choices of notes indicate her willingness to use the graph to extend her technical abilities by producing very high sounds or difficult-to-produce harmonics. Feldman's specifications regarding every aspect of sound (save pitch) marks a similar aesthetic found in works by Cage (*26'1.1499" for a String Player*) and Brown (*Music for Cello and Piano*) that break down and reconfigure every sonic parameter. However, Feldman's affection for slow, quiet sounds distinguishes his work from the more violent and technically deconstructive compositions of Cage and Brown.[15]

With its fixed pitches, Moorman's realization of *Projection 1* seems to trade in the freedom of spontaneity (which would yield a different version in each performance) for the freedom to compose out her own repeatable version. While this might be construed as yet another willful refusal of the "true" revolution initiated by the New York school, it bears noting that Moorman's realization strategy was itself congruent with the performance practice of Feldman's graphically notated works that had, in fact, been initiated by the authority of pianist-composer David Tudor. After performing Feldman's graphically notated piano solos *Intersection 2* (1951) and *Intersection 3* (1953) with the grid scores alone, Tudor made a fully realized version of the latter and left a partial realization of the former that resulted in repeatable versions from performance to performance.[16] Though as Feldman increasingly distanced himself from improvisatory music making and overwhelmingly preferred Tudor's performances, it is likely that Moorman's mode of working out the grid was at least tacitly approved by Feldman. The recorded documentation, however, indicates that she deviated from her realization, altering numerous pitches and making some errors in articulation. Unlike Tudor's fixed *Intersections*, Moorman's *Projection* likely maintained a degree of openness and spontaneity from performance to performance.[17]

The evidence of her score of *Projection 1* also suggests that she contacted the first performer and dedicatee of *Projection 1*, cellist and composer Seymour Barab, who was active in the performance of Feldman's music into the 1970s.[18] With the evidence not only of *Projection 1* but also her realization of scores by Earle Brown, it is clear that Moorman depended on the tenuous but extant cello performance practice tradition that ran alongside and occasionally intersected the pianistic performance practice developed by Tudor. Moorman extended a "tradition of the new" developed in the 1950s by cellists Barab and David Soyer, whose recording of Brown's *Music for Cello and Piano* Moorman studied in preparation for her own performance of the piece with Tudor.[19] Even as Moorman drew upon these precursors, she transformed experimental musical agency into the perfection of "an imagery of personality" that emphasized "the way music spread out into other things," and which Robert Ashley argued was the "inheritance of [Feldman and Cage's] revolution."[20]

The new composer–performer relationship presented new questions about creative agency within experimental performance. The image of personality recognized by Ashley and discounted by Feldman extended beyond the composer to encompass a new conception of theatricality that, although born from the spirit of music, did not aspire to the identity of "composer."

Rather, it required a form of distributed creativity and coauthorship. Though not fully developed until the emergence of Fluxus in the early 1960s, strands of this newly expanded performer role were apparent in the early work of the New York school and were drawn out in Moorman's performance of Earle Brown's *Synergy* (1952). Moorman performed *Synergy* on a solo concert during the second annual avant-garde festival in 1964 along with Giuseppe Chiari's *Per Arco* (which would become a signature work of hers) and others. Brown's performance instructions read:

> To be performed in any direction from any point in the defined space. Tempo—as fast as possible to as slow as possible—inclusion. Lines and spaces may be thought of as tracks moving in either direction and at any speeds—clef signs thought of as floating in the field. This indicates the theoretical possibility of all the attacks occurring at the same instant, or any other expression of simultaneity.[21]

In developing her performance of *Synergy*, Moorman did much more than add exact pitches to Feldman's graph. Brown's instructions afford multiple options for the production of a performable piece. The work of realization involves a high degree of composition to determine what exactly the piece will become. Moorman's decisions seem to have explored the concept of the "floating field" as a compositional ideal. Her performance joined a live reading of the score with two prerecorded tape versions played on loudspeakers that distributed sound across the space of the concert hall and immersed the audience in her imaginative rendering of Brown's score. Most striking is the effectiveness of the spatialization in emphasizing the multiple temporalities sounding out from the one actual and two virtual Moormans. Moorman expanded the sonic possibilities beyond Brown's notation by saturating her *Synergy* with glissandi—bent notes and slid pitches that are not indicated on Brown's score.[22] Brown was unable to attend Moorman's performance, as he was working in

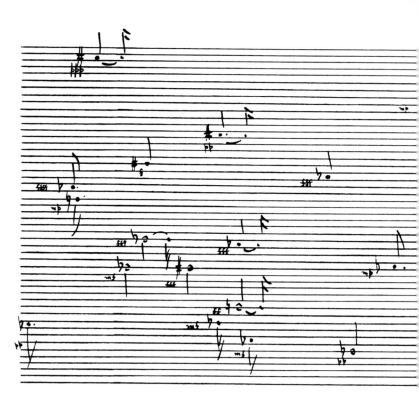

Europe at the time, but he wrote to her on October 2, 1964, with compliments, saying, "So what else is new now that you are the Cecil B. DeMoorman of the music world? I heard good reports from your perf[ormance] of 'Synergy'—thanks piles."[23] Moorman's version of *Synergy* gained currency beyond her performance in the festival, and Brown wrote to her again on February 10, 1965, to inquire after the tapes of her realization:

> [Giuseppe] Chiari did concert here with and wants you to send him y[ou]r background tape of cello "Synergy" over which, I assume, with proper credit he will impose some piano renditions. A guy from San Fran[cisco] may write and ask you the same. How do you feel about that?? I feel o.k.—at least as far as Chiari is concerned—don't knock yourself out for S.F. Play me well, you clown! (that's, CLOWN—in the appreciative sense).[24]

Apparent in Brown's exchanges with Moorman is a more complicated version of artistic agency, one exemplary of the shift within the New York City avant-garde identified by Feldman and Ashley. Brown recognizes her role as impresario, lovingly christening her "Cecil B. DeMoorman" after that director of ostentatious film spectacles, Cecil B. DeMille. He also feels she deserves authorial credit for her work in producing the tapes for *Synergy*, which are taken up into circulation in the transatlantic avant-garde. The version of *Synergy* later performed by Chiari became the product of multiple compositional and performance agents: Brown's production of the score, Moorman's taped realization, and Chiari's real-time piano interpretation. This desire to give credit and recognition to his collaborators was typical of Brown, who, unlike Feldman, valued the chain of mediators his music had to go through for a performance to occur. Musicians were, in the words of

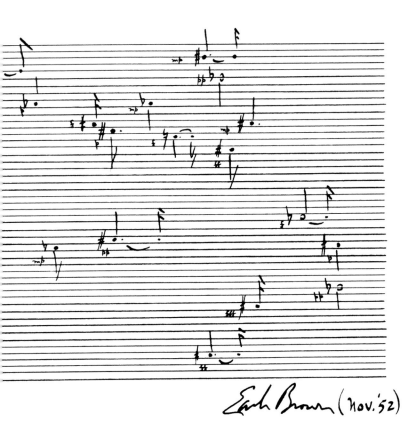

philosopher Adriana Cavarero, "necessary others" coming together to collaboratively produce the work.[25]

Moorman's realizations of Feldman's *Projection 1* and Brown's *Synergy* demonstrate the conflicted lineage of the New York avant-garde, even within its coterie of originators. Sound itself was in tension with the image of personality, and we see Moorman negotiating those poles of aesthetic commitment in these two realizations—a faithful working out of Feldman's aesthetics of sound itself along with the assertion of a creative agency beyond mere executant to one who transformed Brown's notation into vibrating, fleshy, metallic sound. Lukas Foss was correct writing in 1963 that the composer–performer relationship had indeed changed, though what had changed was perhaps the recognition and intensification of the mediations at play in any musical performance.[26] Experimentalism brought the play of forces and relationships to the fore, out from an aged ideology that idealized the role of the composer at the expense of the performer. The newly configured relationship calls to my mind the working relationship between Gertrude Stein and Alice B. Toklas as described by Adriana Cavarero:

As the fruit of a curious fiction that clearly refutes itself, the text [of *The Autobiography of Alice B. Toklas*] is therefore interesting not only as the transgression of the autobiographical genre, but also for the desire that sustains its ingenious mechanism. That this desire is tightly bound to a lesbian relationship has been made clear by feminist literary criticism. What is remarkable, however, is the capacity of the book to stage a relationship between Alice and Gertrude that refigures itself in terms of both a visual and narrative reciprocity. Indeed, the game is found out. The two are accomplices. Alice types— or, rather, first reads, and then rewrites, the pages that Gertrude has written by hand. Alice was not a typist by trade. She had to learn how to use the typewriter in order to support Gertrude's work.[27]

Moorman resembles Toklas in this account. Like that of Toklas, Moorman's collaborative ethos came from a place of love and commitment. She also transformed and made presentable the texts (scores) given to her. Like Toklas, Moorman found a need to extend her abilities, to learn to do what she did not know how in order to realize a vision to which she was essential. Her collaborations with composers and musicians were based on a similar foundation of reciprocal trust, devotion, and commitment. But unlike that of Toklas, Moorman's role was not simply to transcribe but to cocompose, to bring forth her personality as the medium of her collaborative endeavors—be they with Brown, Paik, Cage, or Feldman.

Yet, perhaps she thought herself more like Toklas. Until now, Moorman's agency and creative contribution to the works she herself performed remained suspended between mere interpreter and full collaborator. Despite performing the most radically open and indeterminate works of the time, she often downplayed her creative agency, most famously (and strategically) in her trial on charges of indecent exposure and obscenity resulting from a performance of Nam June Paik's *Opera Sextronique*. She described herself as doing what the composer told her, and as such she seems beholden to a classical music ideology. Yet Moorman's occasional rejection of her creative agency masks a radical practice of freedom that was latent in the first generation of the New York school and became a fully developed performance practice through Moorman's committed labor. She, along with her community of fellow travelers in the avant-garde, practiced a reciprocal self-donation in which they felt each other as necessary to the task at hand.

Notes

Special thanks are due to Scott Krafft, Sigrid Pohl Perry, and Nick Munagian for their help navigating the bountiful Charlotte Moorman Archive in the Charles Deering McCormick Library of Special Collections, Northwestern University Library, Evanston, Ill. (hereafter cited as CMA). The ideas presented in this essay benefited from conversations with Seth Brodsky, Kirsten Speyer Carithers, and Kyle Kaplan. Thanks to Matthew Richardson for editing help.

The epigraph is from Robert Ashley and Morton Feldman, "Around Morton Feldman," unpublished manuscript, March 1963, Morton Feldman Collection, Paul Sacher Foundation, Basel, Switzerland, 6.

1. Ashley and Feldman, "Around Morton Feldman," 1.

2. Morton Feldman, "Liner Notes," in *Give My Regards to Eighth Street*, ed. B. H. Friedman (Cambridge, Mass.: Exact Change, 2000), 6. Feldman's comments were initially published as album notes to *Feldman/Brown*, Time Records 58007/S8007. They also appeared in *Kulchur* 2, no. 6 (Summer 1963): 57–60. *Kulchur* was one of the "little magazines" of the New York avant-garde that published writing by Feldman's friend Frank O'Hara, Amiri Baraka (then LeRoi Jones), La Monte Young, and Feldman himself.

3. See Benjamin Piekut, *Experimentalism Otherwise: The Avant-Garde and Its Limits* (Berkeley: University of California Press, 2011).

4. Christian Wolff, "New and Electronic Music," in *Writings about John Cage*, ed. Richard Kostelanetz (Ann Arbor: University of Michigan Press, 1996), 85–92, at 85. For an exploration of this idea in terms of John Cage's "politics of nature," see Benjamin Piekut, "Chance and Certainty: John Cage's Politics of Nature," *Cultural Critique* 84 (Spring 2013): 134–63.

5. Ashley and Feldman, "Around Morton Feldman," 14.

6. Ibid., 8. Feldman recalled how David Tudor asked for explicit instructions on how to perform his *Piano Piece (for Philip Guston)* that matched both how Feldman composed and how the composer performed in public. Feldman expresses his ethics of "love and interest" on p. 16.

7. See, for example, Lukas Foss, "The Changing Composer-Performer Relationship: A Monologue and a Dialogue," *Perspectives of New Music* 1, no. 2 (1963): 45–53.

8. On the genealogy of this performance mode and its development in Fluxus, see Liz Kotz, *Words to Be Looked At: Language in 1960s Art* (Cambridge, Mass.: MIT Press, 2007).

9. Ashley and Feldman, "Around Morton Feldman," 2.

10. The *Oxford English Dictionary* notes that the earliest use of the word "realization" for this practice is 1911. I am grateful to Kyle Kaplan for reminding me of realization's connection to early music performance.

11. Charlotte Moorman, WBAI broadcast recording, November 2 and 9, 1963, 10.5" reel recording in CMA. Moorman performed *Projection 1* first on April 15, 1963, and then again that year in the first New York avant-garde festival. See Joan Rothfuss, *Topless Cellist* (Cambridge, Mass.: MIT Press, 2014), 60. Feldman, though he later abandoned such indeterminate notation, took every opportunity to position himself as the *originator* of "chance" notation. See Brett Boutwell, "Morton Feldman's Graphic Notation: *Projections* and Trajectories," *Journal of the Society for American Music* 6, no. 4 (2012): 457–82.

12. Morton Feldman, program note for Merce Cunningham Dance Company at Hunter College, New York, January 21, 1951, Merce Cunningham Dance Company Archive, Jerome Robbins Dance Division, New York Public Library, New York.

13. Moorman's manner of realization resembles a style of notation that John Cage turned to in 1979 for his vocal ensemble composition *Hymns and Variations*.

14. My study of the score indicates two primary layers of annotations. The realization was done in graphite pencil indicating specific pitch content along with additional markings and marginalia. A later set of markings in blue pencil indicates notes toward editing a recording of the piece that seems to have never materialized. The live performance broadcast on WBAI is the only extant recording. See Morton Feldman, *Projection 1*, annotated copy by Charlotte Moorman, CMA.

15. On Moorman's performance of Cage's *26′1.1499″ for a String Player*, see Jason Rosenholtz-Witt in this volume and Piekut, *Experimentalism Otherwise*, 140–75.

16. Both realizations are held in the David Tudor Collection at the Getty Research Institute, Los Angeles. Tudor also left a partial realization of the grid notation of Feldman's *Ixion* (1958), which accompanied the touring version of Merce Cunningham's *Summerspace*. Tudor performed *Ixion* for many decades, and pianist Joseph Kubera notes that Tudor would play from the graph notation itself. Joseph Kubera, email with author, June 2007. On Tudor's realizations, see John Holzaepfel, "Painting by Numbers: The *Intersections* of Morton Feldman and David Tudor," in *The New York Schools of Music and Visual Arts*, ed. Steven Johnson (New York: Routledge, 2002), 159–72.

17. I say "likely" because there is only one extant recording with which Moorman's realization can be compared.

18. On the title page of her copy of *Projection 1*, Moorman has written "S. Baron 215 W. 91 St. Apt. 123 (12th floor)." "Baron" seems a likely a mishearing of "Barab," who would have been an important contact for her as she prepared the piece. Barab also recorded Feldman's sound track for Hans Namuth's film *Jackson Pollock Painting* (1951), the first LP of Feldman's music (*New Directions in Music 2*, Columbia Masterworks, 1959), and *The Viola in My Life* (CRI, 1972).

19. "Tradition of the new" is Harold Rosenberg's phrase. See Rosenberg, *The Tradition of the New* (New York: Horizon Press, 1959). For Moorman's references to Soyer, see her extensive annotation and comparisons with Soyer's recording on her copy of Earle Brown, *Music for Cello and Piano*, CMA.

20. Ashley and Feldman, "Around Morton Feldman," 9–10.

21. Earle Brown, performance directions to *Synergy* in *An Anthology of Chance Operations*, ed. La Monte Young and Jackson Mac Low (n.p., 1963). Moorman had two copies of the score to *Synergy* in her possession: one in the printed score of *Folio and Four Systems* and one in *An Anthology of Chance Operations*.

22. A recording of Moorman's performance of *Synergy* is available on *Charlotte Moorman: Cello Anthology*, Alga Marghen, 2006, compact disc.

23. Earle Brown to Charlotte Moorman, October 2, 1964, CMA.

24. Earle Brown to Charlotte Moorman, February 10, 1965, CMA.

25. Adriana Cavarero, *Relating Narratives* (New York: Routledge, 2000), 81–94.

26. Foss, "Changing Composer-Performer Relationship."

27. Cavarero, *Relating Narratives*, 83.

Beyond the Score: Charlotte Moorman and John Cage's *26'1.1499" for a String Player*

Jason Rosenholtz-Witt

My first look at Charlotte Moorman's copy of John Cage's *26'1.1499" for a String Player* was a mystifying experience.[1] Her markings saturate the score's eighty-five pages and include myriad notes in assorted colors, indications for extrainstrumental sound production, directions to hit Nam June Paik, and various ephemera such as an Icelandic lullaby, newspaper clippings, tampon box instructions, a unique tablature system, and phonetically spelled Italian and Japanese words. Indications such as "razar [*sic*] duck," "Big-Ben," and "cat in heat" confuse rather than enlighten. To better understand the questions of interpretation that faced Charlotte Moorman and to internalize the challenging practical decisions this work presents, I attempted a performance of *26'1.1499"* (hereafter *26'*) for double bass.[2] I discovered that Moorman's annotated copy of the score was an edition meant for herself alone—nearly illegible and incomprehensible to other eyes. However, her markings were practical, thoughtful, organized; and her choice of external sound producers signified solutions to open-ended challenges in the score. Cage sought emancipation from what he considered a tyrannical relationship between the composer and the performer, and his style of composition

OPPOSITE
Charlotte Moorman rehearses for her performance of John Cage's *26'1.1499" for a String Player* at the Institute of Contemporary Arts, London. Photograph by Bela Zola. Published in *Daily Mirror*, September 23, 1968. © Mirrorpix.

THIS PAGE
Charlotte Moorman's setup for a performance of John Cage's *26'1.1499" for a String Player,* WNET-TV studio, 1973. Photographer unknown. Courtesy of Charlotte Moorman Archive, Charles Deering McCormick Library of Special Collections, Northwestern University Library.

grants the musician enormous liberties.[3] There were perhaps too many liberties, as Cage was not pleased with Moorman's choices.[4] This particular score allows significant freedom in terms of sound production, though the temporality in which it occurs is

Nam June Paik and Charlotte Moorman perform John Cage's *26′1.1499″* for a *String Player*, ca. 1965. Newspaper clipping with an inscription by Ute Klophaus, dated 1967. Courtesy of Charlotte Moorman Archive, Charles Deering McCormick Library of Special Collections, Northwestern University Library.

a catalyst for Moorman to explore and embrace her agency as an artist. A close reading of her personal score illuminates her artistic and interpretive approach and serves as an archive of its performance history. A lifelong devotee of Cage's music and philosophy, Moorman took full advantage of the intrinsic freedom of the score, even when it surpassed the boundaries envisioned by the composer.

The composition, completed by Cage in 1955 with the assistance of pianist and frequent collaborator David Tudor, incorporated five short earlier pieces.[6] Cage composed *26′* via chance operations and the exploration of imperfections found in the paper on which the work was written, a process he had previously explored in *Music for Carillon* (1952).[7] In addition to indeterminate compositional methods, the piece breaks down traditional string technique and forces performers to approach their instruments in ways that often contradict deeply entrenched training. The musician who plans to perform such a work needs to develop a relationship with the score that may require the invention of new techniques. In the score of *26′*, there is a separate line for each string with a graphic depiction of where on the instrument one should play. An area running along the bottom of the page is devoted to the aforementioned "sounds other than those produced on the strings," and Cage neither stipulated nor restricted their source. There are separate indications for bowings, with fastidious specificity as to placement and pressure. Shorthand symbols represent *sul tasto* (above the fingerboard), extreme *sul tasto*, slight *sul tasto*, *ponticello* (close to the bridge), and so on. In lieu of traditional dynamic markings, bow pressure is graphically indicated on a separate line in the upper section of the score. In addition, the strings are variously tuned up and down, denoted by "increase" and "decrease," respectively. Cage marks precisely what, where, when, and how to play each on-string sound event. *26′* is almost impossible to execute accurately, and, as one performer noted, "the tension in the work arises from a performer's frantic attempts to play every note."[8]

strictly defined. Especially in collaboration with Paik, Moorman increasingly exceeded the confines of the notation and shifted her focus to the section of the score calling for "sounds other than those produced on the strings."[5] She maintained a serious and earnest dedication to Cage's original score, though Moorman's personal markings eventually supplanted the composer's as her performances with Paik became more extravagant and spectacular.

Cage's unconventional notation requires collaboration from the performer, who must complete his compositional process to make the work performable. The piece became

While preparing my performance, I was faced with the same problems as Moorman, starting with the cumbersome score itself. Typical sheet music is 8½″ × 11″ while the pages of *26′* are 18″ × 12″. A single page may last just five seconds, necessitating near constant page turns, or a dedicated assistant. Whereas Moorman used the score itself as a canvas for her realization, I chose to invent my own system of notation to include all of Cage's instructions, a task I approached as an editor.[9] Like Moorman's heavily annotated score, this was an edition for myself alone. James Grier, a scholar of musical notation and editing, aptly sums up the validity of this approach: "music sources are almost always functional, and so the prime concern of the copyist is not necessarily to replicate the text of the piece with exactitude, but often to *create a usable text for the purpose at hand*."[10] As in Moorman's first public performance, I limited myself to the opening nine pages, or 169″.[11] In the score, Cage allows for the performance of shorter excerpts, provided the title is changed to indicate the new duration. I, too, was attracted to external noises and had initially prepared a number of electronic sounds to be generated on my computer as well as on a variety of auxiliary instruments. In practice, the physicality of putting the bow down, pressing buttons, or reaching for supplementary items immediately set me behind. To solve this problem, I explored the percussive nature of my bass and the use of my voice. There are several extended passages in which I did have the chance to use auxiliary instruments, which I restricted to conch shell and mouth harp.

In theory, there is no limit to the sounds a performer can bring to *26′*; in practice, Cage's densely arranged events and exacting temporal demands diminish the possibilities. In Moorman's marked copy of the score, the section of Cage's didactic introduction that she underlined and bracketed refers to the noncello sound events:

> The lowest area is devoted to noises on the box, sounds other than those produced on the strings. These may issue from entirely other sources, e.g. percussion instruments, whistles, radios, etc. Only high and low are indicated.[12]

Aural piquancy was a goal for Moorman, and her wild stage setup reflected this. Program notes from a 1965 concert at the Philadelphia College of Art list a dizzying array of auditory devices.[13] A caricature from a

Charlotte Moorman, cellist: See " Explosion of New Music."

Les Gibbard. Caricature of Charlotte Moorman's performance of John Cage's *26′1.1499″ for a String Player*, Institute of Contemporary Arts, London. Published in *Sunday Telegraph,* London, September 22, 1968. © Estate of Les Gibbard. Courtesy of Charlotte Moorman Archive, Charles Deering McCormick Library of Special Collections, Northwestern University Library.

Johnny Carson assists Charlotte Moorman in her performance of John Cage's *26'1.1499" for a String Player* on *The Tonight Show*, September 25, 1964. Photographer unknown. Courtesy of Charlotte Moorman Archive, Charles Deering McCormick Library of Special Collections, Northwestern University Library.

sul tasto, *arco* up-bow; a quadruple-stop up-bow with normal bow placement; a *sul tasto*, triple-stop, *col legno* (with the wood of the bow) down-bow; and finally a normal *pizzicato* on the D string. The "normal" *pizzicato* is one of four possible *pizzicati*, each with its own graphic indication. This exposition of Moorman's first page serves to demonstrate the enormous complexity of the piece and the extraordinary amount of sensory information to process and enact in an extremely short amount of time. If Moorman is following all of her personal notes, she will fall behind immediately. Though, as discussed above, not all of the markings in her score were necessarily used for every performance.

An examination of Moorman's methods shows that, even when temporal accuracy was sacrificed, she approached every sound event as an individual problem to be solved and gave herself multiple solutions. The first second in time calls for four extra-instrumental sound events—three very short and one slightly lengthened—of varying dynamics. Moorman chose to relay standard dynamic designations interpreted from the upper section (*piano, mezzo forte, forte*, etc.). The first two short events are *forte* and *pianissimo*, respectively—she indicated a loud knock to the body of her cello, followed by a strike to a tin can for the softer sound. Next, there is a short yet sustained sound, which must *decrescendo*, and Moorman wrote "sand" in the score. She had placed sandpaper on the bottom of her shoe, and at that point she scraped it against the floor, a thoughtful and resourceful solution to the challenge presented. On the second page, Cage notates a sustained event lasting six seconds, beginning strongly, and followed by a steady *decrescendo*. Moorman chose a cymbal crash, a loud sound with immediate yet protracted decay. Page twenty-nine of the score calls for a sustained seven-second event at the fullest volume possible. Moorman solved this problem by playing a recording of the departure blast from the *Queen Mary*, a steamship docked in New York City for a time. This seems to have superseded other options listed in her score, such as wasps, foghorn, duck whistle, Big

1968 London *Sunday Telegraph* shows a busy Moorman employing a plethora of objects, including a gun, a skillet, and a live dog. While her annotations appear at first to be overabundant, not all of her markings were followed for every performance. There are numerous venue-specific notations, such as her television appearances on *The Tonight Show* and *The Merv Griffin Show*, the latter including instructions for her fellow guest, Jerry Lewis. Her score represents many years of performance to which she added, rather than replaced. A 1973 Jud Yalkut film of a performance shows pages of Moorman's score in the introductory credits, revealing that some of the markings in its current state were not yet included.[14] The first page consists of five seconds in time, and Moorman has indicated for herself the following instructions corresponding to the lowest area: "RH [right hand] knock; buzzer; glass; chimes; sand rubber; LH [left hand] knock; coke; light bulb; get hammer; HAMMER BULB; LH pluck; RH below." This is all in addition to four "events" on the upper section of the graph: a double-stop, extreme

Ben chimes on tape, [drinking] Coke, or the somewhat cryptic "income tax." On page forty-three, Cage notates a very short, exceptionally loud extrainstrumental event, which Moorman aptly realized as a gunshot. "Kick cowbells" and "buzzer" are two possibilities that had been crossed out in favor of the more dramatic gunshot. Moorman indicated certain multiple-stops for herself using a tablature system—the top representing the nut, the bottom the fingerboard. This visual representation allowed Moorman to accurately reproduce Cage's notations without specifying the notes, thus ensuring that each performance would be unique.

The 1973 Yalkut video is in palpable contrast to Moorman's earlier performances, which were relatively stark and followed Cage's notations more closely. When listening to a complete performance from December 1964, it is not too difficult to follow along with the score, even though Moorman requires more than thirty-two minutes to complete the piece.[15] Moorman and Paik increasingly abandoned the cello in favor of actions such as drinking Coke with a throat mike (an apparent homage to Cage and his thunderous amplified drinking of water[16]), setting the cello aside in favor of performing on a bomb with a saw for a bow, or a sometimes topless Paik as a human instrument. As the human cello, a crouching Paik faced Moorman and held up along his spine an amplified cello string that produced the power and volume of a distorted guitar. They employed numerous prerecorded sounds, extended segments of rock 'n' roll records, and projections of film. In the 1973 video, Paik and Moorman telephoned Cage's home and conducted a conversation with his partner, Merce Cunningham. Paik sprayed shaving cream on both Moorman and a television. A blender was used to mix Coke, ice, and torn-up images of bikini-clad models. "I never was a cook," Moorman says, all under the auspices of a portrait of Cage looming in the background. One can almost hear him clicking his tongue. Every action in this performance was scripted—Moorman was closely following the score, though her annotations supplanted the original. When she replaced the bow with flowers, Cage's

indications of bow pressure were disregarded. When records and blenders were played for extended lengths, any silence inherent in the composition became obfuscated. A five-minute phone call ruptured Cage's temporal borders. This appears to be less a rendition of 26′ than an exploration of new modes of visual-musical performance.

Benjamin Piekut has documented the lenient attention to temporal synchrony and the increasingly lascivious nature of her performances with Paik as the primary reasons for Cage's disdain of Moorman's interpretation of 26′.[17] Cage wanted to grant performers certain liberties, and he imbued himself with authority to bestow these freedoms to individuals he considered worthy:

> This giving of freedom to the individual performer began to interest me more and more. And given to a musician like David Tudor, of course, it provided results that were extraordinarily beautiful. When this freedom is given to people who are not disciplined and who do not start—as I've said in so many of my writings—from zero (by zero I mean the absence of likes and dislikes), who are not, in other words, changed individuals, but who remain people with particular likes and dislikes, then, of course, the giving of freedom is of no interest whatsoever.[18]

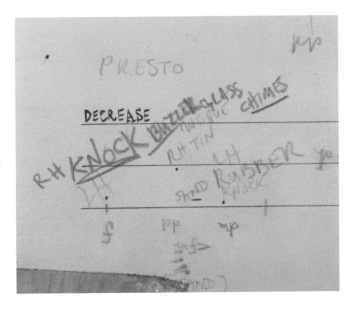

Detail showing the extrainstrumental indications of the first second in time. John Cage. Score for *26′1.1499″ for a String Player*, p. 1, with annotations by Charlotte Moorman. See top of page 34 for the full-page image.

John Cage. Score for *26′1.1499″ for a String Player*, p. 1, with annotations by Charlotte Moorman. © 1960 by Henmar Press, Inc. All rights reserved. Used by permission of the C. F. Peters Corporation. Courtesy of Charlotte Moorman Archive, Charles Deering McCormick Library of Special Collections, Northwestern University Library.

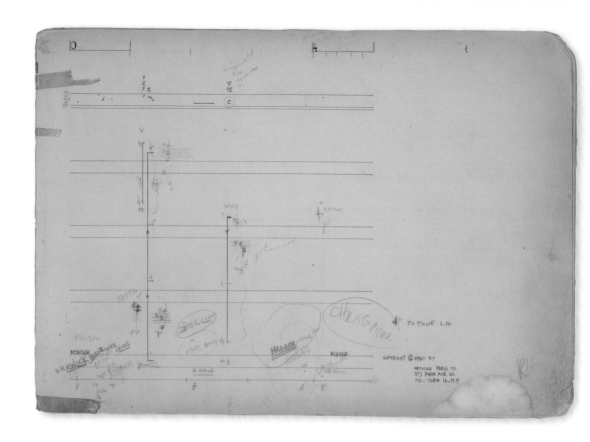

p. 12

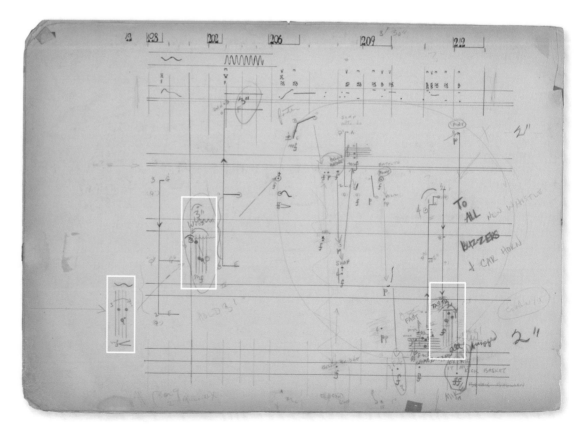

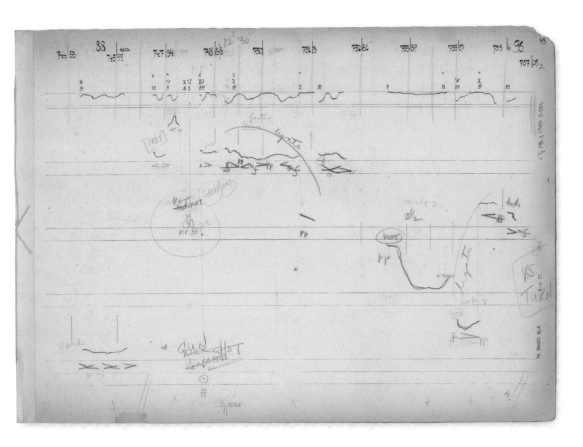

p. 43

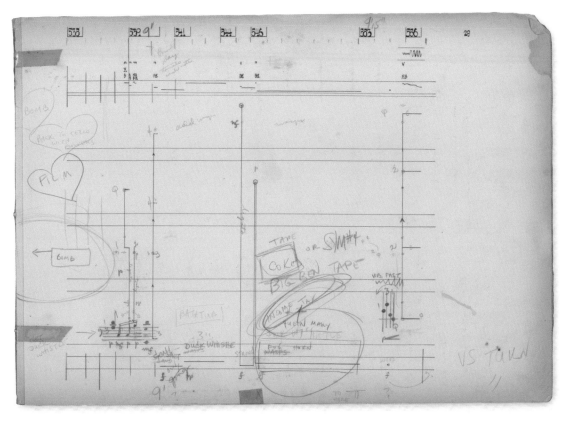

Peter Moore. Charlotte Moorman
and Nam June Paik perform
Human Cello variation as part
of John Cage's *26′1.1499″ for a
String Player*, Channel 13 Studio,
New York City, May 27, 1971.
Photograph © Barbara
Moore/Licensed by VAGA, NY.

Julius Eastman's performance of *Song Books* is another well-documented example of Cage's frustration over an interpretation with which he disagreed. For his realization of *0'00"*, Eastman chose to give a lecture in the form of a mock anatomy lesson, in which he disrobed two assistants (one male, one female), the female assistant resisting.[19] Cage hated this, and he uncharacteristically responded with visible anger and frustration.[20] While he did not have as public a reaction to Moorman's performances, statements in his personal letters reveal his negative feelings.[21]

Additionally, the composer disliked Moorman's interpretation because her performances with Paik became more about *them* and less about Cage, or *26'*. In the documentary *Topless Cellist*, Paik said of Moorman, "Charlotte is always Charlotte Moorman. Whatever she plays, whether she plays with the voice of John Cage, she is Charlotte Moorman . . . She *herself* is interesting."[22] In the graphic scores of the 1950s, a spatial awareness, in an architectural sense, forces the performers to reconceptualize their instruments, contrasting with how standard notation affects brain-body awareness. Cage attempts to displace subjectivity, as one must undo painfully learned technique to follow notation that is often sui generis. Brandon LaBelle writes, "[Cage's] de-centering, indeterminate and chance-oriented strategies open the way for multiplicity and simultaneity to confront us."[23] Instead of decentering the self, here it took over the piece. Even more so, Moorman displaced Cage as the primary artistic agent. A 1973 *New York Times* article mentions Moorman's performance of *26'* "which among other things requires the performer to prepare and eat mushrooms."[24] This is one example of how, to Cage's vexation, observers came to associate Moorman's interpretation with *the work*. While Cage's aversion to recordings is well known, this line of reasoning can be extended to individual performers.[25] There are no instructions "to cook mushrooms" found in the score (other than in Moorman's hand), yet it is reported as such in none other than the newspaper of record. Moorman's decision to do so was an apparent nod to Cage and his interest in mycophagy. There were many similar instances in the popular press. A 1968 *Daily Mirror* article reported, "The composer also requires the player to cook a six-egg omelette for the audience." The April 1969 *American Musical Digest* reported erroneously that Cage wrote *26'* specifically for Moorman.[26]

Moorman was drawn to Cage's ethos because it gave her a new and exciting platform at a time when artists such as Carolee Schneemann and Yoko Ono were exhibiting female agency on stage.[27] She eventually departed from the score's restrictions to enter a realm of visually oriented experimental performance in the spirit of Fluxus. Music as an artistic medium can be in large part visual, in both its performative and written elements, as evidenced by the score itself as a striking object. Moorman was a singular champion of both the visual and musical realms. Literary scholar turned musicologist Lawrence Kramer speaks of the musical score as a continual work in progress that determines a performance to a certain extent without dictating the precision of the result. If the musical work is a message, "its vulnerability to going astray is not a defect but a condition of possibility."[28] *26'* became a vehicle for Moorman to find her artistic voice and to embark on a remarkable career in avant-garde performance.

Notes

1. Moorman's annotated copy of the score for *26'1.1499" for a String Player* is located in the Charlotte Moorman Archive, Charles Deering McCormick Library of Special Collections, Northwestern University Library (hereafter cited as CMA).

2. For those curious, a video of my attempt can be found here: https://vimeo.com/88960450.

3. For the composer's own words on his compositional ethos, see John Cage, *Silence: Lectures and Writings* (Middletown, Conn.: Wesleyan University Press, 1961).

4. For a detailed account of Cage's aversion to Moorman's treatment of *26'*, see Benjamin Piekut, "Murder by Cello: Charlotte Moorman Meets John Cage," in *Experimentalism Otherwise* (Berkeley: University of California Press, 2011).

5. John Cage, *26'1.1499" for a String Player* (New York: Henmar Press, 1960).

6. James Pritchett, "The Development of Chance Technique in the Music of John Cage, 1950–1956" (UMI Dissertation Services, 1988), 243. These included *57½" for a String Player*; *1'5½" for a String Player*; *1'½" for a String Player*; *1'18" for a String Player*; and *1'14" for a String Player*. All were composed between May and June 1953.

7. James Pritchett, *The Music of John Cage* (Cambridge: Cambridge University Press, 1996), 92. *Music for Carillon* was Cage's first such experiment; the composer randomly folded pieces of paper, made holes at the intersections of those folds, and then placed these holes onto a graph where a score could be prepared for performance.

8. Tom Peters, CD liner notes to *26'1.1499" for a String Player and 45' for a Speaker*, Tiger Barb Records 700261251042, 2008, compact disc.

9. Creating separate realizations for performance was common performance practice for artists such as David Tudor. See, for example, David P. Miller, "Indeterminacy and Performance Practice in Cage's 'Variations,'" *American Music* 27, no. 1 (Spring 2009): 60–86, and Philip Thomas, "Understanding Indeterminate Music through Performance: Cage's Solo for Piano," *Twentieth-Century Music* 10 (March 2013): 91–113.

10. James Grier, *The Critical Editing of Music* (Cambridge: Cambridge University Press, 1996), 110, italics mine.

11. Moorman's first public performance of the work was on April 15, 1963, at the loft of Philip Corner (Piekut, "Murder by Cello," 143). For that performance, Moorman performed 162.06", roughly the first nine pages of the score. After many attempts, I managed to record the piece in 180", or eleven seconds overtime. In a letter to David Tudor, Moorman initially stated she would play the first thirty-four pages. Given the difficulty I encountered, it is quite clear to me why she managed only the first nine pages in her 1963 endeavor.

12. Moorman's annotated score, CMA.

13. "Program Notes for a Concert at Philadelphia College of Art," Friday, February 26, 1965, CMA:

   "You will hear a cymbal, garbage can top, guero, contact mike, sand, chains, shoes with sand paper glued to the soles, aluminum sheets, piepans, hammer, drum sticks, snare drum brush, rubber band, glass chimes, wood chimes, balloons, straight pin, oriental bells, cowbells, antique cymbals, woodblock, sleigh bells, beer cans, door bells, door chimes, door buzzer, pistol, light bulbs, waste basket filled with bricks, whistles: police whistle, gym whistle, toy whistle, halloween whistle and siren whistle; animal calls: duck call, crow call, squirrel call, and predator call; tape recorders, mixer, amplifiers, speakers, taped sounds (Queen Mary departure blast, Big Ben chimes, ocean waves, cat in heat, tug boat, wasps, and a bomb exploding); fire engine siren and a plate of glass (which is broken during performance) ETC - plus many new cello sounds all of which Miss Moorman plays in tandem."

14. *26'1.1499" for a String Player*, directed by Jud Yalkut (New York: Electronic Arts Intermix, 1973), DVD, in CMA.

15. Gabriele Bonomo, ed., *Cello Anthology,* disc 2, Alga Marghen, 2006, compact disc, in CMA.

16. At the request of saxophonist Joseph Jarman, who had been influenced by ideas in *Silence,* Cage agreed to a pair of concerts in Chicago's Hyde Park featuring himself on electronics with the Jarman Quartet in a performance titled *Imperfections in a Given Space.* For his part, Cage attached a contact microphone to his throat as he drank water so that it would be thunderously amplified through speakers. See Rebecca Y. Kim, "John Cage in Separate Togetherness with Jazz," *Contemporary Music Review* 31, no. 1 (February 2012): 63–89.

17. Piekut, "Murder by Cello."

18. Richard Kostelanetz, *Conversing with Cage* (New York: Limelight Editions, 1988), 67.

19. Ryan Dohoney, "John Cage, Julius Eastman, and the Homosexual Ego," in *Tomorrow Is the Question: New Directions in Experimental Music Studies*, ed. Benjamin Piekut (Ann Arbor: University of Michigan Press, 2014), 45.

20. Ibid., 39.

21. In a letter to Cage dated October 21, 1967, the double bassist Bertram Turetzky inquires as to whether anyone has performed his *59½" for a String Player*. "I've got it going nicely and on a clean day the timing is right on the nose! It's an exciting piece and joy for the too often abused ears . . . I wonder if it's

been recorded yet?" That Turetzky mentioned hitting the timing right on the nose must have excited Cage. He quickly replied, "Would you consider doing the large work for st[ring] player? The one Charlotte Moorman has been murdering all along ... I'd travel a long way to hear a proper performance" (Northwestern University Library, John Cage Correspondence, Folder 7, Box 13, Sleeve 41). In a subsequent reply letter concerning Turetzky's progress, Cage further disparages Moorman: "Glad you're planning to do Str[ing] Player piece (my enthusiasm had been somewhat dampened by what Charlotte Moorman did with it)." Cage then goes on to discuss logistics and record label contracts, moving toward a professional recording. In his reply, Turetzky treads lightly, making sure to let the composer know that his wishes will be carefully heeded: "My hope was to do a version that pleased you (anything I would send would have to pass my scrutiny) and get it from tape to record. So if you hear *some* of the piece and feel that it's good would you consider offering my work to McClure or is there another artist in mind for this Herculean task? I'm beginning another of the set soon and hope to perform them next year—with click-track and headphones if necessary. (O.K.?)" (Cage Correspondence, Folder 10, Box 6, Sleeve 2). In the end, Turetzky did indeed use a click-track to achieve accurate timing.

22. Howard Weinberg and Nam June Paik, *Topless Cellist* (London: Nexus Productions, 1995), videocassette (VHS). This half-hour documentary is readily accessible on youtube.com.

23. Brandon LaBelle, "The Uses of Cage: Walks, Silences and Other Acts of De-Centering," in *Cage and Consequences*, ed. Julia H. Schröder and Volker Straebel (Hofheim: Wolke, 2012), 254.

24. Michael T. Kaufman, "When Festival Is 10, Is It Avant-Garde?" *New York Times*, December 10, 1973, in CMA.

25. For recent scholarship on Cage and his views on recordings, see David Grubbs, *Records Ruin the Landscape* (Durham, N.C.: Duke University Press, 2014), and Elizabeth Ann Lindau, "*Goodbye 20th Century!* Sonic Youth Records John Cage's 'Number Pieces,'" in *Tomorrow Is the Question*, ed. Benjamin Piekut (Ann Arbor: University of Michigan Press, 2014).

26. *American Musical Digest*, April 1969, in CMA.

27. Carolee Schneemann, an early Fluxus participant later ousted from the group by George Maciunas, described the role of women in the group as "cunt mascots on the men's art team." Carolee Schneemann, *More Than Meat Joy: Carolee Schneemann, Complete Performance Works and Selected Writings* (Kingston, N.Y.: McPherson, 1997), 52. On her relationship with Moorman: "[We] helped each other, called for each other at times of stress, materialized in the wings year in and year out with missing scores, safety pins, tampons, telephone numbers, ambulances, food, dollars. That was the real sisterhood in the stud club" (ibid., 196).

28. Lawrence Kramer, *Interpreting Music* (Berkeley: University of California Press, 2011), 259.

Messy Bodies and Frilly Valentines: Charlotte Moorman's *Opera Sextronique*

Laura Wertheim Joseph

Charlotte Moorman was known to delight in girlish things. Her classmates at Little Rock High School remembered her as the only senior they knew who wore dark lipstick and owned a "risqué" dress.[1] A number of years before earning the moniker the Topless Cellist, she was given the title of Miss City Beautiful, a distinction bestowed on the winner of a beauty pageant held in conjunction with Little Rock's annual beautification campaign. A photograph of Moorman as beauty queen—perched demurely on the hood of a car with a tiara resplendent on her head and a bouquet of flowers splayed across her lap—was the centerpiece of *Room for Charlotte Moorman*, an elegiac installation Nam June Paik created in her honor at the Venice Biennale in 1993. Framing this photograph of a nineteen-year-old Moorman was an arrangement of her formal evening gowns on hangers, including a couture Balenciaga that she had purchased from drag queen and Marlene Dietrich impersonator Alexis Delgado in 1982.[2] These were gowns Moorman loved to wear, and donning formal attire was one of several vestiges of classical musical performance that Moorman maintained after she strayed from her career as a traditional cellist and became known by Edgard

Varèse's description of her as the Joan of Arc of New Music.

Her proclivity for the feminine did not diminish with illness. Even "when she was in the hospital, dying, she was still grabbing for her make-up and hairspray," Barbara Moore recollected in an interview with Gisela Gronemeyer.[3] And she "was big on hearts," Andrew Gurian noted in a video tribute made after her death in 1991.[4] He would certainly know. As the coadministrator of her estate, he was responsible for sorting through hundreds of pieces of

Charlotte Moorman uses a makeshift ladies' room as her dressing room before performing Nam June Paik's *Opera Sextronique*, February 9, 1967, New York City. Photograph by Hy Rothman/ © *New York Daily News* via Getty Images.

feminist contemporaries voiced direct criticisms, which I address shortly, of the ways in which she seemed to embrace signifiers of stereotypical femininity. Yet, as the following statement that feminist artist Martha Rosler wrote in denunciation of Nam June Paik suggests, the disapproval of other feminists who were aware of Moorman's work can often be inferred.[6] Rosler asserts:

> And—oh yes!—he is a man. The hero stands up for masculine mastery and bows to patriarchy. . .The thread of [Paik's] work includes the fetishization of a female body as an instrument that plays itself, and the complementary thread of homage to other famous male artist-magicians or seers (quintessentially, [John] Cage).[7]

Rosler does not bother to mention Moorman by name but rather tacitly implicates her in Paik's masculinist project, as a female body "that plays itself." Although not strictly articulated in response to Moorman's love of cosmetics, evening gowns, or valentines, Rosler's text takes issue with her docility more generally, which feminists of the era argued to be related to expectations not only about conventional feminine behavior but also conventional feminine dress.

To give a broader sense of how seventies-era feminist activists and artists expressed leeriness toward the feminine, if not Moorman's embrace of it specifically, I give the examples of two barometric events in the history of postwar feminism that took place on opposite coasts. First, in 1968, as the feminist movement was gaining momentum, a group of women organized a demonstration against the Miss America Pageant in Atlantic City, New Jersey, during which they threw bras, curling irons, issues of *Ladies' Home Journal*, and other emblems of femininity into a "freedom trash can."[8] In her biography *Topless Cellist*, Joan Rothfuss notes that it was probably not by accident that just after this event, which was one of the first feminist protests to generate national media attention,[9] Moorman started modeling Nam June Paik's *TV Bra for Living Sculpture* around the world.[10]

correspondence, many of which Moorman marked with heart shapes and signed with love. It should not come as a surprise, then, that Valentine's Day was her favorite holiday. But if the dates on her valentines are any indication, she did not confine observance to the day itself.

Moorman's career as an avant-garde cellist coincided with the emergence of what has often been described as "second-wave feminism" in the United States, a complex and heterogeneous movement best known for having developed in California and New York but which rose up in cities across the nation, including Minneapolis and Chicago.[5] To my knowledge, only a handful of Moorman's seventies-era

Nam June Paik. *Room for Charlotte Moorman*, installed in the German Pavilion at the 45th Venice Biennale, 1993. Photograph © Roman Mensing.

Second, several years later, in 1971, the Jack Glenn Gallery placed two consecutive full-page ads in *Artforum* advertising an exhibition of Judy Chicago's work at California State College at Fullerton, Orange County, in Los Angeles. The first featured a head shot of Chicago wearing a headband and dark glasses with a caption that read, "Judy Gerowitz hereby divests herself of all names imposed upon her through male social dominance and freely chooses her own name: Judy Chicago."[11] In the second, Chicago stands with her head cocked and her arms extended out from her body, resting them casually on the ropes of a boxing rink. She wears laced-up black boots, nylon sports shorts, a sweatshirt with "Judy Chicago" printed on the front, boxing gloves, and an intimidating look on her face. An icon of seventies-era feminism, Chicago is famous for her vaginal imagery and the visual celebration of femininity, but ironically

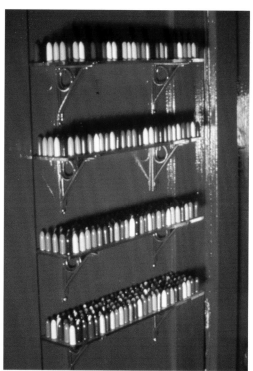

JUDY CHICAGO Exhibition, Cal State Fullerton, Oct. 23 - Nov. 25
Preview 6 - 8 PM, Oct. 23, Faculty Club, Cal State Fullerton
Manager, Jack Glenn Gallery, 2831 E. Coast Highway, Corona Del Mar, Calif. 92625

ABOVE
Judy Chicago. *Boxing Ring Ad*, announcement in *Artforum* for Jack Glenn Gallery, 1970. Photograph by Jerry McMillan. Courtesy of Through the Flower Archives, Penn State University Archives.

RIGHT
Camille Grey. *Lipstick Bathroom* from *Womanhouse*, 1972. Courtesy of Through the Flower Archives, Penn State University Archives.

she began her career by making overt displays of machismo. Art historians often describe the West Coast feminist movement within which Chicago was a central figure as a movement that sought to valorize and redeem those images, materials, and processes that had historically been dismissed as "feminine." Yet, this assertion has at times been based on a misreading of West Coast feminist projects, including one of the most famous, *Womanhouse*, which Chicago worked with Miriam Schapiro and her students of the Feminist Art Program at California Institute of the Arts to create. Although the feminist art installation and performance space made use of feminized materials such as crochet, bras, lipstick, high heels, and aprons, these objects were not celebrated so much as they were suggested to have an oppressive and subjugating effect on women. In Camille Grey's *Lipstick Bathroom*, for example, the artist painted every surface in the room bright red, including not just the walls, ceiling, mirror, and lightbulbs, but also the stockings, bras, panties, and towels that hung from them. Jane F. Gerhard writes that the wall, on which hung two hundred tubes of lipstick, "drew the viewer into the relentless ritual of face painting." She describes the room's overall effect as alternating between "claustrophobia and horror."[12] These two examples—one of which took place on the East Coast when the feminist movement was beginning to take the national stage, and the other of which took place on the West Coast when the movement was at the height of its activity and proliferations—are suggestive of the consistent basis on which feminist artists and activists would have taken issue with Moorman's performance of seemingly stereotypical femininity.

We might expect, then, for Carolee Schneemann—who is widely acknowledged within histories of the period for having pioneered tactics of feminist performance art in the early sixties, before feminism had cohered into a movement—to be one such feminist. But like Moorman, Schneemann had a habit of writing valentines and delighting in the feminine. In fact, a number of these valentines Schneemann addressed to Moorman, with whom she had a long-standing friendship. It is via their relationship that I introduce a famous episode in Moorman's career and, ultimately, that I suggest a means of recalibrating Moorman's relationship to the feminist narratives with which I have begun.

On February 14, 1967, Schneemann wrote a valentine to psychiatrist Joseph Berke. She addressed him "Dear Valentine Mine," but rather than go on to discuss the amorous topics we might expect to follow such a greeting, she reported instead on events that had taken place a few days prior at the now-demolished Wurlitzer Building at 125 41st Street in New York. "Here," she wrote to Berke, who was working in London, "all being arrested." She went on to explain:

> —not development—sequential actions/activities . . . just the FUZZ heavy in 'plainclothes'—long tweed coats grabbing *before* the move is made . . . ; jumping up on the stage in the midst of most tender, courageous and witty performance of Charlotte Moorman (long formal skirt, bare-breasted, playing cello and Paik at the piano, gentle, twitching, incomparable).[13]

In language as evocative as it is idiosyncratic, Schneemann brings to mind an evening that did not transpire according to plan or logical sequence, but rather broke down into a chaotic flurry. "Bumping bodies . . . all jelly and cloudy, milling on stage,"[14] resulted in plainclothesmen hauling Moorman off to the Midtown South precinct police station at 375 West 35th Street.[15] At the police station, she was fingerprinted and then transferred to the Manhattan Detention Complex, where she spent the night, by her accounts, with a colorful and nefarious cast of inmates that included a drug addict, a prostitute, and a murderer.[16]

The piece Moorman was in the midst of performing was Nam June Paik's *Opera Sextronique*, and the arrest that cut her performance short became one of the most famous episodes in her eventful career. Although the ways in which her performance and subsequent arrest influenced the trajectory of her career are complex, these events nevertheless seem to have been defining ones for her. It was not just that she got stuck with what Rothfuss aptly describes as a "ludicrous and reductive" nickname, "Topless Cellist."[17] After her death, her lawyer Jerald Ordover said in an interview that subsequent to having made a splash as the Topless Cellist in the New York City papers, the Board of Education removed her name from the list of classical musicians approved by the state to tour New York City schools.[18] As there is no evidence to suggest that she ever did perform in the New York City schools, this was likely a dramatization passed on to him directly from Moorman. She had a tendency to emphasize the extent to which she had

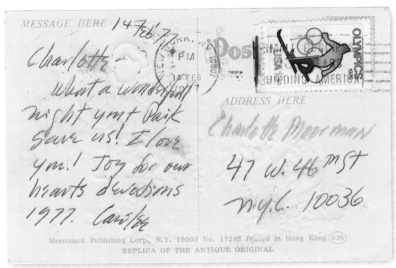

Valentine from Carolee Schneemann to Charlotte Moorman, February 14, 1977. Written after *From Jail to Jungle*, an evening of performances held in commemoration of the tenth anniversary of Moorman's arrest for *Opera Sextronique,* Carnegie Hall, February 10, 1977. Courtesy of Charlotte Moorman Archive, Charles Deering McCormick Library of Special Collections, Northwestern University Library.

sacrificed paid classical music engagements in the service of her avant-garde music, even when such assertions were not always, or at least not clearly, grounded in fact.[19] Yet, what her dramatization suggests is that Moorman identified this moment in her career to be one with far-reaching consequences. And for whatever confluence of reasons, she did not perform much classical work after her arrest.

Charlotte Moorman arrested at the performance of Nam June Paik's *Opera Sextronique,* February 9, 1967, New York City. Photograph by Fred McDarrah. © New York Getty Images.

What might have been a crossroad for Moorman is, for me, an entry point into several inquiries that drive this essay. On the one hand, it is clear, for reasons I've discussed, why the terms of Moorman's avant-garde artistic practice were in tension with the concerns of her seventies-era feminist contemporaries and why, except for Schneemann, New York–based feminist artists were not among those who spoke out against her arrest.[20] On the other hand, her performance bears hallmarks of feminist performance art (namely, a disruption of the structures and assumptions of conventional art forms by means of actions performed by women with their politically charged bodies). Therefore, the question of why her landmark performance was bypassed by Moorman's feminist contemporaries and neglected by subsequent scholars of feminism is one, I argue, that merits further consideration. This question ultimately gives way to another: what insights does feminist thought bring to reading Moorman's performance of *Opera Sextronique*?

To be clear, the question is not whether Moorman identified with any of the feminist ideas that were percolating around her. If this were the heart of my inquiry, this essay would be decidedly short and unrevealing. The extent to which Moorman articulated feminist attitudes was limited, Schneemann explained in a recent interview, to occasional expressions of dismay at the fact that male musicians secured better positions and earned higher salaries than their female counterparts.[21] Moorman made the kind of remark to which Schneemann referred in a 1962 interview for an article in the *Arkansas Democrat*. She stopped short of saying that symphony orchestras demonstrated prejudice against women members and suggested instead that "prejudice is perhaps not the right word. . . . It seems to be a tradition to hire men rather than women players. But women will break through."[22]

In 1963, shortly after Moorman gave this statement, the passage of the Equal Pay Act made it illegal to pay women less than men for the same work, and, in 1964, Title VII of the Civil Rights Act added "sex" to the categories protected by federal law from

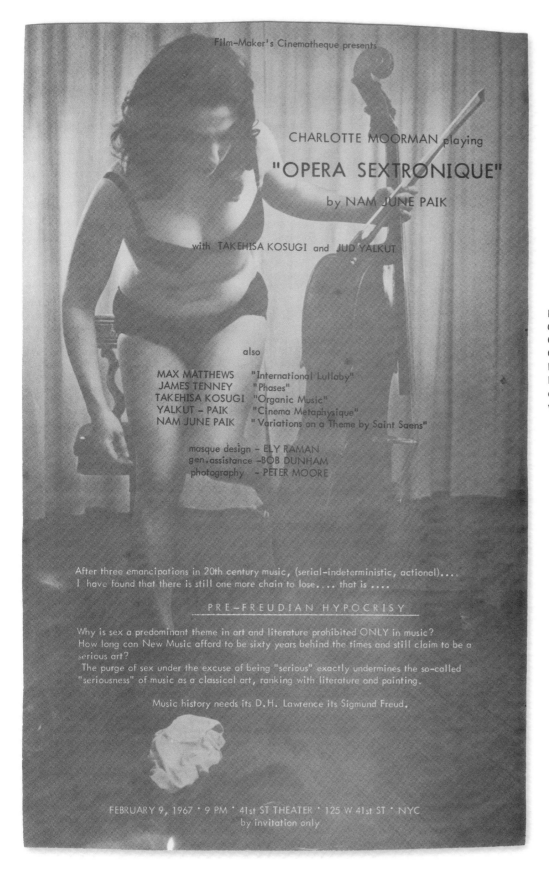

Poster for Nam June Paik's *Opera Sextronique*, New York City, February 9, 1967. Courtesy of Charlotte Moorman Archive, Charles Deering McCormick Library of Special Collections, Northwestern University Library.

employment discrimination.[23] Moorman's suggestion of a need for employment equality suggests that she—like many women in the post–World War II United States—was influenced by arguments raised by women's rights advocates. But she went no further than the occasional comment to advance such causes.

It was hardly because of Moorman's lack of participation in feminist debates and protests, however, that second-wave feminist Andrea Dworkin called Moorman a "harlot" and "declared her career . . . a process of extended rape."[24] As I have suggested, it was Moorman's maintenance of the conventions of Southern femininity, as well as the way in which she deferred to male figures of authority within the avant-garde while capitalizing upon the sexual connotations of her instrument, that incited such criticism. Even Fluxus artist Alison Knowles—a frequent participant in Moorman's (nearly) annual avant-garde festivals—expressed a mix of pity and bafflement at what she perceived to be Moorman's subservience and infantilism. These were impressions Knowles shared with Gronemeyer upon Moorman's death:

> She was always this girl from Arkansas, this wonderful child in a dress, holding flowers—so when someone tells her to take off her clothes, she takes off her clothes, and when someone tells her to go naked into the water, and she'll do it [*sic*]. It was thoughtless. . . . And I find that at a certain point for her to redo those pieces of Paik again and again was a bit sad, or maybe she would just do it because it was the work she was known for.[25]

The implications of these criticisms are contradictory: together they suggest that Moorman was at once a victim and an instigator of sexually driven manipulation. But the consequences have effectively been the same: historians of art and feminism alike have—with one or two very notable exceptions—deemed Moorman and her work unworthy of serious consideration.[26]

By equal measure, evocations of Moorman as promiscuous subject *and* mindless object work to obfuscate the performative strategies through which she navigated the sexual economy of the sixties and seventies avant-garde art scene. Ultimately, I argue that Moorman hovers between two equally credible personas: that of the virtuoso and that of the artist's plaything, refusing to fully associate or disassociate from either. The resulting dissonance produces a rupture that exposes conservative sexual politics that lingered in the art world after the war. As I have suggested, it is via Schneemann—an artist who also navigated that economy, and whose importance in the development of feminist performance strategies is widely acknowledged—that I begin to suggest the strategic possibilities of Moorman's refusal to resolve the tension between decisive artist and manipulated object.

When Bruce McPherson started to organize *More Than Meat Joy*, a midcareer catalog survey of Schneemann's performances and selected writings, he wrote to Moorman requesting that she contribute to the text. Schneemann added a handwritten message to McPherson's typewritten letter. She scrawled:

> Whatever comes to mind—not too long—touching on our long and marvelous shared ventures. Perhaps the story of your initial nudity when I so loosely pinned a sheet around you for the balcony ascent? Whatever you think of! Much love, C.[27]

The "initial nudity" to which Schneemann makes reference occurred at the U.S. premiere of Karlheinz Stockhausen's *Originale*. Nam June Paik actually claimed to have been the first to convince Moorman to appear seminude in the service of his desire to advance music by means of infiltrating it with sex. (In Paris in 1965, she wore cellophane in lieu of a gown for a performance of his composition *Variations on a Theme by Saint-Saëns*).[28] But the year before, at Schneemann's suggestion, Moorman appeared wrapped in sheer gauze during one of the evenings she played the "String Player" in the *Originale* cast.[29] In interviews, Moorman also traced her first experimentation with nudity back to when she "played herself" for a duration indicated by Stockhausen's score. Rather than credit Schneemann for her wardrobe adaptations, however, she reported that it had been Allan Kaprow, director of the U.S. production, who had made the suggestion in an effort to "defeminize" her.[30] Moorman liked to conclude the anecdote by noting how (contrary to expectations!) the sheer fabric turned out to accentuate, rather than divert attention from, her feminine bodily features.

To Schneemann's dismay, this would not be the only occasion Moorman would credit Kaprow for a performance element for which Schneemann had been responsible. The following year, at Moorman's third annual avant-garde festival in 1965, Schneemann directed her own version of Kaprow's happening, *Push and Pull*.[31] According to the piece's instructions, she invited members of the audience to exit Judson Hall and to go out to 57th Street in search of soft materials to use in the making of a mixed-media environment. Schneemann has described the events that followed as a "rampage" during which participants ripped hubcaps from cars, tore street signs from metal posts, dragged bins filled with trash into the installation space, shattered windows, and attracted the attention of the police.[32] To avoid detainment or arrest, Schneemann, along with several other avant-garde festival participants, escaped through a back entrance and jumped in a taxi.[33]

A number of years later, during an interview with Gerald Marzorati for *SoHo News*, Moorman reminisced about the chaotic events of that day, but she claimed it had been Kaprow, not Schneemann, who had been responsible for "the mayhem."[34] After reading the interview, Schneemann wrote a letter to Moorman in which she expressed a number of frustrations and concerns. She admitted that at the time of the event she had been afraid "that if something special developed from [her] direction of *Push and Pull*, it would directly accrue to Allan—more known, respected, male." She argued that by crediting Kaprow with the production, Moorman contributed to what Schneemann described as the "many distortions of our recent history [which] have to do

with old notions of power—individualistic, masculine-heroic traditions by which power accrues to those with power." Schneemann wanted to be sure that Moorman remembered the circumstances clearly: *Push and Pull* was a *collaboration* between herself and Moorman, made possible by the avant-garde festival that *Moorman* had worked to organize.[35]

Carolee Schneemann performs *Eye Body: 36 Transformative Actions for Camera*, 1963. Photograph by Erró © Carolee Schneemann / Artists Rights Society (ARS), New York.

It is both the kinships *and* tensions between Schneemann and Moorman that help give critical structure to Moorman's dismissal on feminist grounds, as well as enable me to establish alternative tactics for reading Moorman's controversial performance of *Opera Sextronique*, to which we will soon return. While Moorman was dubbed the Joan of Arc of New Music, Schneemann has argued that she served only as a "cunt mascot" for the male-dominated movements of Fluxus and Happenings.[36] It is not by accident that the self-appointed father of Fluxus, George Maciunas, excommunicated Schneemann from the Fluxus collective upon her performance of *Eye Body* in 1963. Maciunas deemed the work "too 'messy' for inclusion" in his "Art Stud Club."[37] Historically speaking, Moorman also has significant associations with Fluxus, but she was ejected from the official group even more quickly than Schneemann. In fact, Rothfuss writes that her dismissal was "almost immediate."[38] Maciunas likely objected to

Moorman's work on the same grounds as those on which he had objected to Schneemann's. But he was better known for having disliked Moorman's inclusive—or, to his mind, nondiscriminating—approach to festival organization and her "poaching" of *his* Fluxus artists.[39]

Maciunas's rejection of *Eye Body* warrants further discussion and bears relevance to our subsequent discussions of *Opera Sextronique*. What he implies, but does not state directly, is that "messy" is a stand-in for "sexed" and "bodily." For what Schneemann introduced to her work in *Eye Body* was her own naked body, which she made an integral component of her painting construction by marking it with traditional artmaking materials, including paint, grease, and chalk.[40] The naked female body has a ubiquitous rather than an anomalous presence within the history of art. What is different about Schneemann's *Eye Body* is that in it she operates both as object of the gaze (body) *and* the maker of the image (I/eye), thereby disrupting the duality between male/artist/subject/mind and female/object/body that has long informed Western art making and interpretation. Not only does Schneemann's project make evident the way in which subjectivity and objectivity are "performative rather than fixed,"[41] it also suggests the way in which subjectivity is never self-contained and is always contingent, in flux, and, yes, *messy*. Such insights enabled radical questioning of the disinterested, coherent, and discrete male subject/seer and were thus crucially important to the art-based feminist movement that cohered later in the sixties.

Schneemann's position within the history of feminism and postwar art is now secure[42]—thanks not only to Schneemann's own writings but also to the writings of feminist scholars, including Lucy Lippard, Kristine Stiles, Amelia Jones, Rebecca Schneider, and Jane Blocker. But because Schneemann made her naked body the site of her work, it was initially dismissed as "self-indulgent exhibitionism, intended only to stimulate men."[43] As Lippard, Schneider, and Jones, among others, have noted, male artists have for centuries used the naked female body in their art without resulting in the questioning of their motives or neutrality, but female artists who have used their own bodies in their work have often been met with accusations of narcissism.[44] In fact, the Criminal Court judge who presided over the trial that followed Moorman's arrest during her performance of *Opera Sextronique* justified his guilty sentence with just such an accusation.[45]

While both Paik and Moorman had been arrested on the evening of February 9, at their arraignment the next morning the judge dismissed all charges against Paik on account of the fact that he claimed that a musical composition could not be pornographic.[46] Moorman, on the other hand, was charged with indecent exposure under Section 1140 of the New York State Penal Law, but the standards for defining obscenity upon which she was judged were based on precedent set by the landmark U.S. Supreme Court ruling *Roth v. United States* (1957). According to *Roth*, for something to be deemed criminally obscene, and thus be unprotected by the First Amendment, it must be "utterly without social importance," and "the average person, applying contemporary community standards," must find that "the dominant theme of the material taken as a whole appeals to prurient interest."[47]

When applied specifically to works of visual art, not only does this resolution assume clear and easy distinctions between art and pornography (distinctions that are altogether more blurry in the history of art),[48] it also suggests, relatedly, that sexually charged or controversial subject matter is inappropriate for art. According to the *Roth* obscenity rule, social importance and prurience are assumed to be mutually exclusive, and as a result the prosecution in Moorman's case set out to prove that Moorman's seminude performance was intended to arouse lustful desires in her audience, which would, according to the test, negate the possibility of it also having social importance.

During his direct examination of the arresting officer, Michael Mandillo, prosecutor Gino Gallina posed a number of questions through which he insinuated Moorman's seductive intentions. First, these sexual innuendos came in the form of a series of questions about the sequence of actions during the first aria. Officer Mandillo testified that he had struggled to make out exactly what was happening in the darkened theater (to which he had gained entrance without invitation). He ascertained that the piece had commenced, however, when it seemed that Moorman had entered the stage wearing an "electric bikini" of sorts—three triangles of lights,[49] which he assumed, due to their triangulated positioning, covered her breasts and crotch.

> PROSECUTOR: What was the light doing?
>
> WITNESS: They were [*sic*] on and off, as she played.
>
> PROSECUTOR: In other words, winking, sort of?
>
> WITNESS: Yes.[50]

Via remote control, Paik controlled the "suggestive" flashing lights to which Mandillo refers in his testimony, while Moorman walked, to the rhythm of a slowly beating gong,[51] to the center of the stage. Still in darkness, she must have taken her seat, Mandillo explained, before she began to play a composition on her cello. The officer reported that the piece she performed—French operatic composer Jules Massenet's *Élégie*—was one with which he was unfamiliar. This time, it was Judge Milton Shalleck who posed follow-up questions to the witness:

> COURT: She played cello?
>
> WITNESS: Yes.
>
> COURT: Where did she put the cello?
>
> WITNESS: Between her legs, your Honor.
>
> COURT: You say there was light playing on her vagina as she played the cello?[52]

Officer Mandillo replied that, indeed, "the cello was tilted in such a way," that the twinkling lights between her legs were visible to him. In effect, the combined suggestion of

Peter Moore. Charlotte Moorman in the "electric bikini" during Aria 1 of Nam June Paik's *Opera Sextronique*, New York City, February 9, 1967. Photograph © Barbara Moore / Licensed by VAGA, NY.

this testimony was that Moorman's "vagina" was winking, wantonly, at the members of her audience. The insinuations continued during discussions of the second aria, which followed the first after a brief intermission.

For the second act, Moorman took her seat topless, wearing a formal floor-length black skirt on the bottom. After Paik ran a three-minute cassette tape of computer-generated electronic music by Max Mathews,[53] Moorman performed a variation of Johannes Brahms's sweet bedtime lullaby. As she played, she grabbed various objects from a suitcase propped open on a chair beside her, including a gas mask, sunglasses, a baseball cap, a steel military helmet, and two small propellers that functioned as pasties. Moorman supplemented her concert attire with these props, while also intermittently replacing her conventional bow with substitutions that included a bouquet of carnations, a violin, and a yardstick. In the courtroom, questions ensued about the size of her cello and how widely it required her to spread her legs.[54]

As required by the *Roth* standard, Moorman's defense attorney, Ernst Rosenberger, attempted to discredit the prosecution's claims that Moorman's performance "appealed to prurient interests" by arguing that *Opera Sextronique* had "redeeming social value." Rosenberger's direct

examination of Moorman established not only that had she been formally educated and classically trained but also that she approached her mixed-media work with the same seriousness of purpose as classical musicians were thought to approach traditional musical scores.[55] A reenactment of Moorman's performances of arias one and two—which Jud Yalkut filmed for use in the trial—was intended to give visual evidence of Moorman's concentrated attention to Paik's score.[56] If her primary concern was to adhere to Paik's notations, by logical deduction, it could not also be to stir arousal in her audience. Put another way, if she was a mere vehicle for expression of Paik's vision,

she could not also be, according to the prevailing subject/object divides we have discussed, an agent of sexual provocation.

Because the footage captured a reenactment of the performance for which Moorman stood trial, and not the performance itself, Judge Shalleck did not permit the video to be entered into evidence.[57] Instead, Moorman was left to testify to the importance of following Paik's words and musical notations, several of which she clarified for the judge. The word "green" written above a musical staff in the second aria's score, for example, served as an indication for Moorman to put on a green mask, she explained.[58]

Charlotte Moorman performs Aria 2 of Nam June Paik's *Opera Sextronique,* New York City, February 9, 1967. Photograph by Hy Rothman. © *New York Daily News* via Getty Images.

Rosenberger called a number of "expert" critics to the stand who because of their specialized and rarefied knowledge, he argued, could speak to the social value of Moorman's work as art. Much to District Attorney Gallina's satisfaction, *Village Voice* critic Carman Moore testified, upon cross-examination, that he did believe Moorman's performance served to call into question "community" standards of sexuality and dress. Art critic for the *World Journal Tribune* John Gruen conceded to Gallina that the performance's primary action lay in directing attention to Moorman's "erotic zones."[59]

David Bourdon, assistant editor at *Life*, and Jack Kroll, senior editor of *Newsweek*, were, for the most part, more effective in their attempts to strip Moorman's performance of any sexual charge. Both did so by situating Moorman within a traditional art historical canon. Bourdon drew similarities between Moorman's work and the work of Dadaists of the 1920s, although the judge noted that he was unfamiliar with any such movement. Kroll asserted that he no more questioned the social value of Moorman's seminudity in *Opera Sextronique* than he questioned the social value of a Rembrandt painting in which a nude woman was pictured.[60] To Kroll, both were simply works of art, objects, to which he "as a professional art critic [was] called upon to decide [whether or not they] present[ed] an interesting *formal* pattern [to which] one could react" [emphasis added].[61] Kroll described Moorman as "a kind of living statue" and suggested a comparison between her seminude body and the marbles and bronzes of Rodin.[62] Here, Kroll performs the role of the critic Schneemann called into question in *Eye Body*, the critic whose mastering gaze upon feminized and sexualized objects of art is, according to long-standing art historical myth, disinterested and cerebral, not desirous and bodily. In other words, he was performing being a man who was not aroused by Moorman by virtue of his more sophisticated knowledge of art. Yet this disinterest was something with which Gallina contended during his cross-examination.

Despite Gallina's efforts, Kroll maintained over the course of most of the questioning that Moorman's naked body functioned just as an art object would. He even asserted that he hardly registered the fact that it was a human being sustaining the art object until the second act.[63] When Gallina asked, hypothetically, if Moorman's "derrière" had been exposed, would Kroll have pulled someone in front of him away in order to see it, Kroll responded that yes, he would have, "simply because it was a part of the whole thing." Gallina followed up for clarification: "Not because you're a man?" Kroll gave a definitive reply: "No."[64] Yet, as Gallina pushed Kroll to articulate the difference between Moorman's performance and burlesque, Kroll conceded to the fact that the difference seemed to be one of intent.[65] This conceit provided the district attorney an opportunity to suggest that if the only difference between Moorman's performance and a burlesque is intent, then the *effect* might nonetheless be the same: the arousal of *some viewers*. When Kroll replied that he did not believe that the audience members would have been aroused in the way Gallina suggested, Gallina retorted: "You don't think members in Miss Moorman's audience would have been aroused in an obscene way, at all, while the same amount of taking it off in a burlesque situation would probably so [*sic*] have aroused the audience?"[66] Although at first, Kroll declined to speculate, upon being pressed by the judge, who asked him if he had really felt nothing physical in response to Moorman's performance, Kroll conceded: "Perhaps I could have; there's no need for me to confess this; I was physically aroused by Miss Moorman that night. It might be fifteen years [ago] that I was in the same predicament that I was physically attracted to [the burlesque stripteaser] Lili St. Cyr, and had the same reaction."[67] Although this statement was a coup for the prosecution, Kroll's confession was followed by his attempt to reestablish his argument in a subsequent and somewhat cryptic statement in which he noted, "Needless to say, I couldn't consider myself a human being, other than a professional art critic, it is not true at all, I was not having the same feeling."[68] Although, via the transcription alone, it is difficult to say with certainty on what distinction Kroll is insisting here, it seems to be between his feelings as a man and his feelings as a professional art critic. Perhaps, in this statement, he is attempting to retain the sanctity of his disinterested gaze as an art "expert" while conceding that as a man he was subject to arousals. Crucially, though, for the prosecution, Kroll had already counted himself among *those viewers* for whom Moorman's performance had appealed to prurient interests and thus, according to the law, disallowed the possibility that it could also have social importance.

It should perhaps not come as a surprise, then, that Judge Shalleck did not buy the arguments that placed Moorman on a continuum of beautiful female nudes that have spanned the history of Western art. In his statement of more than one hundred thousand words, he noted that he was familiar with the fact that "the pristine beauty of human female breasts had been immortalized by painters and sculptors and writers of poetry and prose," but that in all these representations he had never seen "a nude or topless cellist in the *act* of playing that instrument" [emphasis added].[69] Clearly, the judge found no issue with the tradition of female nudity within the history of art (within which there are numerous examples of seminude and nude female string players to be found). The problem with Moorman's nudity was rather that it was not "pristinely" confined to objecthood. Instead, Moorman's laboring body messily traversed the space between subjectivity and objectivity, while also confusing other heavily policed but nebulous boundaries, including that between art and pornography.

In his decision, Judge Shalleck asks: "What was the purpose of the exhibition here? Was [it] playing the cello with bizarre nudity for self-aggrandizement with consequent later economic benefit for the purpose of enticement?"[70] This question seems to express Shalleck's hope that he had resolved the crisis of recognition that Moorman inaugurated by unveiling her as a calculating and salacious narcissist. He concluded that

Moorman's work was "born not of a desire to express art, but [rather] to get the vernacular 'sucker' to come and be aroused."[71] As an esteemed and erudite representative of the law, Judge Shalleck asserted that he was no such "sucker."

Although it is clear why Moorman's performance of *Opera Sextronique* poses a threat to the prevailing norms underlying art criticism and history, I want to return, briefly, to the question of why Moorman has not found her place within the history of feminist art. While feminist body art of the era was derided for exhibiting no skill or artistry, oxymoronically, Moorman was criticized by those very feminists because, in her performances, she displays both her body *and* her virtuosity. It seems that Moorman claimed a kind of agency in her labor and virtuosity while also claiming a kind of agency in her performance of femininity by exploiting its quality of masquerade. It is the tension between these two strategies, the way in which they were discordant and rubbed up against each other, that makes Moorman's body—both as laboring and as striking a pose—so vexing to read.

Moorman's concentrated demeanor and her ability to play classical cello have often been dismissed as mere indicators of her submission to gendered hierarchies of traditional music, while her displays of femininity have been assumed to work only in the service of maintaining heterosexual and patriarchal norms. Postcolonial feminist Saba Mahmood argues that Western feminists have tended to overlook the fact that certain strategies of dissent are made possible only by means of what we have traditionally understood to be subordination. She gives the example of a virtuoso pianist who

submits herself to the often painful regime of disciplinary practice, as well as to the hierarchical structures of apprenticeship, in order to acquire the ability—the requisite agency— to play an instrument with mastery. Importantly, her agency is predicated upon her ability to be taught, a condition classically referred to as "docility."[72]

Jim McWilliams. Promotional flyer for *Mixed Media Opera*, 1968. The event was organized to raise funds for Charlotte Moorman's *Opera Sextronique*–related legal fees. Courtesy of Charlotte Moorman Archive, Charles Deering McCormick Library of Special Collections, Northwestern University Library.

Within the traditional concert convention to which Mahmood refers, feminine dress and behavior are completely naturalized elements of a professional female cellist's "repertoire," as is her relationship with the cello itself. In *Opera Sextronique* Moorman makes discernable reference to these conventions—in the trial she emphasizes to the court that her ensembles for both arias should be referred to as concert attire. But as prosecutor Gallina suspected, and witness for the defense Carman Moore confirmed, she also calls into question the naturalization of such musical conventions, not only via her "electric bikini" and toplessness but also via masks and props that make explicit reference to masquerade and performativity. Moorman thus calls attention to the erasure and aestheticizing of the labor of traditional female musicians.

In her discussion of Moore's testimony in *An Artist in the Courtroom*, Moorman offers a point of clarification on which I will conclude. She claims that the intention of her performance was not, as Moore had suggested, to flaunt disregard for society's mores;[73] it was rather to "[satirize] that which is sham and hypocritical." She then goes on to quote him directly: "the juxtaposition of ironies is important to the new [performative] approach," and "these points of irony create . . . artistic tension."[74] Such tensions—between subjectivity and objectivity, virtuoso and plaything, Brahms and bikinis, art and pornography—create messiness that historians are often inclined to straighten up. Instead, I suggest that we linger in the undecidability of those "bumping bodies . . . all jelly and cloudy, milling on stage."[75]

Notes

1. Joann Martin and Julianne Honey in *Topless Cellist: Charlotte Moorman*, directed by Nam June Paik and Howard Weinberg (New York, N.Y.: Electronic Arts Intermix, 1995), videocassette (VHS).

2. Delgado was known also by his stage name, Alexis Bassini. See Gayle M. Skluzacek, *The Estate of Charlotte Moorman: Personal Property Estate Appraisal* (New York: Abigail Hartmann Associates, 1993), 44.

3. Gisela Gronemeyer, "Seriousness and Dedication: The American Avant-Garde Cellist Charlotte Moorman," *Charlotte Moorman: Cello Anthology* (Milan: Alga Marghen, 2006), n.p.

4. Andrew Gurian in *Topless Cellist: Charlotte Moorman*.

5. For a discussion of the ways in which discourses on seventies-era feminism have tended to overlook feminist activity outside of New York and California, see Joanna Inglot, *WARM: A Feminist Art Collective in Minnesota* (Minneapolis: Weisman Art Museum and University of Minnesota Press, 2007).

6. As Joan Rothfuss notes in *Topless Cellist: The Improbable Life of Charlotte Moorman* (Cambridge, Mass.: MIT Press, 2014), 203, the story of Moorman's arrest for nudity in Nam June Paik's *Opera Sextronique* was sensationally but still only briefly featured in New York City papers. "During the spring of 1967, soldiers were dying every day in Vietnam, and the New Left was promoting sedition in protest of the escalating war," Rothfuss writes. The first all-female artists'

cooperative in the United States, A.I.R. (Artists in Residence), opened in New York in 1972 and gives an indication that although the women's movement was gaining momentum in the late sixties, the establishment of formal feminist institutions in the New York art world happened several years after Moorman's arrest. It nevertheless seems safe to assume that many women who participated in the feminist movement, at least in New York, would have been aware of her work and especially of her collaborations with Nam June Paik.

7. Martha Rosler, "Video: Shedding the Utopian Moment," in *Illuminated Video: An Essential Guide to Video Art*, ed. Doug Hall and Sally Jo Fifer (New York: Aperture/BAVC, 1990), 45.

8. Sara M. Evans, *Tidal Wave: How Women Changed America at Century's End* (New York: Free Press, 2003), 40.

9. Bonnie J. Dow, *Watching Women's Liberation, 1970: Feminism's Pivotal Year on the Network News* (Champaign: University of Illinois Press, 2014), 29–51.

10. Rothfuss, *Topless Cellist*, 239–40.

11. Jane F. Gerhard, *The Dinner Party: Judy Chicago and the Power of Popular Feminism 1970–2007* (Athens: University of Georgia Press, 2013), 22.

12. Ibid., 53.

13. Kristine Stiles, ed., *Correspondence Course: An Epistolary History of Carolee Schneemann and Her Circle* (Durham, N.C.: Duke University Press, 2010), 113.

14. Ibid.

15. Charlotte Moorman, *Complete Nam June Paik/Charlotte Moorman Chronology 1964–1981* (New York: s.n., n.d.), 15. Charlotte Moorman Archive, Charles Deering McCormick Library of Special Collections, Northwestern University Library (hereafter cited as CMA).

16. Charlotte Moorman, Nam June Paik, and Frank Pileggi, *An Artist in the Courtroom* (New York: s.n., 1967), 7, in CMA. Fred Stern, interview, April 23, 1980, Baltimore, in *Charlotte Moorman and the New York Avant Garde*, directed by Fred Stern and John G. Rauh (United States: Rainbowmaker.us., 1980).

17. Rothfuss, *Topless Cellist*, 205.

18. Jerald Ordover in *Topless Cellist: Charlotte Moorman*.

19. See Rothfuss, *Topless Cellist*, 144.

20. As Rothfuss notes in *Topless Cellist*, 194, Claes Oldenburg and German artist Tomas Schmit were among artists to write letters to New York's mayor John Lindsay on Moorman's behalf.

21. Carolee Schneemann, interview with Lisa Corrin and Corinne Granof, July 29, 2014, New Paltz, New York.

22. Bobbie Forster, "Little Rock Cellist to Play for Casals," *Arkansas Democrat*, December 27, 1962.

23. For a more extended discussion of women's political activism, see Evans, *Tidal Wave*.

24. As quoted in Brian Morton, "Candy-Coated, Gravity-Defying, Streamline Baby," *Wire*, September 2007, 25.

25. Gronemeyer, "Seriousness and Dedication," n.p.

26. The significant exception is Rothfuss's thoroughly researched and recently published biography, *Topless Cellist: The Improbable Life of Charlotte Moorman*. This publication and increased access to Moorman's archive seem already to have generated increased interest in and consideration of Moorman's work. In *Topless Cellist*, Rothfuss lists several scholars of music history who have also looked seriously at Moorman's performances and collaborations. See Rothfuss, *Topless Cellist*, 381n7.

27. Bruce McPherson and Carolee Schneemann to Charlotte Moorman, undated, in CMA.

28. Rothfuss, *Topless Cellist*, 122–24.

29. In an interview with Rothfuss, Schneemann explained that she suggested Moorman's change in outfit because Moorman "hated her dress" and "didn't know what to wear." Rothfuss, *Topless Cellist*, 102–15.

30. Stern and Rauh, *Charlotte Moorman and the New York Avant Garde*; Charlotte Moorman, interview with Harvey Matusow, 1969, in *Charlotte Moorman Anthology*, vol. 4 (Milan: Alga Marghen, 2006), compact disc.

31. Kaprow first presented *Push and Pull* in April 1963 in connection with MoMA's exhibition devoted to the abstract expressionist Hans Hofmann.

32. Carolee Schneemann, *More Than Meat Joy: Performance Works and Selected Writings,* ed. Bruce McPherson, 2nd ed. (1979; repr. Kingston, N.Y.: Documentext/McPherson and Company, 1997), 92.

33. Schneemann interview.

34. Stiles, *Correspondence Course*, 323.

35. Ibid., 324.

36. Rebecca Schneider, *The Explicit Body in Performance* (New York: Routledge, 1997), 34.

37. Ibid., 35.

38. Rothfuss, *Topless Cellist*, 96.

39. Maciunas forbade Fluxus artists from participating in Moorman's second avant-garde festival. Because many went ahead and participated anyway, for the fourth festival he changed tactics and billed Moorman for the use of his artists. This was one of many bills Moorman failed to pay; see invoices from 1965 in CMA.

40. McPherson, *More Than Meat Joy*, 52.

41. Amelia Jones, *Body Art: Performing the Subject* (Minneapolis: University of Minnesota Press, 1998), 176.

42. Although, as McPherson noted in the introduction to *More Than Meat Joy*, this emphasis on Schneemann's pioneering roles in feminist, body, and performance art of the sixties and seventies has sometimes come at the expense of recognizing her ongoing relevance and contributions to the field.

43. Schneemann quoted in Schneider, *Explicit Body*, 34.

44. Jones, *Body Art*, 151–95.

45. As I discuss subsequently, in his statement the judge asks this rhetorical question: "What was the purpose of the exhibition here? Was [it] playing the cello with bizarre nudity for self-aggrandizement with consequent later economic benefit for the purpose of enticement?" Milton Shalleck, "People of the State of New York v. Charlotte Moorman," *New York Law Journal* 157, no. 91 (May 11, 1967), in CMA.

46. Moorman, Paik, and Pileggi, *An Artist in the Courtroom*, 10–11. Schneider, *Explicit Body*, 40.

47. Roth v. United States, 354 U.S. 475 (1957), accessed September 30, 2014, http://scholar.google.com/scholar_case?case=14778925784015245625&q=Roth+v.+United+States&hl=en&as_sdt=2,37. This ruling was superseded, but largely reinforced, by Miller v. California 413 U.S. 15 (1973).

48. There are a number of scholarly texts that trouble, both directly and indirectly, the supposed polarity of art and pornography, including Schneider's *Explicit Body* and Jones's *Body Art*. See also Kelly Dennis, *Art/Porn: A History of Seeing and Touching* (Oxford: Berg, 2009).

49. This "electric bikini" was made of three triangles of fabric to which a number of six-volt bulbs were attached.

50. Court Reporter's Minutes, *People of the State of New York v. Charlotte Moorman*, February 27, 1967, 11, in CMA.

51. This was a recording. See Court Reporter's Minutes, *People of the State of New York v. Charlotte Moorman*, April 19, 1967, 15–16, in CMA.

52. Court Reporter's Minutes, February 27, 1967, 12–13.

53. The piece was entitled *International Lullaby*.

54. Court Reporter's Minutes, February 27, 1967, 27–28.

55. See Rosenberger's direct examination of Moorman. Court Reporter's Minutes, April 19, 1967.

56. Charlotte Moorman, *Opera Sextronique*, directed by Jud Yalkut (New York, N.Y.: Electronic Arts Intermix, 1967), 16 mm film transferred to videocassette (VHS).

57. Rothfuss, *Topless Cellist*, 197.

58. Court Reporter's Minutes, April 19, 1967, 47.

59. Full transcripts of these examinations are not available in the archive, but Gallina makes reference to Moore and Gruen's testimony when he cross-examines Jack Kroll; see Court Reporter's Minutes, *People of the State of New York v. Charlotte Moorman*, April 20, 1967, 124–30, in CMA.

60. Ibid., 87.

61. Ibid., 99–100.

62. Ibid., 92 and 101.

63. Ibid., 102.

64. Ibid., 113–14.

65. Ibid., 116.

66. Ibid., 121.

67. Ibid., 123–24.

68. Ibid., 124.

69. Milton Shalleck, "People of the State of New York v. Charlotte Moorman," *New York Law Journal* 157, no. 91 (May 11, 1967), in CMA.

70. Ibid.

71. Ibid.

72. Saba Mahmood, *Politics of Piety: The Islamic Revival and the Feminist Subject* (Princeton, N.J.: Princeton University Press, 2005), 29.

73. The actual text reads that Moore saw in the opera an attitude "disregarding, flaunting and putting down society's mores." Moorman, Paik, and Pileggi, *An Artist in the Courtroom*, 18.

74. Ibid.

75. Stiles, *Correspondence Course*, 113.

Live Art in the Eternal Network: The Annual New York Avant Garde Festivals

Hannah B Higgins

Hell's Hundred Acres

For the first half of the twentieth century the Manhattan neighborhood now known as SoHo (*So*uth of *Ho*uston Street) was a light manufacturing and distribution hub, producing and trading consumer goods from fabric to buttons to paper to olive oil and spices. This bustling factory and warehouse neighborhood fell into rapid decline after World War II, collapsing under pressure from competition with the South (especially in textiles) and the rise of the commercial shipping container, which moved light manufacturing and distribution hubs out of cities to suburban and peripheral areas more readily accessible by rail, boat, or highway.[1] In the ensuing two decades, New York City lost a quarter of its factories and a third of its manufacturing jobs to upstate New York, Connecticut, and Pennsylvania.[2] By 1960, the once busy streets of SoHo were nearly empty.

SoHo and parts of the area just south of it, now called TriBeCa (for its location in the *Tri*angle *Be*low *Ca*nal Street), were at the time called Hell's Hundred Acres, a nickname associated with the frequent warehouse fires in the neighborhood. Given the cheap rents and low value of the "dead storage" goods that lay fallow in these moribund factories, vulnerability to arson is hardly surprising.[3] Using statistics from a 1962 City Club pamphlet bearing the proscriptive title *The Wastelands of New York City*, SoHo native, critic, and literary artist Richard Kostelanetz described the neighborhood as blighted, with vacancy rates greater than 15 percent and rents from thirteen to seventy-five cents per square foot per year. Kostelanetz comments, "Need I calculate that $0.75 becomes for 1,600 square feet, say, only $1,200 per year or $100 per month; $0.13 becomes roughly $200 per year."[4] In 2015 dollars, that translates into a monthly rent from about $750 on the high end to $125 at the low end for a large loft.

In the 1960s SoHo became an artists' colony broadly committed to the utopian ideals of liberation from the physical, social, moral, and creative constraints of the so-called establishment.[5] Dancer Elaine Summers had performed in a loft at Canal and Wooster Streets in 1952.[6] By 1958 painter Alison Knowles and writer-sculptor Robert Morris were in the neighborhood. A little later, in 1960, a remarkable list of artist couples, most of whom had direct or indirect ties to the composer John Cage, were living in the general vicinity of SoHo. They included Knowles and Dick Higgins (my parents), Morris and Simone Forti, Yoko Ono

OPPOSITE
Peter Moore. Publicity photograph for Karlheinz Stockhausen's *Originale*, 2nd Annual New York Avant Garde Festival, Judson Hall, August 21, 1964. Clockwise from top center: Moorman, Director Allan Kaprow, Allen Ginsberg, Max Neuhaus, Jackson Mac Low, Robert Breer, David Behrman, Olga Adorno Klüver, Nam June Paik, Gloria Graves, Robert Delford Brown. Photograph © Barbara Moore / Licensed by VAGA, NY. Courtesy of Charlotte Moorman Archive, Charles Deering McCormick Library of Special Collections, Northwestern University Library.

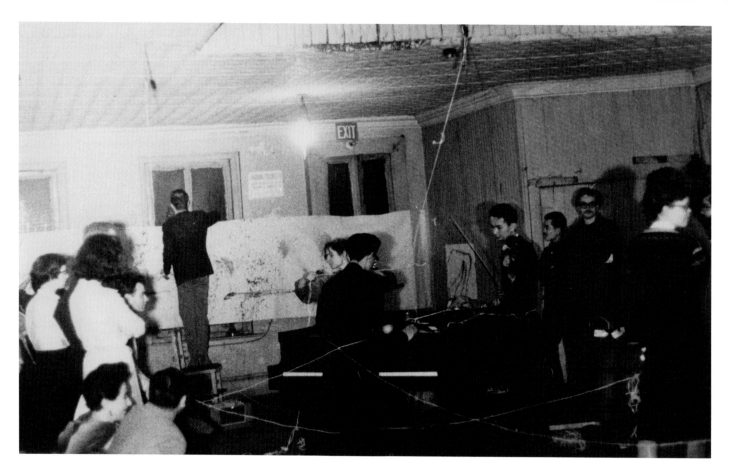

Concert at Yoko Ono's Chambers Street Loft, New York City, 1960. Shown are Richard Maxfield, Yoko Ono, and La Monte Young. Photograph by Terry Jennings. Jackson Mac Low Papers. MSS 180. Courtesy of Special Collections and Archives, University of California, San Diego.

and Toshi Ichiyanagi, and Marian Zazeela and La Monte Young. The cheap rents, open floor plans, and vast square footage of the artists' lofts made them perfectly suited to live performance, to large-scale work, and to emerging technologies, not to mention the possibility of working and living in the same space. In other words, the lofts' barren nature for light industrial users represented a blank slate of sorts for these composers, dancers, artists, writers, and sculptors.[7] James R. Hudson made just this point, describing SoHo in his book *The Unanticipated City: Loft Conversions in Lower Manhattan*, in terms that emphasize the idealism associated with this new arrangement:

> Work and residence, which had become separated as the industrial system become more complex, were reunited in Soho [sic], which became a community for unifying work, residence and ideology. Among Soho residents, personal relations were

directed at unification through mutual support. . . . Artistic ideas were shared, enhancing the feeling that it was here that what was important was "happening."[8]

One early example of SoHo as cultural "unification through mutual support" is a concert series held in 1960 and 1961 by Young and Ono, the former a composer from California, the latter an artist from Japan. The pair curated a concert series of new music in Ono's loft at 112 Chambers Street. The series was a bellwether for collaboration among diverse vanguard sensibilities. For example, the January concert of music by Ichiyanagi included performances by Robert Dunn, Forti, Kenji Kobayashi, Jackson Mac Low, Richard Maxfield, Toshiro Mayazumi, Ono, David Tudor, and Young.[9] This cross section of the avant-garde included associates of John Cage and several of his students as well as future participants in the as-yet-unformed Judson Dance and

Fluxus groups, the emerging concrete and sound poetry movement, and Japanese and American new music scenes.

In addition to this who's who of young artists, the loft space itself was an important contributor to the legacy of the series. As described by art historian Julia Robinson, one of the concerts included Forti's *Five Dance Constructions & Some Other Things*, which used architecturally scaled elements routinely left lying around in industrial lofts, including wide boards, platforms, and hangers (ropes from the high ceiling), which Forti used to generate movement when, for example, dancers pulled their way up a slanted board using ropes or, on another occasion, unwound on a rope and listened intently to a recording of Young's durational tone piece *Two Sounds*.[10] Forti implicitly situates the piece in the vast once-industrial room: "The sound fills the space. . . . The rope unwinds, then rewinds on its own momentum, unwinds and rewinds on and on until, finally, it becomes still. The unwinding ends many minutes before the tape is over. The person remains on the rope, hanging plumb and listening."[11] Among Morris's contributions to the concerts was a fifty-foot gray corridor that gradually narrowed, sounding a beating heart. The corridor originated at the entrance to Ono's loft.[12] The experience of both works, to state the obvious, is inextricably tied to their being situated in the industrial loft.

Furthermore, the series fundamentally shifted the way SoHo was viewed by music audiences.[13] Musicologist and composer Kyle Gann credits the series with opening up the downtown music scene: "The Ono/Young/Maxfield concert series was the first to draw adventurous music lovers downtown, and it offered wild new avenues of endeavor that the uptown classical concertgoers wouldn't have considered music, or at least not 'serious' music."[14] The series was followed by others in rapid succession. Most famously, Fluxus cofounder and impresario George Maciunas ran a related series uptown at his AG Gallery at 925 Madison Avenue (between 73rd and 74th Streets) in early 1961. Later (following his return from Europe, in 1963), he hosted a series of Fluxus events at his loft in SoHo, on Canal Street near Broadway, and on nearby streets. Related concert series grew from dance groups, such as Judson Dance (which worked out of the Judson Church, a block north of Houston Street) from 1962 to 1964. Another example, James Waring, a dancer and choreographer who worked periodically with Judson dancers and poets, programmed a 1962 series at the Henry Street Playhouse in the Village that included dance (Waring, Yvonne Rainer), Fluxus (George Brecht), and new music (Terry Jennings of the ONCE Group and composer Richard Maxfield, who is best known for his work with magnetic tape).[15]

The Judson Hall Festivals (1963, 1964, 1965)
Even though Charlotte Moorman never lived in SoHo, her Annual New York Avant Garde Festivals provided a roving venue for this emerging SoHo output. Her working relationship to the extended community of experimental artists living there and her use of the city radiated from the idealism of this urban artists' colony, with its distinctly experimental identity. Virtually every artist mentioned previously as early settlers of SoHo and performers in the downtown scene produced work in Moorman's now legendary festivals, which took place fifteen times from 1963 to 1980. The first three were coproduced with Norman Seaman and held at Judson Hall at 165 West 57th Street, far from Judson Church.

Among the many planning scribbles and organizing notes in Moorman's archive, one rough sketch is especially useful as a loose diagram, in nascent form, of what the festival would become. Composers are emphasized, in green and pencil letters across the top, including "[Morton] Feldman, Earle [Brown], Frederic [Rzewski], [David] Tudor, [David] Behrman and, to the right, the twelve-tone and magnetic tape composer [Richard] Maxfield." "[John] Cage," whose music Tudor was famous for performing, appears in the middle of the page. "[Giuseppe] Chiari, [James] Tenney, and [Toshi] Ichiyanagi" also appear on the page, but are smaller and not overwritten, perhaps as less established in the vanguard music world.[16] "SIX

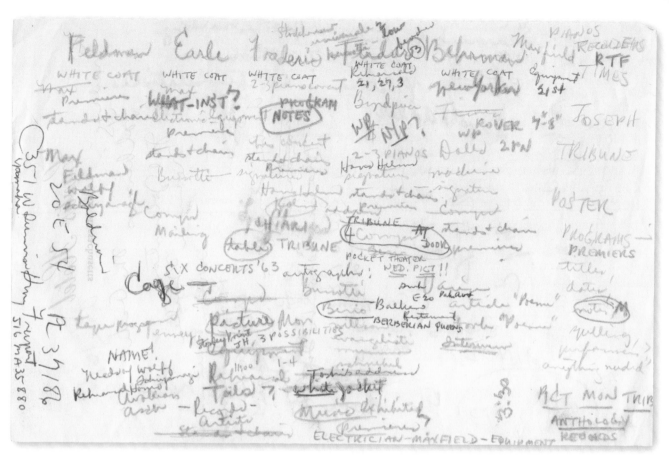

Charlotte Moorman. Preliminary Notes, 6 Concerts '63. Courtesy of Charlotte Moorman Archive, Charles Deering McCormick Library of Special Collections, Northwestern University Library.

CONCERTS '63" appears near the middle of the page, crisp, clear and all in capital letters with nothing around it, establishing the unified field of the page, upon which the copious details of the actual event took shape. Unsurprisingly, the most prosaic aspects of planning appear on the note alongside Moorman's grand vision.

One can readily imagine this homely piece of paper evolving on a table as Moorman pondered her remarkable program, writing and overwriting the names of the key participants on the small sheet while thinking through the logistics. At this early stage, she seems to have imagined everyone in white jackets, which would maintain the dignity of the series as "serious music" while establishing distance from the black ties and ball gowns of the uptown music scene. The equipment needs of each concert appear near each name, with Maxfield requiring "ELECTRICIAN and EQUIPMENT," Tudor "2–3 PIANOS" and "stands and chair." Piano brand names Yamaha and Baldwin

and possible rental company addresses run up the left side of the note. Publicity makes an appearance in the form of the *New York Tribune*, *Times*, and *New Yorker*. On this scribbled sheet, in other words, the majestic festival of the future appears in all its style, ambition, technical detail, commercial savvy, and inhomogeneous glory.

By the time this modest scrap metamorphosed into a formal program, the composer list had expanded, resulting in overlapping categories that included, for example, an "Electronic Concert" and an "Ensemble Concert" as well as concerts headlined by performers, some of whom appear in more than one. Moorman's design of the final program names the performers by signature at the left, as if to emphasize the uniqueness of each in the open field of the page. She collected the signatures by asking each composer for his or her autograph, which she then added to the design. These signatures would remain part of the poster design until the 1970s.[17] In contrast to the smooth sweep of a group arguably implied by a typeset list of participants neatly represented in uniform type, the autographic element presents each performer and composer as unique, despite the shared spine that organizes the names down the page. Karlheinz Stockhausen's carefully regulated signature, Cage's all-embracing C, and Ornette Coleman's calligraphic marks at the end of his name demonstrate something essential about the work of each of them; the first is associated with a meticulously calibrated serialism in music, the second with accepting what sounds the world offered his "silence," and the third with the spontaneous utterances of free jazz.

Moorman's performance on September 3, 1963, is something of a benchmark, as it was the first of many times she performed John Cage's *26′1.1499″ for a String Player* in totality in public. By virtue of the open space of the sheet and Moorman's colorful calligraphy, her copy of the score bears a marked resemblance to the planning scrap. Reproduced in Jason Rosenholtz-Witt's essay in this book, the score is formed by a rectangular grid of six wide bands (four representing each string, a fifth the bow, and a sixth the box of the instrument), which are vertically cut into irregular sections by time intervals refined to unplayable fractions of a second. Treating the score as a kind of

Charlotte Moorman. Paste-up and preliminary program for 6 Concerts '63. Courtesy of Charlotte Moorman Archive, Charles Deering McCormick Library of Special Collections, Northwestern University Library.

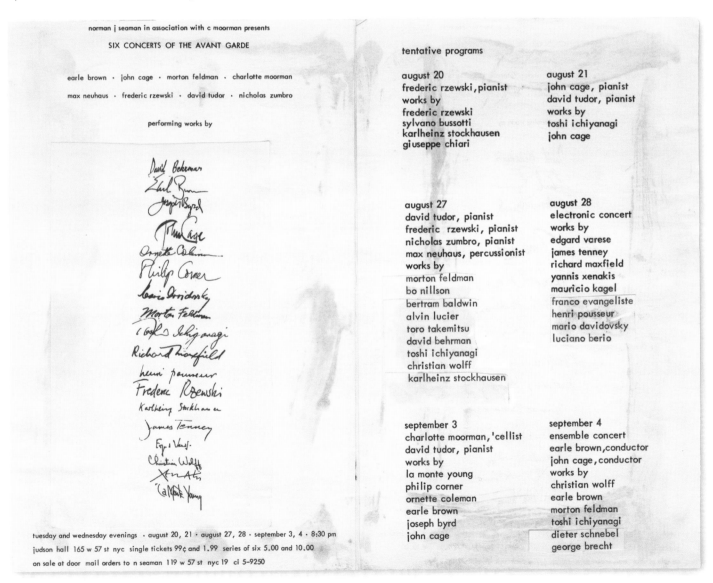

Peter Moore. Nam June Paik's *Robot K-456* performs *Robot Opera* outside Judson Hall, 2nd Annual New York Avant Garde Festival, August 31, 1964. Photograph © Barbara Moore/Licensed by VAGA, NY.

"open plan," to borrow a term from architecture, Moorman's annotations are written in multicolored pencil in and around these rectangles. Demonstrating the aesthetic potential in unusual uses of musical instruments as well as everyday things, Moorman would mark up and perform from this score for decades, including a list of eggs, whistles, wood, hair, tin cans, balloons, buzzers, and boat bells governed by such instructions as "put logs on," "tend eggs," and "flowers bomb."

These instructions were performed to Cage's chagrin, not for their noninstrumentality (which he valued and the zest for which

Moorman clearly shared) but for the improvisational, even theatrical, features of Moorman's performance, which came complete with party dress.[18] On this first occasion, she performed simultaneously with pianist David Tudor performing another piece, Cage's *34'46.776"*.[19] Winthrop Sargeant reviewed the duet in the *New Yorker*:

Technologically, like most Cage works, this one was a lulu. Mr. Tudor, reading from a score that resembled a checkbook, was equipped with fifteen or twenty varieties of drumstick, and his piano with rocks—or objects that look like rocks. Every once in awhile, he would rise and peer into its interior, like a truck driver looking for a defective sparkplug. Both he and Miss Moorman blew whistles from time to time, and several children's balloons were burst with loud pops. At one point, Miss Moorman hurled a cymbal into the middle of the stage floor with an imposing crash.[20]

The review is rife with the predictable ridicule reserved at the time for experimental and avant-garde work. Instead of engaging with the experience of noninstrumental sound, with the harsh clatter of a rock as against the hushed thump of a mallet or the startle caused by a popped balloon or a dropped cymbal, the reader is treated to the usual dismayed accusations of charlatanry. The noble pianist is demoted to truck driver and the Juilliard-trained cellist to cymbal hurler; the motley pair joins the bizarre marching band of Cage and his "lulu" followers.

For the second festival, in 1964, Moorman expanded the network of artists involved while staying close to the European-American avant-garde scene, bookended at the time by Cage's compositional indeterminacy on one side and Stockhausen's carefully calibrated serialism on the other. The resulting realization of Stockhausen's benchmark *Originale* (*Originals* in English) famously used people in their authentic roles (as actual poets, painters, musicians, models, children, camera operators, composers, animal handlers, etc.), not character actors.[21] Allen Ginsberg and Jackson Mac Low (a beat poet and a visual and sound poet, respectively), appeared alongside Robert Delford Brown (performance artist and cofounder of the First National Church of the Exquisite Panic), Allan Kaprow (cofounder of happenings), and Olga Klüver (sometime Judson dancer, happenings), David Behrman (minimalist composer), Nam June Paik (video artist, Fluxus), Gloria Graves (No! artist), and Charlotte Moorman (experimental artist, classical cellist, festival organizer), an image of whom appears in a gauze wrap in Laura Joseph's essay in this

book. The program also included Robert Breer (experimental filmmaker), Dick Higgins (Fluxus, happenings, publisher), Michael Kirby (New York University theater professor), Billy Klüver (Bell Labs engineer), Alvin Lucier (composer), James Tenney (electronic composer), Marjorie Strider (painter), and Ay-O (Fluxus, painter).

Photographer Peter Moore's film of the event, *Doubletakes*, depicts a packed room. Bird whistles seem to hail from some long-ago place and time, maybe the woods or a field. Precisely clipped string sounds cut through the idyll, staunchly defending a new musical sensibility. Max Neuhaus plays carefully calibrated percussion. Exquisitely beautiful models (Olga Adorno and Letty Eisenhauer) pose before a mirror, then walk as if on runways. One examines herself in a pocket mirror while sauntering before the crowd. Moorman plays cello while lying on her back. Paik pours a pail of water over his head. Again. Again. Overtones. Microtones. James Tenney is playing electronic music. One poet reads. Another poet reads. Or maybe it's the academic. They overlap. Then don't. Robert Delford Brown appears in a papier-mâché costume with an enormous (plastic tubing or hose) penis dangling almost to his feet. Recorded and live music sounds. Allen Ginsberg sings "Hare Krishna" and plays an Indian sarod or sarangi. The sounds seem to come from everywhere while the building surfaces disappear and reappear at the whim of glaring lights, television sets, and mirrors. Through it all, musicians are depicted time and again carefully following the score in front of them.

While the eighteen "scenes" of *Originale* could be overlapped or performed in sequence, the work was bound together by Stockhausen's fastidious, serialist music. Despite superficial resemblances to the everyday elements and apparent chaos of happenings, in other words, the experience of *Originale* unfolded according to a tight musical sensibility. This internal structure sets *Originale* apart from happenings, a performance format which empowered the viewer with decision-making in the construction of her or his own experience.

For the performers the difference occurred at the level of assigned task and musical structure and for the audience at the level of passive viewership. Despite these important distinctions, *Originale* was entirely consistent with the emerging ethos of avant-garde, multidisciplinary concerts, including performers (friends) from across the spectrum of movements then active downtown.

Notably, several of these artists both performed in *Originale* and protested against it. Picketing Judson Hall on the evening of September 8, 1964, the protestors added considerably to the drama of the festival and were presumed by many to be a proscenium-blasting street-based extension of the work. Far from it. Despite early sympathies with Stockhausen generally, Fluxus impresario George Maciunas had organized this "Action Against Cultural Imperialism" to protest Stockhausen's rejection of jazz and folk music as racist imperialism, his essentially conventional use of the proscenium format, and (equally important for Maciunas) the festival's apparently one-upping of Fluxus. Maciunas wrote as much in a letter to George Brecht: "Upon arrival here she [Charlotte Moorman] . . . frantically rushed to put together her own festival a few weeks before Flux—even though it fell in a bad season."[22] What was rivalry for some was clearly an opportunity for collaboration and gentle teasing for others. Among the protestor-performers were Higgins, Kaprow, Ginsberg, by some accounts Moorman, and Brown, who functioned as a saboteur on the inside, lighting a smoke bomb from inside his papier-mâché and soft-pipe (penis) costume, which resulted in an evacuation of the hall.[23] Brown was replaced in subsequent performances by the Japanese Fluxus artist and painter Ay-O.

Peter Moore. Meredith Monk performs one of Jackson Mac Low's scores from *The Pronouns— A Collection of 40 Dances—For the Dancers*, 3rd Annual New York Avant Garde Festival, Judson Hall, September 10, 1965. Photograph © Barbara Moore / Licensed by VAGA, NY.

The 1965 festival was larger still, with more than eighty participating artists, poets, dancers, filmmakers, jazz musicians, and performance artists. Performance pioneer Carolee Schneemann, who participated in the festival with her generative instrumental performance *Noise Bodies*, recalls the presentation of Allan Kaprow's *Push and Pull* (original 1963) in her book *More Than Meat Joy*:

> I requested the audience to use a forty-minute [intermission] by going out to 57th Street to bring back soft materials with which to construct an environment of two rooms. The artists at the festival erected two three-sided rooms with windows cut in them while the audience was away.[24]

The intent is clear in this description; by inviting the audience to awaken to the underutilized materials and spaces of the urban environment outside the hall, they would learn something essential about the city: The city contains untold interest. The city is dynamic. The city can be touched. The city isn't always texturally hard (buildings and sidewalks), but can be soft (food, wrappers, a discarded scarf, a piece of a plant, a lost toy, mud). The assumption was clearly that the city dwellers were ready for such an exploration since, as Kaprow wrote in 1961, "The most intense and essential Happenings have been spawned in old lofts, basements, vacant stores, natural surroundings and the street."[25]

Peter Moore. Nam June Paik performs in John Cage's *Theater Piece*, 3rd Annual New York Avant Garde Festival, Judson Hall, September 7,1965. Photograph © Barbara Moore/Licensed by VAGA, NY.

Peter Moore. Yvonne Rainer performs her *Three Satie Spoons*, 3rd Annual New York Avant Garde Festival, Judson Hall, August 26, 1965. Photograph © Barbara Moore/Licensed by VAGA, NY.

Instead, according to Schneemann:

The next thing I knew someone was running up the back stairs yelling, "There's three paddy wagons out front and forty police coming through the box-office." The audience had gone on a rampage, pulling hubcaps off cars, tearing at neon signs. To give people permission to do something we considered inventive and constructive was for them the freedom to attack the ordinary fixtures of their culture.[26]

More mayhem ensued, with audience members breaking the mirrored panels inside the venue.

As recounted by Moorman's biographer, Joan Rothfuss, "Moorman convinced the lawyers and managers to let the show go on, but she had to sign a document promising not to 'perform any act or theatre piece that will provoke disturbance in the audience leading to an undisciplined or uncontrollable situation.'"[27] Accounts vary as to whether the festival was permanently expelled from Judson Hall, but whatever ensued legally or contractually between the producers Moorman and Seaman, the police, and Judson Hall, clearly the liberating intent of Kaprow's piece was ill suited to the venue.[28] As Kaprow later lamented, the public wasn't ready for truly participatory art.

Given free rein, it is difficult to predict what an audience will do. Will it become a self-regulating system or a mob? The title of *Push and Pull* implies a tug of war. A push, a pull, a push again, pull again: the words describe a sequence of actions and reactions that result in either an exhausting stasis or a breakthrough when one side yields and the whole thing falls over. Now familiar

Peter Moore. Publicity photograph for 3rd Annual New York Avant Garde Festival, Judson Hall, August 26, 1965. Left to right: Nam June Paik, Charlotte Moorman, Takehisa Kosugi, Gary Harris, Dick Higgins, Judith Kuemmerle, Kenneth King, Meredith Monk, Al Kurchin, Phoebe Neville. In front, kneeling, Philip Corner and James Tenney. Photograph © Barbara Moore/Licensed by VAGA, NY.

Peter Moore. Children play inside dome donated by the Walter Kidde Company, 4th Annual New York Avant Garde Festival, Central Park, September 9, 1966. Photograph © Barbara Moore/Licensed by VAGA, NY.

with total destruction, of joy given over to anger, frustrations with daily life percolating up through a public situation. Subsequent years would usher in similar situations at Haight-Ashbury's 1967 Human Be-In, in Chicago in 1968, and at the famous Woodstock festival in 1969. Moorman learned from the experience, moving the annual avant-garde festival into increasingly "public" spaces while at the same time working closely with the regulatory agencies that could guarantee some semblance of public order.

Scaling Up (1968, 1971, 1975)

1st	1963	Judson Hall
2nd	1964	Judson Hall
3rd	1965	Judson Hall
4th	1966	Central Park
5th	1967	Staten Island ferryboat *John F. Kennedy*
6th	1968	Parade, Central Park West
7th	1969	Wards Island and Mill Rock Island
8th	1971	69th Regiment Armory
9th	1972	Hudson River excursion boat *Alexander Hamilton*, South Street Seaport
10th	1973	Grand Central Terminal
11th	1974	Shea Stadium, Flushing Meadows, Queens
12th	1975	Gateway National Recreation Area / Floyd Bennett Field, Brooklyn
13th	1977	World Trade Center
14th	1978	In conjunction with Second Annual Cambridge River Festival, Cambridge, Massachusetts
15th	1980	Passenger Ship Terminal[29]

oppositions that characterize the 1960s are embedded in the logic of the work: destruction and creation, revolution and counterrevolution, anger and joy, thoughtfulness and hedonism, and a precise sense of place and transience. The risk of overreach is palpable, of freedoms gone dangerously far, of flirting

Following her expulsion from Judson Hall, Moorman's use of public sites ranged from entertainment and tourist destinations

(Central Park, Shea Stadium, the World Trade Center) to transit hubs (Grand Central Terminal, South Street Seaport, Gateway National Recreation Area / Floyd Bennett Field, the 69th Regiment Armory in Manhattan) to the transportation system itself (the Staten Island Ferry, a parade down Central Park West, and a boat trip past Wards and Rock Mill Islands in the East River). Participants at the festivals hailed from virtually every continent and, whether participating in person or by proxy (artists proposed work to Moorman for someone else to execute), the festival demonstrated the communitarian spirit of both the international avant-garde and the downtown scene. The 1968 festival parade down Central Park West, for example, included artists from Japan, Denmark, Chile, Hungary, West Germany, Italy, Bulgaria, Canada, Turkey, Greece, and the United States (to name only a few in the long list of participating artists' countries of origin). Like the early festivals, the 1968 parade combined overlapping movements (happenings, events [meaning Fluxus], experimental film, environments, computer art, jazz, new music, painting, sculpture, and kinetic light art). Many of the artists were active in several of the groups.

In addition to a prodigious letter-writing campaign, Moorman did extensive work preparing the police department and Con Edison for the kinds of activity imagined for the parade, effectively providing them the educative framework that would make a general public open to the work and less likely to

Peter Moore. Robert Watts performs *Oraculum*, 4th Annual New York Avant Garde Festival, Central Park, September 9, 1966. Photograph © Barbara Moore / Licensed by VAGA, NY.

Peter Moore. Takehisa Kosugi's *Piano '66,* 4th Annual New York Avant Garde Festival, Central Park, September 9, 1966. Photograph © Barbara Moore/Licensed by VAGA, NY.

JAZZ FLOAT ONE
DON HECKMAN GROUP
ED SUMMERLIN GROUP

CHARLOTTE
MOORMAN
SKY KISS
No 4

BKLYN
JOE JONES
MUSIC BIKE
COMPOSITION

JAZZ FLOAT TWO
ROBIN KENYATTA QUINTET
SUN RA SOLAR ARKESTRA

FILM FLOAT JUDD YALKUT
& CAR   DICK PRESTON
         JOYCE WEILAND

AY-O (JAPAN) ORIENTAL
FLOAT

NAM
JUNE
PAIK
WORLD'S
LARGEST
T-V

GILLES LARRAIN
CLEAR VINYL SCULPTURE
ON FLOAT

ALLAN
KAPROW
METALLIC
BALLET

WALKING
POEMS

FLOAT
MOBILE KINETIC ENSEMBLE
ENVIRONMENTAL ART
DICK HOGLE
PRESTON MCLANAHAN
JOHN VAN SAUN

Strobes, elect. sounds,
chroma lux.

CHRISTO JAVACHEFF
WRAPPED TRUCK

CHAMBER
ARTS
WOODWIND
QUARTET
PERFORMING
JOHN CAGE'S
SILENT PIECE

BELL LABS FLOAT
COMMUNICATION
THROUGH
COMPUTERS
13' MURAL, MUSIC,
4 MILE POEM BY
EMMET WILLIAMS

WALKING
POEM

WILLOUGHBY SHARP
40'x 80' BUBBLE
. TO PROJECT ON.

FILM FLOAT
CAR

LES LEVINE
NEON SCULPTURE
FLOAT

WALKING
POEM

JAZZ FLOAT THREE
MARK LEVIN ENSEMBLE
ROSWELL RUDD GROUP

WILLOUGHBY
SHARP
PROJECTOR
VEHICLE

WALKING
POEMS

BLUE BIRD
CON EDISON ELECT.
CAR

JEAN
TOCHE
CARCAN

CAROLEE SCHNEEMAN
FLOAT EVENT
COLUMNS, FOAM LIGHTS

JOSEPH BEUYS

POETRY FLOAT
JOHN GIORNO
CAROL BERGE .
JACKSON MACLOW
LARRY FREIFELD
HANNA WEINER
BLUEBIRD BANNER

WALKING POEMS
HANDED OUT POEMS

THIS IS NOT
A FLOAT
DITER ROT
100 CHILDREN
BOOK

THIS NOT A
FLOAT
AL HANSEN
BALLOON
SCULPTURE

endanger the project by going on the kind of destructive spree that nearly ruined the festival's prospects in 1965. Toward this end, with Al Hansen she constructed Styrofoam models of the floats, including a hand-size model of Joseph Beuys's felt-wrapped piano and a blue toy police car, whose benign form stands in stark contrast to the violent relationship normally depicted between the police and the counterculture in 1968, and most specifically at the Democratic National Convention in Chicago, whose violence erupted just three weeks before Moorman's parade. The models would, almost by definition, generate a playful atmosphere, with Moorman, Hansen, and a scattering of interested artists playing in the proverbial sandbox of official culture, alongside city management reviewing the sequence of floats and activities.

Beginning sometime after 7:00 P.M. September 14, the floats and artists lumbered down tony Central Park West, which is adjacent to the park. But for the leisurely pace, the scene suggests something from *And to Think that I Saw It on Mulberry Street*, Dr. Seuss's fantasy tale of floats and acrobats, exotic animals, and thundering instruments. Allan Kaprow's metallic ballet kicked the thing off: oil drums were rolled down the street with the help of local students, making a great, metallic crash and boom. A few floats down, Sun Ra's orchestra played loosely structured, poetry-infused "Infinity Music." In contrast, Les Levine's *Photon Two* float would have streamed past, a ghostly grid of neon tubes in lockstep coming down the avenue, its blue haze wafting quietly past accompanied by the hum of

Peter Moore. Charlotte Moorman performs Jim McWilliams's *Sky Kiss*, 6th Annual New York Avant Garde Festival, Central Park West, September 14, 1968. Photograph © Barbara Moore/Licensed by VAGA, NY.

the generators. Photographs depict Joseph Beuys's mute piano loosely wrapped in gray felt. Jean Toche's *Carcan*, described in the press release as "a 'medieval rack' of human activity, kinetic lights and speed," bundled the mediated and live art aspects of the multitiered mobile spectacle, with the artist tied to his sculpture and accompanied by "three sirens," which could refer to women or live police sirens—probably the former. At the tail end, Bell Labs and Experiments in Art and Technology (EAT) hooked up a printer (apparently, though there may have been boxes of preprinted material also dispensing) that spewed out a steady stream of computer printout with a thirteen-foot-long mural by Ken Knowlton and A. Michael Noll,

computer music by Max Mathews and John Pierce, as well as a "five mile poem," computer-generated poetry by engineer Peter Neumann and concrete and sound poet Emmett Williams. Back and forth along the parade route, Fluxus artist Joe Jones could be seen pedaling his large tricycle, a three-wheeled geared whirligig of an instrument hooked up with self-playing drums, cymbals, strings, and horns that played when he rolled, a one-man mobile band. For a finale, Moorman performed Jim McWilliams's *Sky Kiss*, the cellist playing and floating aloft, borne by the effort of scores of white balloons.

In addition to the New York Police Department and the Department of Parks, and Marine and Aviation, Moorman sought out other unexpected alliances. As ambassador for experimentalism with regard to the general public, Moorman clearly hoped to interest new audiences in the cutting edge of culture, tapping into the sports and entertainment industry. One example: in addition to WBAI (public radio), information about the Central Park West Parade was announced at two Yankees games and a Mets game, at Shea Stadium, on September 10 and 13.[30] Leon Leavitt, the chairman of the board of Con Ed, who provided power for the parade, described in some detail the potent, affirmative experience of the fair by nonartists. Referring to the assassinations of Robert Kennedy and Martin Luther King and the general unrest of 1968, his statement inheres the values of shared human experience: "After a year of mass assassinations, riots, political mayhem, and international disorder, New York City took time to show the world that life is the important thing. . . . This is the most beautiful free show I ever witnessed in my many years in this city."[31]

Moorman had clearly mastered the public spectacle in terms of the administration that made such a thing possible. Large scale and technologically saturating experiences were almost mandatory in the enormous festivals of the later years. Moorman's fibroid tumor or the need for a break from organizing, or both, meant there was no 1970 festival, but the 1971 festival at the 69th Regiment Armory, for example, expanded further the legacy for large-scale work. The spectacular EAT-sponsored *9 Evenings: Theater and Engineering* of 1966 took place at the same site five years earlier. The Armory festival was festooned with a towering inflatable (*Red Rapid Growth* by ZERO artist Otto Piene), an enormous, spinning video Ferris wheel (by filmmaker Shirley Clarke), and the presence of superstars John Lennon and Yoko Ono. A funhouse for perceptually tuned-in adult visitors, Ono's Plexiglas maze would have captured visitors in midmotion and mild spatial confusion, while Lennon's *Baby Grand Guitar* clearly took the issue of scaling up as a point of amused departure. Scaled beyond reach, the instrument is unplayable.

Some artists responded to the challenge of the carnivalesque atmosphere by slowing down or creating meditative or quiet moments inside the melee. At the geographic center of the Armory, for example, Fluxus artist Geoffrey Hendricks sat in quiet, twelve-hour meditation atop an earthen mound placed in the exact center of the room; inside the mound were his wedding ring and other relics of his recent *Flux Divorce* from the artist Bici Forbes (now Nye Ffarrabas). The two had cut most of their possessions in half. He sat, quietly taking periodic notes about his interactions with passersby, in full coat and tails.[32] What was

Peter Moore. Geoffrey Hendricks performs *Ring Piece,* 8th Annual New York Avant Garde Festival, 69th Regiment Armory, November 19, 1971. Photograph © Barbara Moore/Licensed by VAGA, NY. Courtesy of Charlotte Moorman Archive, Charles Deering McCormick Library of Special Collections, Northwestern University Library.

Peter Moore. 8th Annual New York Avant Garde Festival, 69th Regiment Armory, November 19, 1971. Photograph © Barbara Moore/Licensed by VAGA, NY. Courtesy of Charlotte Moorman Archive, Charles Deering McCormick Library of Special Collections, Northwestern University Library.

Peter Moore. Shirley Clarke's *Video Ferris Wheel*, 8th Annual New York Avant Garde Festival, 69th Regiment Armory, November 19, 1971. Photograph © Barbara Moore/Licensed by VAGA, NY.

John Lennon with *Baby Grand Guitar* that appeared in the 8th Annual New York Avant Garde Festival, 69th Regiment Armory, November 19, 1971. Photographer unknown. © The Museum of Modern Art/Licensed by SCALA/Art Resource, NY.

Peter Moore. *Autumn Piece*, attributed to
Rochelle Steiner, 9th Annual New York Avant
Garde Festival, *Alexander Hamilton* riverboat,
South Street Seaport, October 28, 1972. Photo-
graph © Barbara Moore/Licensed by VAGA, NY.

Peter Moore. Robin and Rebecca Moore
participate in Liz Phillips's *Tuned Electric
Spaghetti*, 9th Annual New York Avant Garde
Festival, *Alexander Hamilton* riverboat, South
Street Seaport, October 28, 1972. Photograph
© Barbara Moore/Licensed by VAGA, NY.

Peter Moore. John Cage creates
Work in Progress, a composition
derived from Henry David Thoreau's
Journal, 10th Annual New York
Avant Garde Festival, Grand Central
Terminal, December 9, 1973.
Photograph © Barbara Moore/
Licensed by VAGA, New York.

Peter Moore. Charlotte Moorman
and Nam June Paik in *Music Is a
Mass Transit Too—So Is the Bra,*
10th Annual New York Avant Garde
Festival, Grand Central Terminal,
December 9, 1973. Photograph ©
Barbara Moore/Licensed by VAGA,
New York.

Peter Moore. Nam June Paik performs *Violin to be Dragged on the Street*, 12th Annual New York Avant Garde Festival, Gateway National Recreation Area / Floyd Bennett Field, Brooklyn, September 27, 1975. Photograph © Barbara Moore / Licensed by VAGA, NY.

kept from view in the box remains unknown. George Maciunas handed Hendricks a card that effectively doubled Hendricks's silence:

COMPOSITION 1971

BY GEORGE MACIUNAS

DEDICATED TO ALL THE AVANT-GARDE ARTISTS WHO REFUSED TO PARTICIPATE IN THIS AFFAIR.

George Maciunas shall avoid all visual and oral contact with any of the participants in the so-called avant-garde festival until the next one comes along.[33]

A few years later, in 1974, Danish intermedia artist Eric Andersen asked Moorman to spray paint a chair that read, "Become a member of Eric Andersen's Random Audience." "Make the chair very attractive," he wrote, and asked that Moorman bring it with her wherever she performed during the festival that year, at Shea Stadium, the Queens-based home of the Mets baseball team.[34] It is impossible to know whether the chair was fabricated or not, although it appears in the final program. But the idea, like Hendricks's, was to provide the possibility of watching.

Larger in physical size but smaller in public impact (if the near absence of newspaper coverage is any indicator), the 1975 festival at Gateway National Recreation Area / Floyd Bennett Field in Brooklyn took place in a defunct military airfield. The physical scale was so large that most encounters were completely intimate, as the vast asphalt tarmac provided a seemingly boundless open space for walking in costume, performing small gestures, and arranging simple materials. John Cage appeared with a basket full of his fabled wild mushrooms, as a "work in progress." Dick Higgins rode a horse backward for the day, speaking with passersby and other artists. Alison Knowles's *Bean Garden* consisted of a large, wooden tray on a raised platform whose microphones produced whooshing sounds as visitors shuffled across it. Moorman's longtime collaborator Nam June Paik could be found somewhere on the vast concrete plane of the field pulling a violin by a string. Like an errant pet, the belly of the instrument would have skated across the tarmac, its finish, then the wood itself, slowly worn away, the vibrating body of the instrument generating a corresponding hum of the strings. Perhaps he passed Stephen Varble dressed in a wig and gown. A man sitting on a bucket. Someone reading poetry. A few kids eating ice cream. Another picture shows Paik sitting in this nearly lunar, unpeopled, and unvegetated landscape playing an upright piano.

The most spectacular event at the field was produced by Marilyn Wood, a choreographer and onetime Merce Cunningham Dance Company dancer and designer, who arranged for her Celebration Group to dance in front of an old hangar holding great swaths of bright orange nylon attached to the bowed roofline.[35] These streamers captured the light, vividly glowing against the blue sky. As color complements (blue and orange), the strips of cloth formed giant cuts in the flesh of the sky, tethered, however improbably, to the rusty, dull exterior of the outscaled empty airplane garage. This remarkable fabric was making a return appearance in the art world, as it was made of the leftovers from Christo and Jeanne-Claude's recent *Valley Curtain*, where it was likewise paired with a luminous sky at an improbable location.

The last years of the festival could be characterized as a winding down. In 1979, Moorman began her decade-long battle with cancer, although she continued to perform alone and with Paik. The 1979 festival was cancelled, but there would be one more, at the Passenger Ship Terminal in 1980. The correspondence record indicates that few of the original artists were interested in participating in the festival, even as friends rallied to her aid. Longtime friend and festival contributor Yoko Ono, for example, assisted Moorman in funding her cancer treatments by periodically and anonymously paying the substantial bills in arrears to Moorman's oncologist.[36]

By 1980, SoHo, too, had changed, as had the needs of its ever-expanding roster of artists, many of whom now enjoyed

Peter Moore. Marilyn Wood and Celebration Group perform *Sun Struck,* 12th Annual New York Avant Garde Festival, Gateway National Recreation Area / Floyd Bennett Field, Brooklyn, September 27, 1975. Photograph © Barbara Moore / Licensed by VAGA, NY.

official acclaim. Hell's Hundred Acres had revealed itself to be a fertile field for its artists and (eventually) galleries, artist-run noncommercial spaces, performance venues, and, finally, the shops and restaurants that support a wealthy infrastructure. The artist colony of SoHo had become a founding myth in the development of a delocalized "Soho," one more stop on the tour bus of manifest destiny, the artists displaced even as the desire for their utopian aspirations became reified in the fashions and storefronts of this now established neighborhood.

The Eternal Network

In *Outside the Gates of Eden*, cultural historian Peter Hales described the 1960s counterculture as characterized by a combined sense of place and placelessness: "place" describing a locale with unique social and physical features (Haight-Ashbury, Woodstock, Chicago, SoHo), and "placelessness" a mind-set and set of practices through which the local utopian experiment is exported, reproduced as generalizable to a greater world (Ken Kesey's bus, the Woodstock film).[37] Moorman's festival, with its migrations around the city and use of the transportation systems of New York, deployed just this sense of duality as both an exported version of "downtown" and a roving mechanism for promoting an international community of artists.

From the beginning, participants came from places whose official art worlds (commercial or governmental) did not recognize or support them, amplifying SoHo's early sense of shared values, mutual support, social affinity, and trust that is described in network theory as "social embeddedness."[38] In his synthesizing book on networks, Mark Buchanan writes:

> Social capital is the ability of people to work together easily and efficiently based on trust, familiarity, and understanding. Its importance lies in its power to create efficient networks for transactions. For example, in a network of companies [substitute artist groups here] that involve people linked through networks endowed with social capital, the costs associated with forging legally binding contracts are reduced. Decisions are made more readily and quickly because of shared norms and goals, and so on.[39]

With a few notable exceptions, artists participated in Moorman's festivals without legal contracts or fees, relying instead on goodwill, barter, and donations, those features of an informal economy long associated with utopian living in the 1960s in general and with the artists' colony in particular.

Through her network of contacts, in other words, Moorman effectively shrank the size of the global avant-garde by dispensing invitations, requests for donations, letters of gratitude, and public relations in

Ay-O. *Rainbow Environment no. 11*, 13th Annual New York Avant Garde Festival, World Trade Center, June 19, 1977. Photograph © Ay-O.

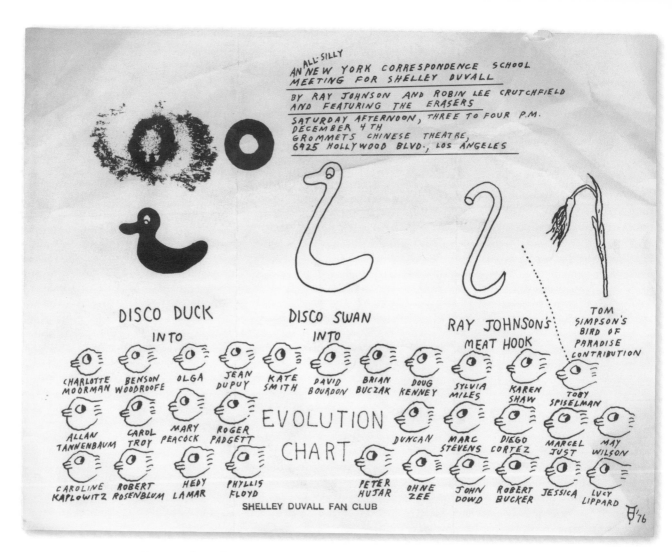

Ray Johnson. *Disco Duck for Shelley Duvall Fan Club*, 1976. © The Ray Johnson Estate at Richard L. Feigen & Co. Courtesy of Charlotte Moorman Archive, Charles Deering McCormick Library of Special Collections, Northwestern University Library.

the service of new and experimental art. Over the course of almost twenty years, she penned thousands of personal letters, encouraging each artist to participate in person or by proxy and to recommend others. She was directed to each participant by a friend of that participant or by reputation, through a growing team of informal advisers whose opinions she respected. The system of friends and, later, friends of friends, and (finally) friends of friends of friends reached by mail means that Moorman's network was structurally eternal, or never-ending, a point made especially clear in larger festivals, which had more than 250 participants, most of whom participated for free.

The terminology for this network as "eternal" first appears in March 1968 in the context of the closing of a tiny antistore, a casual, open-only-on-request nonshop of the experimental arts located in the French seaside town of Villefranche-sur-Mer. The *Cédille qui sourit* (the Smiling Cedilla, named for the hanging diacritical mark below the French ç) was operated by French and American Fluxus artists Robert Filliou and George Brecht, the latter a longtime associate of John Cage and participant in the festivals and the early SoHo concerts.[40] On that sad day in 1968, these erstwhile shopkeepers would go their separate ways, with Filliou remaining briefly in Villefranche and Brecht moving on to London. Filliou was optimistic: "The artist must realize also that he is part of a wider network . . . going on around him all the time in all parts of the world."[41] He later demurred, "We may need to meet at certain times, to gather information at certain places."[42] Charlotte Moorman's Annual New York Avant Garde Festival provided just such a periodic space for the interaction of live artists (including Filliou in 1967) in the newly named "eternal network" of international experimental artists.

Significantly, the term was applied retroactively to describe the constellation of artists associated with New York–based collagist Ray Johnson's mailing list, which had long since made its first public appearance in the inaugural issue of the *Village Voice* in 1955.[43] Johnson's New York Correspondance [*sic*] School linked artists to nonartists in its conception and execution and included Moorman and many others of the participants in her festivals as well as the greater infrastructure of the arts. Mail art deployed an inherently dynamic, spatial instrument, the postal system, as enveloped and stamped artworks were mailed, altered, and reposted among senders. Envelopes, cards, and letters were added to, subtracted from, torn, cut, stamped, glued, and repaired as they moved from person to person or back and forth between people, two-stepping in Johnson's New York Correspondance [*sic*] School.

Moorman appears in several of Johnson's mail art diagrams, and she and Johnson enjoyed a rich exchange of letters and artworks, with Johnson famously dropping foot-long hot dogs from a helicopter over the festival at Wards Island in 1969. Clearly, the live art of the festivals took place in and because of the "eternal network" in both senses of the term; Moorman's festivals expressed the network of live artists connected through human contact and through the post.

The mail played a significant role in the means used by these artists to support one another in nonart endeavors as well. For example, with artists leading the effort, culture makers banded together in a 1972 letter-writing campaign against the much-publicized effort by the U.S. government to deport John Lennon and Yoko Ono from the country for their antiwar activities. Among the letter writers were singer-songwriters Joan Baez and Bob Dylan, beat poet Gregory Corso, composer Leonard Bernstein, and novelists John Updike, Joyce Carol Oates, and Joseph Heller.[44] Along with art activist Jon Hendricks and others, Moorman collected signatures for the cause from her roster of artists and official supporters: they included a WBAI radio engineer (Shuya Abe), the prominent wife of a pop artist (Patty Oldenburg), New York's mayor (John Lindsay), and several festival artists.[45] A letter from Moorman to Ono written from New York Hospital room 1201–1 depicts the "eternal network" in full force as a hybrid space of artistic and general support and resistance:

> Congratulations on the "Aliens of Artistic Merit" Battle! I hope this will stop the other proceedings of deportation or that it will at least help you win. As you know, Doug Davis (Newsweek), Dick Cavett (TV) and Tom Hoving (Metropolitan Museum) want to help if they're needed. . . . Inge Becker or Werner Ruhemann from the Olympics in Munich will contact Mr. Wilder. . . . Also Allan Kaprow promised he'd send signatures of prominent people at California Institute of the Arts.[46]

Emerging initially in the service of promoting music, in other words, this network of engaged artists was also committed to one another socially, politically, and economically.

It behooves us today to remember that Moorman's festivals offered a situation of live art in this eternal network of people with shared cultural and social concerns. Moorman's vivacious and effective idealism models usefully and differently from today's many large-scale, seemingly similar, spectacles of the art marketplace. The publicness, open access, no admission fee, and public use of public space and media were fundamental to Moorman's sense of purpose. Moorman's network was, in a phrase, motivated by her love of art and artists.

Notes

1. Malcom McLean, a Texas-based trucker, moved the shipping container into widespread use beginning in 1956. The collapse of the industrial core occurred in many cities and was not unique to SoHo in Manhattan, since shipping containers could be loaded (once) at the factory and sent across the continent or ocean, where they were unpacked (once) at the final destination.

2. It is no accident that at exactly this time, the zoning laws were in place to construct the Lower Manhattan Expressway, a vast highway conceived by master builder Robert Moses, which would have obliterated much of Lower Manhattan's industrial loft district and divided upper Manhattan from the financial district. The idea was, obviously enough, to bring the highways to the manufacturers—or what remained of them. Moses was trying to save the neighborhood for its original use: manufacturing. Though the Lower Manhattan Expressway was opposed by dozens of public figures and more than two hundred community groups, the efforts of the South Houston Artist Tenants Association and "a handful of artists stepped in and stopped it cold" at the east end of Chinatown, where the partially completed highway exists to this day. For details, see Robert Stern, *New York 1960: Architecture and Urbanism between the Second World War and the Bicentennial* (New York: Monacelli, 1995), 259–77.

3. Similarly, cast-off industrial materials became working materials, not to mention the quiescent plastics, baubles, electronics, and obscure mechanical tidbits awaiting repurposing in the open bins along Canal Street, some lucky few of which would find permanent homes in George Maciunas's Fluxkits a few years later.

4. Richard Kostelanetz, *SoHo: The Rise and Fall of an Artists' Colony* (New York: Routledge, 2003), 3.

5. For an especially detailed exploration of the idea of SoHo as an artists' colony, see ibid.

6. Ibid.

7. For the observations regarding the emergence of SoHo and the sense of aesthetic and social freedom that accompanied the empty spaces of SoHo, I am deeply indebted to my conversations and interview with Mitchell Schwarzer from 2004 through 2006.

8. James R. Hudson, *The Unanticipated City: Loft Conversions in Lower Manhattan* (Amherst: University of Massachusetts Press, 1987), 81.

9. See Gerard Forde, "Plus or Minus 1961—A Chronology 1959–1963," in *+/- 1961: Founding the Expanded Arts*, ed. Julia Robinson and Christian Xatrec (Madrid: Museo Nacional Centro de Arte Reina Sofia, 2013), 255: "The first concerts (December 18 and 19) are devoted to music, performed by the composer . . . Scott LaFaro, and Young. The concert also features compositions written for [Terry] Jennings by Richard Maxfield, Terry Riley, and Young, performed by Jennings, Toshi Ichiyanagi, Kenji Kobayashi, and Young."

10. Forti quoted in Julia Robinson, "Prime Media," in *+/- 1961: Founding the Expanded Arts*, 29.

11. Ibid.

12. Ibid., 38.

13. It should be noted that artists had been active in the area prior to the concert. For example, in in 1959, Dick Higgins and Al Hansen, both students of John Cage's famous course in experimental composition at the New School, organized a concert series in the village, calling themselves "The New York Audiovisual Group," and La Monte Young and the poet Jackson Mac Low assembled "An Anthology," a compilation of instructional scores, visual poems, and conceptual objects. Albeit important precedents to the Ono/Young loft series, these functioned on an admittedly smaller scale. See Jackson Mac Low and La Monte Young, eds., *An Anthology of chance operations concept art anti-art indeterminacy improvisation meaningless work natural disasters plans of action stories diagrams Music poetry essays dance constructions mathematics compositions* (privately printed, 1961). This self-published artists' book was designed by George Maciunas.

14. Kyle Gann, *Music Downtown: Writings from the Village Voice* (Berkeley: University of California Press, 2006), xiii.

15. Program, Charlotte Moorman Archive, Charles Deering McCormick Library of Special Collections, Northwestern University Library (hereafter cited as CMA).

16. It is unclear why some performers appear by their first or last names. Brackets appear around those parts of names that do not appear on the note.

17. Joan Rothfuss, note to the author, January 15, 2015.

18. For details, see Joan Rothfuss, *Topless Cellist: The Improbable Life of Charlotte Moorman* (Cambridge, Mass.: MIT Press, 2014), 77.

19. Ibid., 73.

20. Winthrop Sargeant, "Musical Events: It Just Is—or Is It?" *New Yorker* 39, no. 30 (September 14, 1963): 122. Quoted in Rothfuss, *Topless Cellist*, 75–76.

21. Photographer-filmographer Peter Moore's excellent documentation of the piece can be seen on UbuWeb at http://www.ubu.com/film/stockhausen_originale.html.

22. George Maciunas to George Brecht, August 28, 1965, Archiv Sohm, Staatsgalerie Stuttgart. Quoted in Owen Smith, *Fluxus: History of an Attitude* (San Diego: San Diego State University Press, 1998), 159.

23. For details, see "Charting Fluxus, Picturing History," in Hannah Higgins, *Fluxus Experience* (Berkeley: University of California Press, 2002), 69–77.

24. Carolee Schneemann, quoted in Rothfuss, *Topless Cellist*, 138. Originally in Bruce McPherson, ed., *More Than Meat Joy: Performance Works and Selected Writings*, 2nd ed. (Kingston, N.Y.: McPherson, 1997), 92.

25. Allan Kaprow, "Happenings in the New York Scene" (1961), in *Essays on The Blurring of Art and Life*, ed. Jeff Kelley (Berkeley: University of California Press, 1993), 17.

26. Rothfuss, *Topless Cellist*, 92.

27. Ibid., 139.

28. This event is beautifully laid out in all its complex detail in ibid., 138–40.

29. "Moorman, Charlotte; Annual Avant Garde Festivals," Fondazione Bonotto, accessed May 29, 2015, http://www.fondazione bonotto.org/fluxus/moor mancharlotte/document/ fxc1656115.html.

30. The publicity can be found in the festival files CMA.

31. Con Ed, statement by chairman of the board Leon Leavitt, festival files, 1968, CMA.

32. Geoffrey Hendricks, *Ring Piece* (Barton, Vt.: Something Else Press, 1971).

33. Ibid., 13.

34. Eric Andersen to Charlotte Moorman, October 1974, Hervé Fischer Archive, Bibliothèque Kandinsky, Centre Georges Pompidou, Paris.

35. Wood was renowned at the time for activating the entire forty-four-story facade and plaza of the Seagram Building on Park Avenue with dancers in 1972. She was made an honorary member of the American Institute of Architects for the effort. Building on the environmental theater of Anna Halprin, Wood frequently integrated architecture and dance beginning in 1968. Her *SoHo Fire Escape Dance* and dance using the facade of the Seagram skyscraper (both 1972) belong to a tradition of situating dance outdoors, in a broadly conceived built environment. It should come as no surprise that the tradition took root in SoHo, the same environment that had been so hospitable for Elaine Summers's and Simone Forti's early works, which were similarly site specific. In *SoHo Fire Escape Dance* the industrial facade effectively tips up the traditional dance floor, the fire escape and ladders providing a site-specific armature, the sidewalk a site-specific standing area for the audience, the cars and people passing below an urban symphony. A year later, San Francisco Dancers' Workshop cofounder Trisha Brown's better-known *Roof Piece* spread the audience across two rooftops and the dancers across four more buildings in SoHo. Like the other participants in the festival, by the middle 1970s, each of these dancers had long since found ways to thrive, or at least survive, as culture makers. The Celebration Group, for example, would perform public-space dance in collaboration with communities across the United States and in Berlin, Singapore, Tehran, Hong Kong, and Rio de Janiero, to name just a few destinations.

36. A letter dated August 14, 1971, from Moorman to Yoko Ono, in CMA, contains the following statement of gratitude: "I know I should have gone to Dr. Dillon regularly, but I was ashamed to since I hadn't paid him. He thought I was going to faint when he told me you had paid the entire bill! The way you saved me is too beautiful and too unbelievable."

37. This argument is laid out explicitly in "Counter-Landscapes" in Peter Bacon Hales, *Outside the Gates of Eden: The Dream of America from Hiroshima to Now* (Chicago: University of Chicago Press, 2014), 311–46.

38. Stanley Milgram, *Obedience to Authority* (London: Tavistock, 1974), 151.

39. Mark Buchanan, *Nexus: Small Worlds and the Groundbreaking Theory of Networks* (repr., New York: Norton, 2003), 201.

40. Robert Filliou, *Teaching and Learning as Performing Arts* (Cologne: König, 1970), 198.

41. Ibid., 204.

42. Robert Filliou, *PORTA FILLIOU*, produced by Filliou, Clive Robertson, and Marcella Bienvenue (Calgary, Canada: Artons Video, 1977), videocassette (VHS). Elsewhere, Filliou described a system of equivalences, in which the well-made, poorly made, and not made art are "equivalent."

43. See John Wilcock, "The Village Square," *Village Voice* 1, no. 1 (October 26, 1955): 3. This example is taken from John Held, *Mail Art: An Annotated Bibliography* (Metuchen, N.J.: Scarecrow Press, 1991), entry no. 686, 145. Examples of the use of the term "eternal network" to describe the mail art network include chapters by Michael Crane, Dick Higgins, and Steve Hitchcock in *Correspondence Art: Source Book for the Network of International Postal Art Activity*, ed. Michael Crane and Mary Stofflet (San Francisco: Contemporary Arts Press, 1984). See also Chuck Welch (aka Crackerjack Kid), *Eternal Network: A Mail Art Anthology* (Calgary, Canada: University of Calgary Press, 1995), and the Artifacts of the Eternal Network mail art collection at the University of Iowa in Iowa City.

44. Jon Wiener, "John Lennon and Yoko Ono's Deportation Battle," *Los Angeles Times*, October 8, 2010, http://articles.latimes .com/2010/oct/08/opinion/ la-oe-wiener-john-lennon-deportation-20101008.

45. Alison Knowles, Allan Kaprow, and Emmett Williams also signed on behalf of Moorman, but it is unclear whether their signatures were included. Materials in CMA.

46. Charlotte Moorman to Yoko Ono, CMA.

Festival Posters

Introduction by Joan Rothfuss

Charlotte Moorman's fifteen avant-garde festivals, which took place from 1963 to 1980, were seminal events in the history of intermedia and public art. The posters made to promote them are important documents of what took place at each one, but they also comprise a visual history of the festivals' evolution from a ticketed concert series, held at a midtown recital hall, to immersive, all-day events staged in public spaces that presented hundreds of artists working in dozens of media.

For the first three years, Moorman produced simple, inexpensive pieces that reflect the festivals' conventional structure. She designed, typed, and pasted them up herself, making new versions as needed when performers or compositions changed. The main visual element in each is a column of the featured composers' autographs, which Moorman selected from sheets of sample signatures she collected from them. These "posters" served as both folded mailers for advance publicity and programs for the day of the concert.

In 1966, Moorman moved her festivals out of the concert hall and into iconic public spaces throughout New York City. The poster for that year's festival, held in Central Park, reflected this seismic shift immediately. A map of the park provides the background for the column of artists' signatures, a design that both visualizes the presence of artists in the park and signals the new importance of site to the festivals' mission. That year, the poster and program functions were separated: posters were mailed out in advance to Moorman's ever-expanding list of contacts, while a typed list of works being performed was handed to visitors as they arrived at the festival.

The 1966 poster was designed by Jim McWilliams, an artist who was a friend of Moorman's and a frequent collaborator during the 1960s and 1970s. He taught graphic design, industrial design, book arts, printmaking, and typography at the Philadelphia College of Art. He went on to design all the rest of Moorman's festival posters, gradually transforming them from the functional but conservative designs Moorman had used into exuberant, often chaotic images that mirrored the liveliness, color, and complexity of the events themselves.

His first departure from Moorman's formula was in 1971. That year's festival, the eighth, was held in Manhattan's 69th Regiment Armory and largely devoted to electronic and video art. McWilliams designed a silver-and-black poster featuring two TV sets, which manages to evoke the glare of video monitors in a darkened interior. His poster for the fourteenth festival, held on the banks of the Charles River in Cambridge, Massachusetts, is a collage printed in layers of cyan, yellow, magenta, and silver that seems to shimmer like sunlight on rippling water. In these designs, style was more important than readability. "The information was there," McWilliams says, "but not in a conventional order. I just put things where I thought they made the most annoyance." But what was lost in legibility was gained in high spirits, and Moorman never asked him to make any changes.

By contrast, some of the posters McWilliams made during the mid-1970s reflect the period's vogue for the orderly column-and-grid style of classic Swiss design (as well as the ethos of his relatively conventional job as an art director for the Port Authority of New York and New Jersey). For the twelfth festival, held at Floyd Bennett Field in Brooklyn, he arranged the copy in neat columns, on top of which he placed a large number "12" made up of colored circles set in twelve vertical rows. Each of the circles contains an aerial photograph of the field shot by McWilliams from a Port Authority helicopter. His poster for the thirteenth festival is just as visually clean, with a series of strong verticals that allude to that year's site, the World Trade Center towers and plaza.

McWilliams did not charge Moorman for his graphic work, and through his connections in the design community he was able to get most of the posters printed for free. With her shoestring festival budgets, Moorman surely needed this help. But perhaps more important, McWilliams's distinctive, highly original posters did much to reinforce the avant-garde identity of the festivals.

All fifteen designs are reproduced on the following pages, along with a new poster created by McWilliams especially for this book. Additional comments by McWilliams, excerpted from emails to the author in April and June 2015, appear in italics near some of the images.

norman j seaman in association with c moorman presents

6 concerts '63

earle brown · john cage · morton feldman · charlotte moorman

max neuhaus · frederic rzewski · david tudor · nicholas zumbro

performing works by

[signatures]
David Behrman
Earle Brown
Joseph Byrd
John Cage
Ornette Coleman
Philip Corner
Lucia Dlugoszewski
Morton Feldman
Toshi Ichiyanagi
Richard Maxfield
Henri Pousseur
Frederic Rzewski
Karlheinz Stockhausen
James Tenney
Edgard Varèse
Christian Wolff
La Monte Young

august 20, 21 · august 27, 28 · september 3, 4 · 8:30 pm
judson hall 165 w 57 st nyc single tickets 99¢ and 1.99
on sale at door mail orders to n seaman 119 w 57 st ci 5-9250

august 27

frederic rzewski, piano
david tudor, piano
nicholas zumbro, piano
max neuhaus, percussion

sonata	christian wolff
f rzewski, d tudor, n zumbro	
two piano piece	morton feldman
f rzewski, d tudor	
schlagfiguren	bo nillson
n zumbro	
quantitaten	bo nillson
n zumbro	
music for piano #2	toshi ichiyanagi
f rzewski, d tudor, n zumbro	

intermission

zyklus	karlheinz
m neuhaus	stockhausen
*from place to place	david behrman
f rzewski, d tudor	
**nursery fable with exegesis	bertram baldwin
f rzewski	
**action music for piano	alvin lucier
f rzewski	
**coronata for pianists	toro takemitsu
f rzewski, d tudor, n zumbro	

*world premiere
**american premiere
†new york premiere
  baldwin piano

august 28

electronic concert

*bhagavad gita symphony: chapter XI	richard maxfield
†scambi	henri pousseur
study no 2	mario davidovsky
omagio a joyce	luciano berio

intermission

*ergodos /3 /4	james tenney
**antithese	mauricio kagel
incontri di fasce sonore	franco evangeliste
**orient occident	yannis xenakis
interpolation of deserts	edgard varese

grateful acknowledgement to:
bell telephone laboratory
c f peters corporation
columbia university music department
franco colombo inc
harvey radio and television service

sept 3   charlotte moorman, cello
david tudor, piano

sept 4   ensemble concert
john cage, earle brown, conductors

6 Concerts '63, Judson Hall, New York City,
August 20, 21, 27, 28, September 3, 4, 1963.
Poster/mailer, design by Charlotte Moorman.

2nd Annual New York Avant Garde
Festival, Judson Hall, August 30, 31,
September 1, 2, 3, 8, 9, 11, 12, 13, 1964.
Two posters/mailers, design by
Charlotte Moorman.

Festival Posters   95

3rd Annual New York Avant Garde
Festival, Judson Hall, August 25,
26, 27, 28, 29, 31, September 2, 3,
7, 8, 9, 10, 11, 1965. Poster design
by Charlotte Moorman.

3RD ANNUAL NEW YORK
AVANT GARDE FESTIVAL

JUDSON HALL (165 w 57 st)
AUG 25 – SEPT 11 1965

AUG 25 – PAIK action music

AUG 26 – ALL SATIE program

AUG 27 – ELECTRONIC music

AUG 28 – DANCE evening

AUG 29 – ENSEMBLE concert

AUG 31 – FILM night

SEPT 2 – POETRY program

SEPT 3 – JAZZ concert

SEPT 7 – CAGE "Theater Piece"
          KAPROW participation happening

SEPT 8 – HIGGINS choreographic theater
          CAGE "Theater Piece"

SEPT 9 – CORNER compositions
          KOSUGI events
          CAGE "Theater Piece"

SEPT 10 – MAC LOW play
          CAGE "Theater Piece"

SEPT 11 – HANSEN time-space drama
          CAGE "Theater Piece"

"Theater Piece" performed by
corner · hansen · harris · kaprow
kosugi · moorman · paik · tenney

performances at 8:30 · tickets 99¢
& 1.99 · series 8.00 & 15.00 · on
sale at hall · mail orders : c moorman
judson hall · 165 w 57 st nyc

c moorman
third annual new york
festival of the avant garde
judson hall
165 west 57 street

OPPOSITE LEFT
4th Annual New York Avant Garde
Festival, Central Park, September 9,
1966. Program.

OPPOSITE RIGHT
4th Annual New York Avant Garde
Festival, Central Park, September 9,
1966. Poster design by Jim
McWilliams.

c moorman presents

4th annual new york avant garde festival
september 9,1966 · 6am 'til midnight
central park · conservatory pond

program

sunrise event	yoko ono
it's vital!	benjamin patterson
cut piece	yoko ono
please	larry loonin
zoological gardens	frederic rzewski
sfm2	pietro grossi
aurora	leo nilson
e m s no i	ralph lundsten
jazz morning improvisation	don heckman
danger music no. 2	dick higgins
composition 1960 #13	la monte young
dick higgins, singer	
park music	robert moran
?	philip corner
environment	toshi ichiyanagi
c moorman & t kosugi	
burton greene group	
fahem aniesgwow	hans g helms
asymmetries,gathas & sounds	jackson mac low
from everywhere	
(electronic poetry with 5 live people)	
j mac low · spencer holst · david hazleton	
emmett williams · mordecai-mac low	
we hardly had...	richard huelsenbeck
r huelsenbeck · david anton · jerome rothen-	
berg · j mac low	
poems	carol berge
c berge	
manifesto	diter rot
duet	emmett williams
vol	ludwig gosewitz
visual poetry	lamberto pignotti
spatial poem no 3	chieko shiomi
me	bazon brock
...	tomas schmit
class class struggle opera	kurt schwitters
allan kaprow · alison knowles · takehisa kosugi	
charlotte moorman · .benjamin patterson · bob	
watts · emmett williams · commissioner	
thomas hoving (if possible)	
towers	allan kaprow
empaquetage of a statue	christo
second piece for violin alone(1966) stefan wolpe	
kenji kobayashi, violin	
form	"
howard lebow, piano	
lecture	"
howard lebow	
cecil taylor group	
c taylor, piano;jimmy lyons & ken mc intyre,	
reeds;mike mantler,trumpet;henry grimes&	
allan silva,strings;tony williams,drums	
cross-cut east	jacob glick
j glick, saw · shigeko kubota, reader	
dick & his little wagon,	dick higgins
emmett williams & his japanese tools,	
alison knowles & her all girl team,	
jerry agel & his slide projector	
manodharma concert	takehisa kosugi
t kosugi · shigeko kubota · charlotte moorman	
james tenney · emmett williams	
cello sonata	joseph beuys
charlotte moorman, cello	
telemusic	karlheinz stockhausen
manzit	karl erik welin
don heckman, clarinet, c moorman, cello,	
george jeffers, trombone, james tenney, piano	
?	earle brown
fuori	giuseppe chiari
several performers	
phases	james tenney
ergodos i	"
ergodos ii	"
dew horse	music-bill dixon
ballet-judith dunn	
from morning glory	wolf vostell
heckman-summerlin quintet	
the marion brown ensemble	
sunny · murray's unlimited acoustical unit	
a man & his dog out for air	robert breer
jamestown baloos	"
inner & outer space	"
homage to jean tinguely's homage to n y	"
horse over teakettle	"
blazes	"
pat's birthday	"
breathing	"
fist fight	"
night kite	benjamin patterson
staccato en plein air	gary harris
(a non chamber work for 4000 watts)	
i allegretto; ii vivace; iii largo-presto	
ballet in the park	elaine summers
e summers & clyde heriltz	
ghosts before breakfast	hans richter
rhythms	"
dada '62	takahiko iimura
why don't you sneeze	"
usco	

continuous pieces

symphony #4 by george brecht	
realized by the composer	
variations iii	john cage
music bike	joe jones
toy	charles frazier
shoes of your choice - alison knowles	
picnic jim mcwilliams & robert burridge	
oraculum	bob watts
counting song no ii	emmett williams

at some opportune moment

a slice of life 1962	robert ashley
3 events	al hansen
if & washing event	bici hendricks
sky kite & dumping	geoffrey hendricks
peeping into the balla	shigeko kubota
a museum	larry loonin
blessed event	barbara & peter moore
atlantic city 1962	gordon mumma
american can	max neuhaus
zen smiles	nam june paik
curtain events	lil picard
beethoven's head	raffaele
floating light	ely raman
something	carolee schneemann

grateful acknowledgement to :

carroll musical instruments service
c f peters music corporation
fluxus inc
ken werner
michael kaye - audio consultant
new york city department of parks
peter moore
something else press
steinway pianos
walter segal
walter kidde company inc - plastic dome

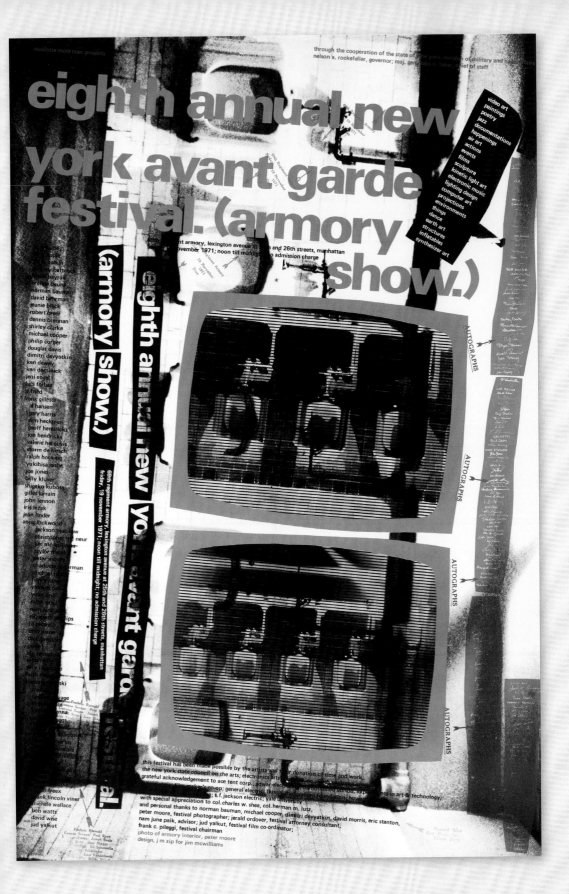

5th Annual New York Avant Garde Festival, Staten Island ferryboat *John F. Kennedy,* September 29–30, 1967. Poster design by Jim McWilliams.

6th Annual New York Avant Garde Festival, Central Park West and Central Park Drive, September 14, 1968. Poster design by Jim McWilliams.

7th Annual New York Avant Garde Festival, Wards Island and Mill Rock Island, September 28–October 4, 1969. Poster design by Jim McWilliams.

LEFT
8th Annual New York Avant Garde Festival, 69th Regiment Armory, November 19, 1971. Poster design by Jim McWilliams.

The story is told and retold at random angles in repetitions of typography and photos of the urinals in the Armory men's room, which I shot with a Polaroid camera. The logical image to use would have been one of the many beautiful carved details on the Armory walls. The most illogical image was the urinals, silent sentinels waiting to become fountains.

9th Annual New York Avant Garde
Festival, Hudson River excursion
boat *Alexander Hamilton,* South
Street Seaport, October 28, 1972.
Poster design by Jim McWilliams.

*This poster was made from a single
printing plate and used a split ink
fountain technique. One color, in this
case blue, was put on the right side
of the ink fountain, and green was
put on the left side, and the oscillat-
ing ink rollers mixed the two, which
merged into a third color. This
was fun because no two posters
are exactly alike.*

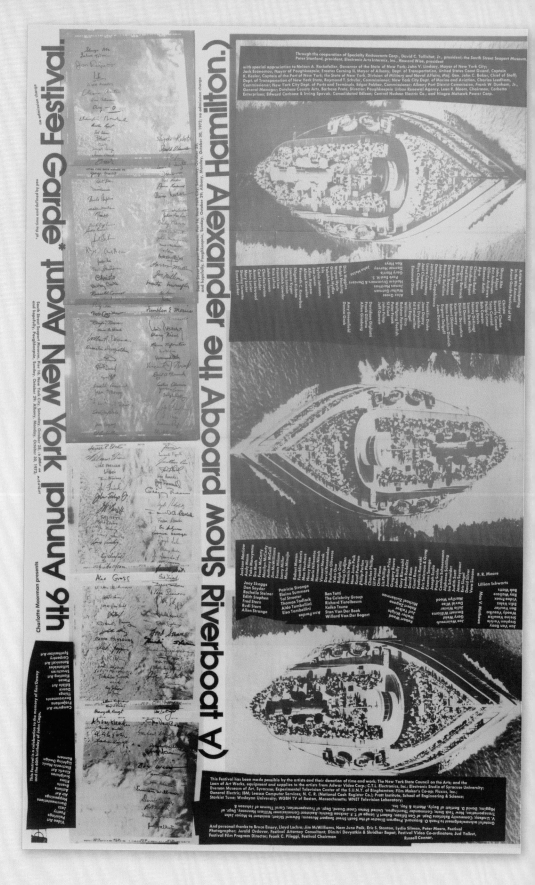

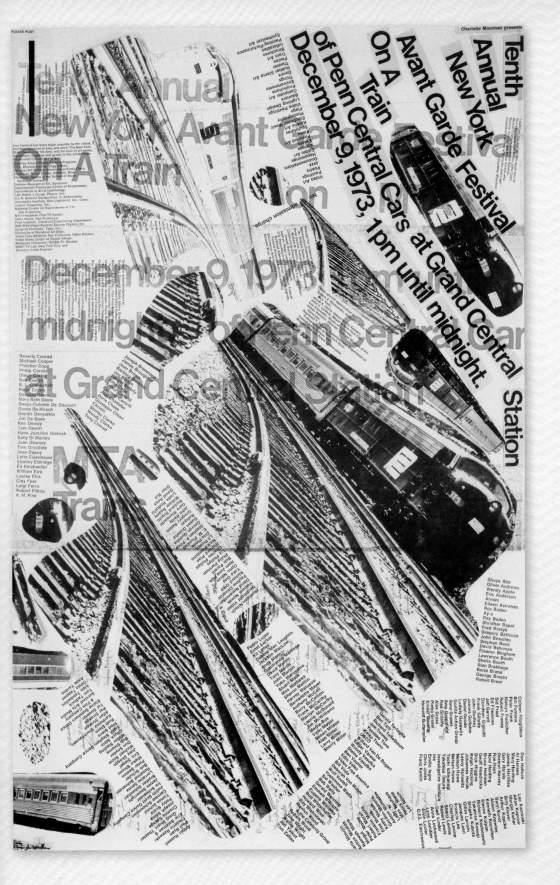

10th Annual New York Avant Garde Festival, Grand Central Terminal, December 9, 1973. Poster design by Jim McWilliams.

A poster of utter confusion because my life in 1973 was utter confusion. The only person who really liked this one was Charlotte. She was my defense against all of those who said, "But you can't read anything." That was the main idea! She got it.

11th Annual New York Avant Garde Festival, Shea Stadium, Flushing Meadows, Queens, November 16, 1974. Poster design by Jim McWilliams.

A rich, full-color circuslike poster that you could actually read. The small pictures of the stadium at the bottom of the poster show all the images used. I spent a lot of time copying and recopying them on the Xerox machine, with its color brilliance setting turned up on high. The background is made up of repetitions of the overhead images from large to small. Each of the cyan, magenta, yellow, and black printing plates was exposed many times.

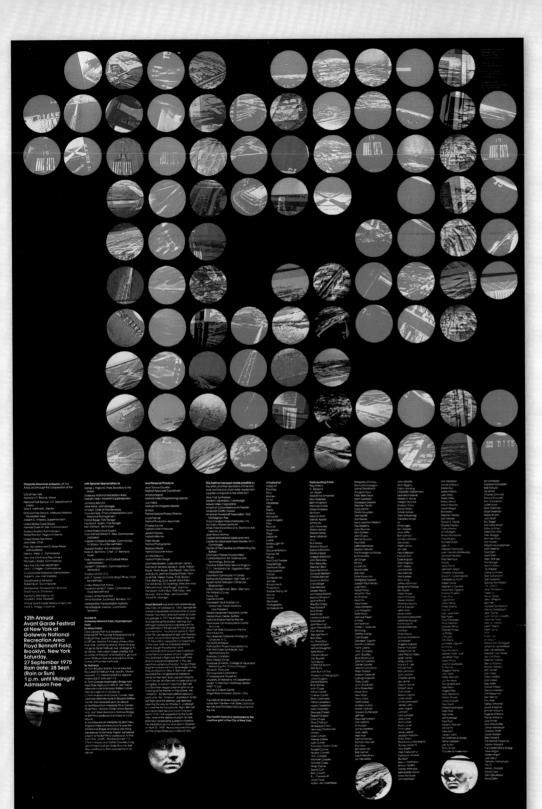

12th Annual New York Avant Garde Festival, Gateway National Recreation Area / Floyd Bennett Field, Brooklyn, September 27, 1975. Poster design by Jim McWilliams.

This one was printed by a company in North Carolina, I think. They brought them up on a Sunday night, and Charlotte had a check from John Lennon to pay for it. They didn't believe it was a real check and wouldn't take it, so we had to get Charlotte's lawyer to come over and verify it. The black-and-white pictures at the bottom are of Floyd Bennett. I wrote the copy for this poster and decided to include a bio of Bennett, a fellow treated hard by life.

13th Annual New York Avant
Garde Festival, World Trade Center,
June 19, 1977. Poster design by Jim
McWilliams.

The images for this poster were again
made on a color Xerox machine. This
time I moved the originals as they
were being scanned, which created
a moiré effect. This poster has more
significance since the 9/11 disaster
because I made the buildings appear
to be crumbling. I had spent five
years working for the Port Authority
on the seventy-third floor of the North
Tower, swaying in the wind and, on
many days, above the clouds.

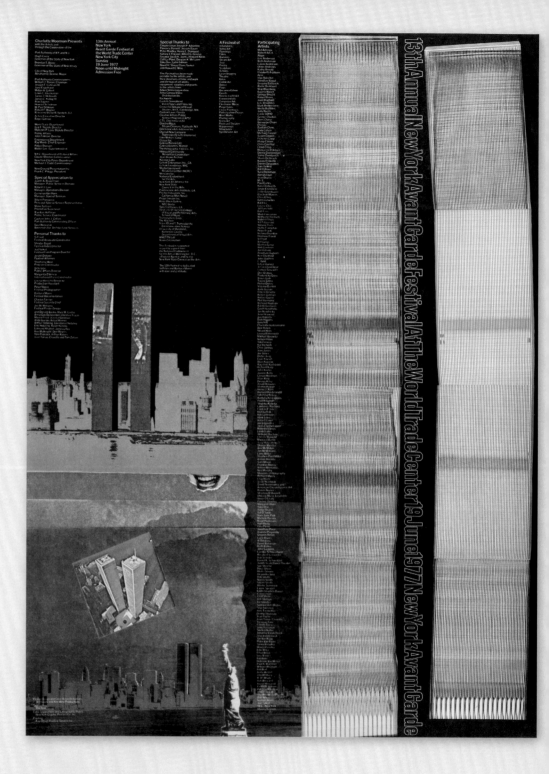

14th Annual New York Avant Garde Festival, north bank of Charles River, Cambridge, Massachusetts, in conjunction with the Second Annual Cambridge River Festival, May 20, 1978. Poster design by Jim McWilliams.

The basket of apples symbolizes all of the Big Apple artists going up to Massachusetts to work by the Charles River. The tire was just a cool object to float the apples in.

15th Annual Avant Garde Festival of New York, Passenger Ship Terminal, July 20, 1980. Poster design by Jim McWilliams.

This one was produced while I was vice president, sales manager, and creative director of the Linweave Paper Company in Holyoke, Massachusetts. I was able to make the poster serve as a promotional sample for a new paper that Linweave was introducing. At this time I was also upgrading a line of their paper called Mardi Gras, which is why I used the confetti and streamers in the design. I threw in a few ships for good measure.

Commemorative poster for *A Feast of Astonishments: Charlotte Moorman and the Avant-Garde, 1960s–1980s*. Design by Jim McWilliams. Published by the Mary and Leigh Block Museum of Art, 2016.

First row: Photographer unknown. Courtesy of Kaldor Public Art Projects. Second row: Photograph by Catherine Skopic. Third row: Photograph by Kerry Dundas © Art Gallery of New South Wales. Fourth row: Photographer unknown. Courtesy of Kaldor Public Art Projects. Fifth row: Photograph by Thomas Tilly. Courtesy of AFORK (Archiv künstlerischer Fotografie der rheinischen Kunstszene), Museum Kunstpalast, Düsseldorf, Germany. Background: Photographer unknown. Private collection of Leon Amitai. Courtesy of Galeria Jaqueline Martins.

Noise Bodies and Noisy Women: A Conversation with Carolee Schneemann

Lisa G. Corrin

On February 7, 1966, Carolee Schneemann wrote to artist Jean-Jacques Lebel, "Things brightened to hysteria for Charlotte's Festival."[1] This "hysteria" was the unique, consciously unpredictable energy of Charlotte Moorman's Annual New York Avant Garde Festivals, making for truly astonishing feats of the imagination. Moorman actively encouraged artists to think freshly and fearlessly, to embrace uncertainty, and to indulge in freewheeling aesthetic border crossings—unexpected couplings among music, dance, visual arts, poetry, and film. It was this "co-mingling of group process" which Schneemann wrote to Moorman's husband, Frank Pileggi, in her condolence letter that "anticipates the only meaningful direction for the future."[2]

"Co-mingling" certainly describes Schneemann's own approach to art making, especially in the early years in which she transitioned from making paintings on canvas to extending that practice into space, time, action, and the body. During the fifteen years of the avant-garde festivals, Schneemann, like Moorman, was an interpersonal collagist, assembling creative partnerships across media to liberate her work from the limitations of artistic homogeneity. For Schneemann, to liberate one's art was to liberate one's self.

A number of Schneemann's radical "cominglings"—works combining object making with movement, sound, and participatory experience—are documented to have been part of the festivals. Among these are *Noise Bodies*, Allan Kaprow's *Push and Pull* (1965) in Judson Hall; *Nightcrawlers II* (1967) on the Staten Island Ferry—"small caves from pink foam rubber"; *Rainbow Blaze* (1971)— "a ritual painting event to enclose/expand, to sanctify, and purify the Armory"[3]; and *Trackings* in Grand Central Terminal (1973).[4]

ABOVE
Peter Moore. Publicity photograph for 5th Annual New York Avant Garde Festival, Staten Island ferryboat *John F. Kennedy*, 1967. Nam June Paik, Don Heckman, Carolee Schneemann with pink foam rubber from *Nightcrawlers II*, Charlotte Moorman, and Jud Yalkut. Photograph © Barbara Moore/Licensed by VAGA, NY.

OPPOSITE
Peter Moore. Carolee Schneemann performs her *Noise Bodies*, 3rd Annual New York Avant Garde Festival, Judson Hall, August 28, 1965. Photograph © Barbara Moore/Licensed by VAGA, NY.

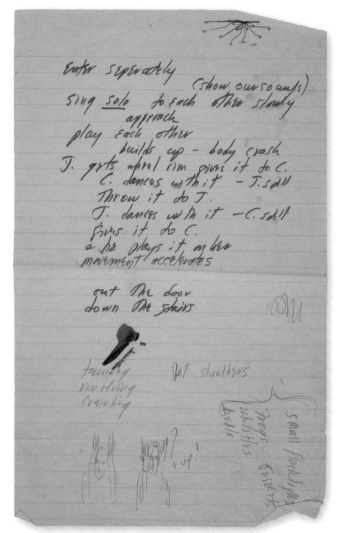

Carolee Schneemann. Handwritten notes on *Noise Bodies,* ca. 1965. © Carolee Schneemann / Artists Rights Society (ARS), New York. Courtesy of Getty Research Institute, Los Angeles (950001).

of collaborative, intermedia works for which the avant-garde festivals became known and which Moorman actively encouraged. The piece called for Schneemann and composer James Tenney, costumed in "sound making debris," to enter the darkened stage with small penlights, "lighting ourselves briefly (like fireflies)" and making occasional noises with squeakers. A handwritten text from the artist's notebook describes the basic sequence of actions for the choreography of *Noise Bodies.* The top has a "doodle" and drawings at the bottom left show pictograms of each performer with their hands up in "gestures for the headdresses."[6] The text reads as follows:

> Enter separately
> (show our sounds)
> Sing <u>solo</u> to each other slowly
> Approach
> play each other
> builds up—body crash
> J. gets wheel rim gives it to C.
> C. dances with it—J. still
> Throw it to J.
> J. dances with it—C. still
> Gives it to C.
> & he plays it on her
> Movement accelerates
> out the door
> down the stairs
> turning
> revolving
> crawling
> pat shoulders [7]

Trackings later became better known as *Up to and Including Her Limits,* one of Schneemann's most iconic works. Suspended by rope, the artist tracked her body's movements on the walls and floor "like a seismograph" with a piece of handheld chalk.[5] The first iteration of the title *Trackings* also connects the work to its initial performance context—an open boxcar on the tracks of the train station.

Noise Bodies premiered on Saturday, August 28, 1965, before an audience including Meredith Monk, Yoko Ono, Yvonne Rainer, Elaine Summers, and Malcolm Goldstein. It was performed only one other time, in Dance at the Bridge at 4 St. Marks Place on November 28–30, 1965. It is in many ways an exemplar of the kinds

In a diary entry of August 27, 1965, Schneemann described the preparations for the evening at Judson Hall: "Went up at 2 p.m., tangled pile of my clattering 'costumes' for 'Noise Bodies'; setting up for rehearsal, chaos—everyone running around, carting cable, testing amplifiers, speakers, dancers practicing . . . hollering for quiet. Good rehearsal; simple, clear shape of piece carries directly; but Jim resisting, re-formation, definition of sequence. Helping Charlotte and Philip."[8]

And in the next day's entry, "To Judson Hall 4:30 with last minute supplies. Beverly Schmidt and I go over lighting for our pieces. *Noise Bodies* so uncomplicated—just Jim &

me—own body-sound system. Crazy dressing each other in all the metal parts; hooking on the refrigerator tubes, ice trays, carburator [sic] vents around our legs . . . balancing the noise squeakers, flashlights, tea pot top 'breasts'. . . .Moving in costumes as we walk the length of the darkened hall . . . audience an intense mass, heat of them, silence . . . the two spots flash on—the audience roars. We begin to touch and 'play' the sound of our 'debris bodies.' Furious cacophonous exit totally concentrated on pitch and timbre of our strikes, moving fast through tripods, crouching photographers—applause over our din."[9]

We are fortunate that the costumes for this little-known early performance were recently rediscovered in Schneemann's attic. Along with a handful of photographs taken at Judson Hall on the evening of its performance, these wearable sculptures provide a rare opportunity to piece together what one would have seen and heard during a typical night of an avant-garde festival.

Noise Bodies had the charming, low-tech simplicity featured in so many festival works. Makeshift, do-it-yourself efforts made from discarded urban detritus elevated the experiences and materials of the ordinary and everyday and closed the gap between art and life, an aesthetic goal for many of the participating artists. Ice trays, hubcaps, party razzers and horns, smashed cans, torn hosiery, gnarly bunches of colored wire, a plastic Wiffle ball, a rusty tin can once containing English fruit-flavored hard candy, fake pearls—whatever Schneemann found in old garages or while foraging for materials in the streets was harnessed as costume material, transforming the performers into colorful, clanging "debris sculpture."

Peter Moore. Carolee Schneemann and James Tenney perform Schneemann's *Noise Bodies*, 3rd Annual New York Avant Garde Festival, Judson Hall, August 28, 1965. Photograph © Barbara Moore / Licensed by VAGA, NY.

Lit only by small flashlights, a neon orange label on an empty Birds Eye "Awake" juice can, a red logo signaling Rheingold beer, or a crushed, bright blue metal lid made flickering arcs of color in motion. This sensitivity to the vibrancy and behavior of color has the sensibility of a painter, which is how Schneemann has always identified herself, but a painter "extending visual principles off the canvas."[10] Taking delight in all this flotsam and jetsam, Schneemann also fashioned a mobile—a hanging bicycle wheel of "junk" strung like a colorful charm bracelet with a license plate, pots and pans, kitchen utensils, and empty oilcans. This sculpture added its own choreography to *Noise Bodies* in the form of kinetic, cinematic shadows that mingled with those cast on the stage wall by the performers like a second, simultaneous performance. The wheel bears comparison to Schneemann's *Fur Wheel* (1962), a motorized, wall-hung construction combining painting and a rotating wheel of fur from which colorful, jangling, squashed tin cans are suspended.

Carolee Schneemann performs her *Noise Bodies*, 3rd Annual New York Avant Garde Festival, Judson Hall, August 28, 1965. Photograph by Ted Wester. © Carolee Schneemann/Artists Rights Society (ARS), New York. Courtesy of Getty Research Institute, Los Angeles (950001).

That the visual, audio, and choreographic elements of *Noise Bodies*, taken together or separately, should evoke painting—along with sculpture, film, dance, and sound—is consistent with the radical art Schneemann began creating at that time, such as *Eye Body: 36 Transformative Actions for Camera* (1963) and the performance *Meat Joy* (1964). In these works, as in *Noise Bodies*, she explored the dynamic possibilities of blending, extending, and activating the full range of artist media with "the body's energy in motion."[11] As art historian Maura Reilly has observed, Schneemann's paintings and drawings are best appreciated as "important corollaries to the kinetic theater, Judson Dance Theater performances, and films that she was producing simultaneously."[12] The converse may also be said— *Noise Bodies* may be seen as a corollary to Schneemann's objects.

Schneemann's purposeful collapsing of artistic boundaries was a critical feminist act, challenging the primacy of the canvas, especially the heroics and "hypermasculinity of action painting," as it was particularly inflected in the work of Jackson Pollock and his male contemporaries.[13] *Noise Bodies* also performs her feminist perspective. The formfitting, jangling metal costumes included gendered headgear—a feminine "diadem" and male "helmet." Equally strong, each performer was endowed with a conducting rod—a piece of a carburetor gear cable from a '57 Chevy—in order to "play" the other. And play the other, they did. One can imagine percussive sounds emanating from the deliberate striking of tin cans, which, in turn, might knock against iron chains and aluminum ice trays; or the sweetly sensual, softer sounds made by the conducting rod tenderly stroking a teapot lid nipple, gently brushing their small attached bells.[14] The costumes were tuning forks, turning each performer into an instrument of the other's desire.

That each performer would be an equal partner in this erotic, "ear-ogenous" composition was an eloquent artistic expression of the rising tide of the sexual liberation and feminist movements of the mid-1960s.[15] Like Schneemann, Moorman deployed her own body as creative material and as a vehicle for breaking pioneering artistic ground. However, Moorman's partnerships with male artists, especially Nam June Paik, would be mostly dismissed by feminists and treated with ambivalence by art history for many years. Yet, for Schneemann, Moorman's project was a profound contribution to the advancement of art as it was informed by the feminist ethos. In a letter to Moorman dated September 26, 1980, Schneemann wrote,

Carolee Schneemann. *Fur Wheel*, 1962. Construction on lampshade base, with fur, tin can mirrors, glass, oil paint, mounted on turning wheel. © Carolee Schneemann / Artists Rights Society (ARS), New York. Generali Foundation Collection. Permanent loan to the Museum der Moderne Salzburg.

Peter Moore. Carolee Schnee-
mann and James Tenney perform
Schneemann's *Noise Bodies*, 3rd
Annual New York Avant Garde
Festival, Judson Hall, August 28,
1965. Photograph © Barbara
Moore / Licensed by VAGA, NY.

There are currently so many distortions
of our recent history being declared
publicly; it seems to have to do with
old notions of power—individualistic,
masculine-heroic traditions by which
power accrues to those with power.
This I always felt was one of your
particular gifts—and one which has
never been sufficiently appreciated:
to establish a community to have
given us all a focused *communality*,
an equity in which we shared, participated, developed a body of mutual
concerns, aesthetically, personally.[16]

In the interview that follows, Schneemann recalls the *Noise Bodies* performance
but also this spirit of "communality" as the
ultimate feminist gesture by Moorman. While
the hysteria and chaos that led up to and
often characterized the festivals resulted in

Schneemann repeatedly vowing to never
do it again, she remained a "regular" and
one of Moorman's lifelong allies.[17] These
two outspoken women raised their artistic
voices to challenge conventional hierarchies
and boundaries and to embrace women's
right to self-determination and agency in art
as in life. To challenge traditional art forms
was, for them, a transformative political act.
To make, to organize, to participate in the
cacophony of the avant-garde festivals was,
to use Schneemann's words, a "powerful
feminist statement."

LISA CORRIN: How and when did you and
Charlotte Moorman first meet?

CAROLEE SCHNEEMANN: My partner, Jim
Tenney, and I were probably introduced
through the composers Philip Corner or

Malcolm Goldstein. I just remember one of them being very excited about what Charlotte was proposing—what became the avant-garde festivals. It was a great experiment—untried—and that's what we all approved of then.

LC: What were your first impressions of Charlotte?

CS: She was such a nice southern girl. And warm. I was just drawn to her. I loved her right away. She couldn't be your best friend because she was so focused on some dynamic that she was pursuing. But you really wanted to be part of it and to be close to it. Every time there was an event she would call and ask my advice and would usually do the opposite of what I suggested and then call back and we'd celebrate that.

I remember when she wanted to do the avant-garde festival in Central Park. She called me and said, "Carolee, I want to talk to that mayor because I want him to give me Central Park for my avant-garde festival. I want all the artists to be there. Do you know him?" I said, "No, Charlotte, I don't know the mayor. He's very busy. We have a transportation strike happening. I don't know how you're going to get to him." I really discouraged her. I said, "Maybe there's another way to do this." She called back in an hour or so and said, "He is such a charming gentleman. He was so very gracious and said, 'Well, Charlotte, I'll be happy to assist you in any way I can.'" I thought, "Yeah, he wanted to get rid of this lady!" She sounded like she would drive him crazy, and so he has given her Central Park for the avant-garde festival.

LC: In 1965 you said, "After a hard year, things brightened to hysteria for Charlotte's festival. Every year everyone saying no I will never work with her again, and every year we were all drawn in and out." Can you talk about the attraction and why people couldn't say no to Charlotte?

CS: Once Charlotte told you who she was inviting, you thought, "Well I should be with that group." It was like a vortex. You were suddenly drawn into a kind of fantasy, and you thought, "She'll probably make this happen." But it would happen in a very chaotic way. Rehearsals overlapped or misaligned, or rehearsal spaces weren't available when we got there and we had to leave. It was always chaos, and Charlotte was infamously late, so she would say we're all coming together at Judson Hall at noon, and we'd all be there, no sign of Charlotte, or it might be a space where we all gathered and she had the keys, and we knew we should just go out and get lunch because who knew when she would turn up.

LC: What do you remember about her performing?

CS: She was wonderful at performing. Utterly concentrated even if she was sitting on a block of ice. That perfect concentration which a musician has to have, connected to an interior score. She would shape her event as if it were prescribed music.

LC: You participated in the second avant-garde festival in the performance of Stockhausen's *Originale* making costumes for Max Neuhaus and James Tenney. You transformed Tenney into a wolf. In the third festival, in 1965, you and James Tenney collaborated on *Noise Bodies*. How did the piece develop?

CS: I was living with Tenney, a remarkable composer. We were very young when we were first together. We were both struggling with our materials. Once we were together, we melded our processes. I would hear him practicing sections of a sonata on his upright piano over and over and over again and he would take a break and come in, and I was shredding papers and building these rhythmic collages. Fragmentation and harmonization—the fracture through which there is an incremental aspect of image or sound—we had really parallel aesthetic dilemmas. How to perfect a form and how to release it. How to keep it from being predictable while establishing a rigorous structure. We were reading Pound and Proust to each other. We were dancing all the time to popular music. I had blue suede shoes, and we danced to Elvis Presley. There was this constant sense of an interchange of materials happening. Our first major collaboration is the self-shot erotic film *Fuses* in 1964.

LC: What led to *Noise Bodies*?

CS: In 1963 I created *Eye Body: 36 Transformations for Camera*, in which I became an extension of my painting construction materials. The body is collaged, and painted, and draped, and stripped, and positioned within the painting constructions, and then photographed only one time, only for a few hours. Those images took me in a very significant direction against the stultification and fetishization of the female body that was taking place in pop art. I had discovered that if you want to paint it, go paint it, but then the nudity becomes the subject rather than the material of the work.

LC: You began to see the body as a material itself?

CS: Yes, that's part of the concept behind *Noise Bodies*. Movement, physicality, and the fun of the noise made from pots and pans and the refrigerator and all the junk we had in our shed.

LC: So you bring the banality of the everyday . . .

CS: . . . and make it outrageously ecstatic and transformative.

LC: You also turn it into music.

CS: We played each other. It's very sensitive, not aggressive. We had these little wands that are part of carburetors. They were pulled out of an old car and they are like conducting rods. We played each other's materials. We started slowly and made a sensitive exploration of what's on each other's bodies.

LC: Almost like a courtship ritual.

CS: It's a courtship of sound debris extending our bodies to each other, and then striking that big wheel, the hanging sculpture on the set, was the crescendo,

the orgasmic element of this play. Towards the end, I recall, Jim shook it intensely.

LC: Like a tambourine?

CS: Like a huge, cumbersome, crazy tambourine.

LC: What is the yellow disk?

CS: Some of those come from kinetic circles I was building, and they didn't get into the sculptures.

LC: They are the debris of your own artist practice?

CS: Yes.

LC: What was it like to put the costumes on?

CS: Tedious. You know there are metal rungs on the thighs. They were not comfortable but we had fun dressing each other.

LC: I can imagine putting them on was quite an experience with the clattering and jangling of all the whistles, horns, razzers, beads, a harmonica, an ice tray, the teapot lids as breasts.

CS: They had little bells hanging off that could be gently stroked and played.

LC: Like pasties?

CS: No. They're really physical and such a strong material. They're enamel.

LC: All the materials are pretty strong. The male and female performers are also both strong. They're both covered in armor that both adorns and protects.

CS: It's not armor. It's collaged debris. Armor belongs to a systematic intention of protecting yourself against aggression.

LC: There was no need to protect yourself. The relationship in real life and in the performance allowed for vulnerability between a man and a woman. Once turned into a costume, the collaged debris became gendered. The teapot lids are no longer teapot lids. We read them as breast with nipples. The tangles of wire and steel wool became brushlike pubic areas.

cs: He had a horn that I could blow. That was funny. It gave it some genital energy. He had more wavy aluminum and chain and tin cans and balls. There are also simple Mexican instruments that made metal music.

lc: There was an equal strength and sexual energy emanating from each of you, a real sense of equality that is an apt metaphor for your creative and personal life together.

cs: What guy in the 1960s would let his girlfriend cover him in metal debris and play him? That's already a very far-reaching adventurous, trusting sensibility.

lc: So there is an intentional double entendre in the work, that is, "to play

someone," to have the upper hand, to have power over, to take advantage? That really upends what was then the accepted order of things.

cs: We would become instruments of each other's intention.

lc: And pleasure?

cs: Yes.

lc: You have these gentle sounds which are very fragile and not necessarily magnified in the space because they're very quiet and yet they come from playing these very hard bodies.

cs: It makes noise, but it's subtle noise until you get to some of these larger sound elements.

lc: How did the approach to sound in this piece relate to Tenney's approach to composing at that time?

cs: It was inspired by the festivity and freedom of our connection to each other where we could try anything and propose anything and find the ways that it was connected to our larger bodies of work.

lc: Where does *Noise Bodies* fit into your work at that time?

cs: I made a series of sculptures using music boxes and music box music. There's also *Fur Wheel* from 1962. I was doing these motorized pieces that had these clanking tin cans in them. It's also motorized, and spinning with all its cans clicking and clanking. The cans were run over by trucks. I would put them out on Sixth Avenue and wait for something to crush them in a strong-looking way.

lc: Your work of that time involves movement—the movement of bodies and the movement of objects. Urban detritus and debris are important materials. You were interested in the sound of the debris as the bodies move, and how the pieces of debris interact with one another.

cs: *Musique Concrete*.

lc: Can we think about *Noise Bodies* as a pas de deux?

Carolee Schneemann and James Tenney perform Schneemann's *Noise Bodies*, 3rd Annual New York Avant Garde Festival, Judson Hall, August 28, 1965. Photograph by Ted Wester. © Carolee Schneemann / Artists Rights Society (ARS), New York. Courtesy of Getty Research Institute, Los Angeles (950001).

cs: No, I don't like the classical association. I would want to chop that to bits. We were working against those perfections and habits, and all of Judson was premised on imperfection, new forms, and the unpredictable.

LC: Tell me about *Noise Bodies* in relationship to collage.

cs: I was engrossed, devoured by collage process, and part of that has to do with the richness of juxtaposition that I'm hearing in the music. When Jim looks at the collage he begins to fragment his compositions, or reinterpret phrasing in the piano works that he's mastering. Collage has the complexity of layers and rhythms, and then the coherence between this unlikely—the confabulation of unlikely—materials that are speaking to me.

LC: In *Noise Bodies* the debris is dangling off the armor and gives a sense of fragmented movement because the objects are inevitably going to move in different ways. There is no possibility of unifying movement.

cs: But there is a unifying movement. There is the curvature of the hanging prop. Everything is fit within that larger rhythm.

LC: The bodies on which the costumes lay were like the central, stable forces in *Noise Bodies*. The fragmentary movement was what happens as those objects extend off of the central body and move.

cs: They become one with it.

LC: They're also playing the body. They have a life of their own.

cs: Yes, that's why they're in it.

LC: The piece embraces the idea of improvisation. Just glancing at this score, there are instructions for how to come out onto the stage, or how the lighting will look, but not for the sound, something one usually finds in a musical score.

cs: We had rehearsed with those materials. The "composition" is to explore what sounds they make. Jim discovered certain sounds, and I would think there was

something else that was a good contrast. In rehearsal we had already played out the potentials of the sounds and then improvised again in the performance, so that we were always a little startled by what happened. That made it fresh.

LC: What was the role of light in the piece?

cs: We entered in the dark. That was very important that the audience didn't see us. They'd hear clanking. I think we had little flashlights that we could point to each other. They were like fireflies.

LC: How long did the performance last?

cs: Thirty-eight minutes.

LC: Not very long. What was the response from the audience?

cs: People were enthralled. They loved it. It was enticing, it was sexy, and it was funny.

LC: Do you think that the photographs of performances in the avant-garde festivals such as *Noise Bodies* capture the spirit of the festivals?

cs: You can't really say "capture the festival" because there was the crazy audience and all the surrounding configurations of time, process, delay, and event.

LC: There are extraordinary photographs of you in the 1973 avant-garde festival at Grand Central Terminal performing *Trackings*, which became *Up to and Including Her Limits*, in a freight car. Can you fill in the gap between that image and the experience of being there?

cs: It was wonderful but cold and dirty. I had Yoshi Wada in the next freight car. He was blowing through plumbing pipes. It became like an accompaniment. I was so connected to it, hanging on my rope inside the space with things happening everywhere outside.

LC: You only performed *Noise Bodies* a few times. Why?

cs: What was going on around us—Vietnam, for instance. It was hard to be playful, to work . . . at all. I could hardly sleep. I could see those houses and children burned up. I think we would have gone back to it if we weren't so engaged with what the Vietnam War was bringing into our work.

LC: Speaking of politics, what contributions, if any, do you think that Charlotte made to feminism?

CS: Women were not very fond of her. Some of them called her a narcissist. If you are a woman artist and use your body in your work, you're immediately subject to that criticism. Charlotte was not a diva.

Nobody was supporting her. She made everything happen. She didn't have enough money to feed their dog. But she was such a powerful central figure in the experimental artist community.

In the festivals we were contentious, and wild, and challenging traditional forms. Charlotte is a pioneer of feminist principles by making this free radical community, by being central to it, imagining in it, constructing it, sustaining it, and extending *it* into a larger public. The Annual New York Avant Garde Festival has to be understood as a powerful feminist statement.

Carolee Schneemann premieres *Trackings* (also known as *Up to and Including Her Limits*) in a baggage car, 10th Annual New York Avant Garde Festival, Grand Central Terminal, December 9, 1973. Photograph by Ivan Spane. Courtesy of Charlotte Moorman Archive, Charles Deering McCormick Library of Special Collections, Northwestern University Library.

Notes

1. Schneemann quoted in Kristine Stiles, ed., *Correspondence Course: An Epistolary History of Carolee Schneemann and Her Circle* (Durham, N.C.: Duke University Press, 2010), 99.

2. Ibid., 413.

3. Carolee Schneemann, *More Than Meat Joy: Performance Works and Selected Writings*, ed. Bruce R. McPherson, 2nd ed. (1979; repr., New York: Documentext/McPherson and Company, 1997), 214. In the publication, Schneemann refers to the piece as *"Rainbow Blaze."* In her proposal to Moorman for the festival, the work is titled *"Rainbow Splatter."* Charlotte Moorman Archive, Charles Deering McCormick Library of Special Collections, Northwestern University Library.

4. Joan Rothfuss, *Topless Cellist: The Improbable Life of Charlotte Moorman* (Cambridge, Mass.: MIT Press, 2014), 209.

5. Schneemann, *More Than Meat Joy*, 227.

6. These descriptions of the drawings are the artist's in a phone interview with Corinne Granof on April 6, 2015.

7. Several descriptions of *Noise Bodies* exist. A typewritten conversation with the artist can be found in the Getty Research Institute, Los Angeles. A similar version is published in Schneemann, *More Than Meat Joy*, 93. The version published here, also from the Getty Research Institute, is from undated, handwritten notes that appear to be from the time of the work's conception. All three documents contain similar instructions, although the later versions are much more elaborate. The handwritten score also has small, loosely rendered drawings and is reproduced here.

8. For the unedited diary text, see Schneemann, *More Than Meat Joy*, 93.

9. For the unedited diary text, see ibid.

10. Schneemann quoted in Maura Reilly, "The Paintings of Carolee Schneemann," *Feminist Studies* 37, no. 3 (Fall 2011): 621.

11. Ibid., 647.

12. Ibid., 621.

13. As Reilly so eloquently points out; ibid., 647.

14. Making a new kind of music from the sounds of everyday materials and actions would similarly inform Moorman's own performances, such as her rendition of John Cage's *26′1.1499″ for a String Player*. The audience was treated to a composition of grease spitting in a hot frying pan, a cap gun pop, and the snap of rubber as Moorman prepared to blow up a balloon.

15. "Ear-ogenous" is a word used by Schneemann to describe *Noise Bodies* in the score located in the Getty Research Institute.

16. Schneemann quoted in Stiles, *Correspondence Course,* 323.

17. Carolee Schneemann, interview with the author, July 29, 2014, New Paltz, New York. Quotation from 1965 taken from Stiles, *Correspondence Course,* 100: "Every one saying no, no I'll never work with her again and every year we all are drawn in and out."

Sky Kiss

Joan Rothfuss

The History of an Idea

She hung in the air, suspended by sixteen balloons in red, orange, white, yellow, and blue. Her cape was white satin trimmed with marabou feathers. It glinted in the Australian sun as it swirled around her dangling legs and black-slippered feet. On the cello that was strapped to her body, she played snippets of the pop tune "Up, Up, and Away." Above her, the southern sky was deep blue; below, hundreds of spectators watched as three assistants holding guylines maneuvered her around the plaza outside the Sydney Opera House. She laughed with delight as she blew kisses to the audience.

This was Charlotte Moorman performing *Sky Kiss* in Sydney on April 11, 1976. Of the many compositions written for her, it was her favorite. Between 1968 and 1986, she performed it eight times—not an insignificant number, considering its technical complexity and the physical effort it required. She considered the Sydney *Sky Kiss* her best realization. She had a gorgeous site, an extravagant costume, and a successful flight in fine weather, as well as an audience of hundreds that included writers from every newspaper in the area. One of them declared the event's finest moment a visual one. "Before rounding the western corner of the Bennelong Restaurant . . . Miss Moorman, silhouetted against the sun and the Harbour Bridge, was suddenly escorted by four seagulls and two blue and red kites, streaming tentacles at their tails."[1]

Sky Kiss was written in 1968 by Jim McWilliams, Moorman's friend and frequent collaborator during the 1960s and 1970s. An artist, designer, and performer who taught at the Philadelphia College of Art, McWilliams wrote the piece for himself because, as he told a reporter, he wanted to "go up in the air and dance."[2] He debuted it at Philadelphia's Rittenhouse Square on March 9, 1968, with Moorman's assistance. As she strolled through the crowd playing "The Daring Young Man on the Flying Trapeze" on a cello suspended from a bunch of helium-filled balloons, McWilliams harnessed himself to his own balloon bouquet and stepped off the edge of an eight-foot platform. Instead of rising into the air, he dropped to the ground. (Too few balloons.)[3] That summer, after a second attempt failed, he decided to give *Sky Kiss*, along with his parachute harness, to Moorman.[4]

McWilliams and Moorman met in October 1964 when she and Nam June Paik performed in Philadelphia during an exhibition of work by the Swiss artist Dieter Roth.

OPPOSITE
Charlotte Moorman performs Jim McWilliams's *Sky Kiss*, Sydney, Australia, April 11, 1976. © Estate of James Ashburn. Courtesy of Charlotte Moorman Archive, Charles Deering McCormick Library of Special Collections, Northwestern University Library.

123

Charlotte Moorman performs Jim McWilliams's *Sky Kiss*, assisted by Henry Niese, Baltimore, Maryland, June 4, 1980. Photograph by Joseph A. DiPaola, *Baltimore Sun*.

wrote for her. *Ice Music* (1972), for example, required Moorman to play an instrument made of ice for as long as it took for the ice to melt; its thematic components were water and time. In *Candy* (1973), Moorman's naked body and her cello were coated with fudge the color of rich, dark soil or even excrement, transforming her into a sort of fertility figure just emerged from the primordial sea. And in *Sky Kiss*, Moorman-Cello was completely enveloped by air.[6] In other compositions, McWilliams envisioned Moorman-Cello as a queen, a ship's figurehead, and an angel—in other words, as an icon or an object. In his compositions, she often did not act; she simply presented herself for contemplation.

Moorman made her first performance of *Sky Kiss* on September 14, 1968, in her own 6th Annual New York Avant Garde Festival, a parade down Central Park West in New York City. She did not spend much time in the air. McWilliams, who served as her technical adviser, once again underestimated the number of balloons needed, so Moorman bobbled more than she flew. She used her feet to push off the pavement whenever she got too close to the ground, and every time she encountered an overhead power line or traffic light, her assistants had to pull her down and under it.[7]

For the same parade, McWilliams wrote two pieces for himself: *Street Kiss* (he would apply a continuous line of paint to the pavement) and *Body Color Kiss* (spectators would use a system of pneumatic colored vinyl tubes to paint the bodies of three actors).[8] Along with *Sky Kiss*, they were part of his search for new ways to visualize what he claimed was the most-often-depicted sex act in the history of art. "All artistic contact [is] equal with the physical act of kissing," he wrote. "When two objects come together and make contact, it can be termed a kiss. When two cars collide it can be a metal kiss. When a bomb drops from an airplane it is a kiss of war. When membranes contact [one another] it can be an orgasm." Here, McWilliams reimagines kisses as intrinsically creative acts and proposes an erotics of daily life in which we continually make "delicious," generative contact with our surroundings.[9]

McWilliams responded strongly to what he later called Moorman's "unique, tough style,"[5] and by 1968, when he began composing works for her, he had come to regard her as a unique entity: not just a musician who would interpret his works but a visual leitmotif for his performative ideas. "She and the cello became an object to me," he has said. "It wasn't her *and* the cello. They were one. [Moorman-Cello] was the object that I was working with." Over the next decade he came to regard her as near elemental, an idea reflected in many of the pieces he

After she debuted *Sky Kiss* in 1968, Moorman performed McWilliams's version three more times. In 1975, she traveled to her hometown of Little Rock, Arkansas, to take part in a citywide festival and parade organized by the choreographer Marilyn Wood.[10] It was only her second realization of the piece, and its technical aspects were still unresolved. During a trial run, some of the balloons burst in the strong July sun, while others escaped into the atmosphere. But on the evening of July 26, Moorman was launched and pulled along the parade route by her assistants without incident. News reports were bemused, but appreciative.

The third performance, in Sydney, was a triumph. But her fourth attempt, in 1980, failed completely. At the invitation of the artist Fred Stern, she had traveled to Baltimore to perform the piece in a park near the city's Inner Harbor. She arrived a full day late, by which time the balloons had leaked so much helium that they could not lift her. Stern was unable to get more of the gas on short notice, so Moorman tried to salvage the performance by climbing onto a friend's shoulders and playing her cello as he carried her along the promenade. But their awkward coupling was mocked the next day by the Baltimore *Sun*, which ran a photograph captioned, "Aim for High Note Misfires."[11] Soon afterward, Moorman contacted the German artist Otto Piene and asked for his help.[12]

•

A founding member of the avant-garde group ZERO, Otto Piene had long been engaged with air, light, and sky as materials for his utopian, ephemeral artworks. In his writings, he cast artists as explorers and "frontier poets" who reach into space to extend humankind's imagination, creativity, and self-knowledge.[13] Piene's earliest sky works were inflatable sculptures, first shown in 1967 at the Museum am Ostwall in West Germany. After relocating to the United States in 1968, Piene began appending human beings to his inflatables. In the fall of that year, he debuted *Flying Girl Sculpture*, in which a young woman was harnessed to a bundle of clear polyethylene tubes filled with helium and floated into the night sky over Boston.[14] During the next fifteen months, Piene repeated the piece twice, under different titles: *Lift and Equilibrium* was performed over an athletic field on the Massachusetts Institute of Technology (MIT) campus in Cambridge, and *Manned Helium Sculpture* took place during a citywide festival in Pittsburgh.[15] It can be inferred from their titles that Piene understood these pieces as primarily sculptural and concerned more with issues of physics and technology than with their potential as performances. Susan Peters, the "flying girl" who "manned" both sculptures, served as a humanizing element in Piene's aesthetic-technological exploration of space, but she never had a job to do, not even the bestowal of a conceptual kiss. She was simply attached to the sculptures, like a garnish. Most of Piene's later Sky Art did not involve human beings at all, except as audience members, who were necessary witnesses to his spectacles.

For Piene was devoted to spectacle. He believed that an artist's job included "preparing, maintaining, and regenerating occasions of pageantry."[16] His events often were staged at night in dramatic public sites and featured multiple inflated, flying sculptures. But his pageantry was not merely beautiful and entertaining. It was meant to be "an effective pageantry of protest, a pageantry of constructive criticism."[17] With Sky Art, Piene wanted to take back the heavens for art. "Why do we have no exhibitions in the sky?" he wrote in 1961. "Up to now we have left it up to war to light up the sky."[18] Sky Art offered freedom—from gravity, from spiritual darkness, from "the ulcers of memory, the superfluities of time past, and the suppurations of the psyche."[19] Through freedom comes enlightenment: Sky Art would lead humankind to utopia.

Charlotte Moorman could have gone on performing *Sky Kiss* without Piene's help. She and McWilliams had overseen successful realizations in Sydney and Little Rock, and even Baltimore would likely have been a success had she arrived in Maryland on schedule. Moreover, she had known Piene since the late 1960s and had included his work in several of her festivals

Charlotte Moorman with Otto Piene before performing *Sky Kiss: A Sky Event by Jim McWilliams, Charlotte Moorman, and Otto Piene*, Sky Art Conference '82, Linz, Austria, September 25, 1982. © Schaffler Design. Courtesy of Charlotte Moorman Archive, Charles Deering McCormick Library of Special Collections, Northwestern University Library.

said that Federal Aviation Administration regulations and "the MIT campus patrol" had prevented her from going higher.[20]) In 1982 and 1983, Piene staged his second and third Sky Art Conferences in Europe and invited Moorman along to perform *Sky Kiss* at both. In Linz, Austria, she rose high over the Danube River; the next year she "flew into the sunset" over a park in central Munich.[21] She performed her final *Sky Kiss* at night, at the edge of the Mojave Desert, in late 1986, as part of Piene's fourth and last Sky Art Conference. Piene was in awe of Moorman. He saw her as "an image like no other" and understood *Sky Kiss* as forceful, truthful, visual music. "She was not just making noise, or doing an avant-garde performance, but playing music," he said. "And the music became more intense every time we did *Sky Kiss*."[22]

Although Otto Piene and Jim McWilliams conceived their sky artworks almost simultaneously in 1968, their aims were radically different. Piene's Sky Art evinced a polemics of exploration that equated space travel with artistic work, and his "manned" sculptures express a profound yearning with swaggering machismo. For McWilliams, *Sky Kiss* was an existential exploration of spirituality, joy, and sex. His was a gentle, quiet work. Moorman's performances of the piece during the 1980s began with the basic situation as imagined by both men—a woman flies, an audience watches—and were embellished according to her own style, which was warm, earthy, and a touch flamboyant. She insisted on a flashy costume, often in purple or red satin, and she preferred brightly colored balloons to the white or transparent ones used by McWilliams and Piene. (She agreed to use transparent tubes only after Piene convinced her, in 1982, that they would take her higher into the sky.) Rather than hang motionless in the air like an inanimate object, she waved, smiled, chatted with the audience, and played a cello.

of avant-garde art. So why did she wait until 1980 to call on him for help? Perhaps it was because she, too, was devoted to spectacle and the production of pageantry. But because of ill health, she had discontinued her annual festival series—and her own, dramatic festival performances—in 1980. Piene, as the director of the Center for Advanced Visual Studies at MIT, was in a position to realize grand, visually spectacular projects that required many assistants and commanded large audiences. It would have served both Moorman's interests and her mission to be a part of them.

So Moorman brought McWilliams's piece to Piene. Their initial collaboration took place at Piene's first Sky Art Conference, a five-day, multimedia event held at MIT in September 1981. Dressed in the black bodysuit and white, feathered cape she had used in Sydney, and harnessed to sixty weather balloons in white and cherry red, Moorman rose to an altitude of ten feet over an MIT athletic field. (Piene later

In Moorman's hands, *Sky Kiss* became both more sumptuous and more accessible than either Piene or McWilliams had conceived it. At the same time, her costumes, carefully arranged coiffure and makeup, and

Charlotte Moorman prepares to perform *Sky Kiss: A Sky Event by Jim McWilliams, Charlotte Moorman, and Otto Piene*, Sky Art Conference '81, MIT, Cambridge, Massachusetts, September 27, 1981. © Catherine Skopic.

abundant personal charm strengthened the work's visual and erotic appeal. Moorman was more than a mere interpreter. She was also more than a "living aerial sculpture by Otto Piene and floating cellist by Jim McWilliams," as she was identified in the program notes for the Munich Sky Art Conference.[23] Rather, she was a creative force whose performative energy, ideas, and audacity were as critical to the success of *Sky Kiss* as were Piene's and McWilliams's concepts.

She knew this. Moorman took formal ownership of the work beginning in 1980, when her letters and notes begin to refer to it as *Sky Kiss: A Sky Event by Jim McWilliams, Charlotte Moorman, and Otto Piene.*

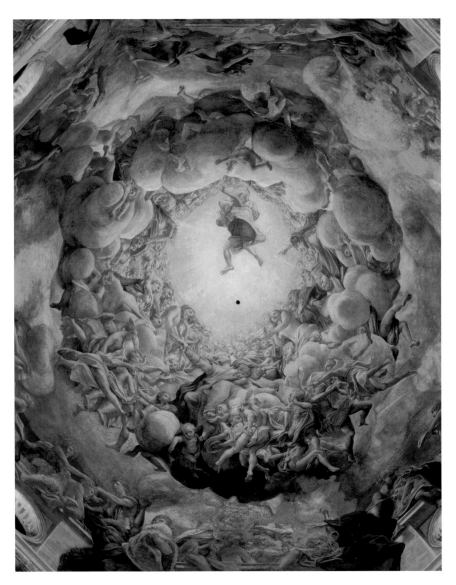

Correggio. *Assumption of the Virgin,* detail, fresco (ca. 1520-1530), Duomo Parma. Alinari / Art Resource, New York.

Theater, Ecstasy, and Wonder: The Further History of an Idea

Those who witnessed Moorman's Linz and Munich *Sky Kiss* events might have been reminded of certain other images in which a woman takes flight: the elaborate ceiling paintings that decorate many of Europe's baroque churches. In these works, architecture seems to open to the sky so that the Virgin Mary could be assumed into heaven or saints beckoned home. These painted illusions are so skillfully integrated into three-dimensional architectural detail that, gazing up at them, worshippers could almost imagine themselves witness to the actual, tumultuous moment in which a body made its passage from earth to heaven. Awe-inspiring, certainly. But many baroque ceiling paintings are also oddly unpretentious. Populated by angels and saints as fleshy and familiar as one's neighbors, they can even seem friendly. In Correggio's celebrated *Assumption*, painted on the domed ceiling of the Cathedral of Parma, the Virgin Mary's limbs flail awkwardly and her billowing robes reveal an immodest amount of leg as she tumbles into a golden sky. The look of surprise on her face is so believably human that she might have been plucked from among the congregation below.[24]

In photographs and videos of *Sky Kiss*, Moorman, like Correggio's Mary, exudes a presence that is both earthy and otherworldly. Is there anything to be learned from thinking about Moorman's *Sky Kiss* as a neobaroque work of art? The comparison might seem fanciful, but it is not entirely superficial. The baroque period in Europe, which stretched roughly from the mid-sixteenth through the late seventeenth centuries, produced an art that is dramatic and sensual, full of curves and color and movement. Erotics are often implied, if not overt. The sky was the venue for many of the era's spectacular images, from church decoration to operas, outdoor festivals, and even sculpture. In Gian Lorenzo Bernini's Cornaro Chapel, to cite an iconic example, Saint Teresa's rapturous swoon is enacted on the bed of a cloud.

Moorman's *Sky Kiss* has striking visual affinity with both Correggio's painted

Æole descend avec huit vents le Tonnerre commence à voûte accompagné dé clairs, deux Venis fondent sur Andromede l'enlevent Jusques dans les nües

Assumption and Bernini's sculpted scene of saintly rapture. As a performance, though, *Sky Kiss* is closest in form to theater. Both incorporated actual movement in real time and required live performers. Beyond these obvious correspondences, both also were heavily dependent on technology. Baroque operas, plays, and outdoor urban festivals all used machinery to simulate the arrival of gods from the heavens, the appearance of a crowded heavenly host, or the Assumption of the Blessed Virgin. In Giacomo Torelli's design for Pierre Corneille's *Andromède* (1650), King Cepheus and his attendants wait on a bank of clouds as the doomed princess is spirited to the skies amid a wild storm of thunder and lightning. His design for Francesco Sacrati's *La Finta pazza* (1645) featured a three-tiered cloud machine of wood and rope on which Jupiter

and his court of nineteen appeared over a city square.[25]

What did it take for Moorman to fly? Enough balloons to hold 3,500 cubic feet of helium, five assistants to fill the balloons, and 900 feet of nylon rope to attach them to her harness. Three 200-foot-long guywires and three men to handle them. An audio technician to connect a wireless microphone, battery pack, and speakers to make audible whatever sound might issue from her cello. For night flights, a handheld spotlight.[26] Although *Sky Kiss* was rather low-tech for its time, it could be argued that, with its machinery, flamboyant costumes, and minimal sound, Moorman's piece was the direct descendant of *festa teatrale*, a seventeenth-century Venetian operatic form that privileged visual magnificence and complicated special effects over music.[27]

Giacomo Torelli. Set design for Pierre Corneille's *Andromède* (Paris, 1650), act 2. Engraving by François Chauveau. Collection Bibliothèque Nationale de France.

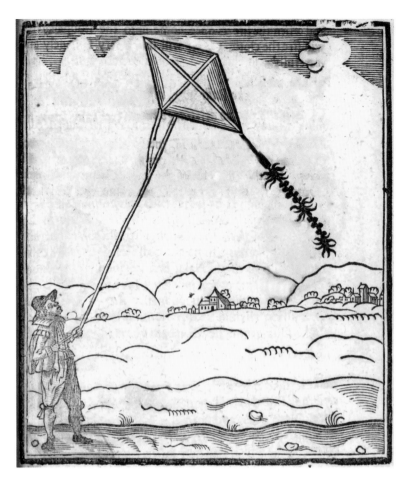

"Fire Drake," in John Bate, *The Mysteries of Nature and Art*. Woodcut, printed for Ralph Mabb, London, 1635. Courtesy of Charles Deering McCormick Library of Special Collections, Northwestern University Library.

Donato Creti. *Astronomical Observation of the Moon*, Pinacoteca, Vatican Museums, Vatican State, 1711. Scala / Art Resource, New York.

Any history of baroque theatricals and public celebrations will give the lie to Otto Piene's claim that humanity had "left it up to war to light up the sky." During the baroque era, European skies were regularly animated by elaborate displays of fireworks celebrating religious festivals, military victories, and royal coronations, marriages, and births. Technical manuals such as John Bate's *The Mysteries of Nature and Art* (1635) offered detailed instructions for individuals wishing to create such low-altitude amusements as self-propelled mechanical dragons that spit sparks from both ends, and "fire drakes," or kites with tails of firecrackers. Even the baroque fascination with astronomy can be related to *Sky Kiss*. During the seventeenth century, scientists first speculated that the earth was not the center of the universe and that the skies expanded into an infinite, unknowable space. The art historian Robert S. Huddleston has suggested that seventeenth-century men and women were both exhilarated and terrified by this idea and that both emotions suffuse much art of the baroque era.[28] Perhaps the dichotomy can be felt in paintings such as Donato Creti's *Moon* (1711), in which the awesome celestial body hangs huge in the night sky, dwarfing two men who have ventured out with their telescope to gaze at the sight. Moorman often spoke about *Sky Kiss* as a glorious, intensely pleasurable experience. Since she had an acute fear of heights, it must also have been a frightening one.

·

It has been said that baroque style "was at root about performance, made to persuade as well as to impress. . . . It was a rhetorical style that aimed to engage the senses, as much through the emotions as through the intellect."[29] This would not be a bad description of Charlotte Moorman's entire artistic practice. Like that of the baroque, her rhetorical style was not verbal but visual and enacted. It engaged the senses with its theatrics, dynamism, and pure charm, and it aimed to persuade the public that experiencing the art of one's own time was both illuminating and essential. This goal was her life's mission. She pursued it in each festival she organized and every performance she made. But it was not until the end of her career that *Sky Kiss* emerged as emblematic of that mission. As conceived by Jim McWilliams, it was erotic, spiritual theater for an ethereal stage. As elaborated by Otto Piene, it was a joyous mix of technology and metaphysics. As performed by Moorman, it was flamboyant and colorful as well as thrilling and unnerving. *Sky Kiss* was the ideal vehicle for her enacted rhetoric of accessibility and engagement. It was also perfectly aligned with baroque sensibility. That was never clearer than on the April day she performed the piece in Sydney.

It was Palm Sunday, one week before Easter. As Moorman hung from her brightly colored balloons above the Opera House, an orchestra indoors was playing J. S. Bach's *St. Matthew's Passion*. Through music of sweeping intensity and forceful beauty, the oratorio relates the story of the events leading up to Jesus Christ's crucifixion. Near its end, the principal storyteller, the Evangelist, sings of a miraculous occurrence: "And the earth was filled with quaking, and the cliffs split asunder, and the graves themselves opened up, and there rose up the bodies of many saints who were sleeping." Here again is that familiar baroque motif, the assumption of saints into heaven, this time rendered in language and sound.

To Moorman, the alignment in time and space of *St. Matthew's Passion* and *Sky Kiss* had produced a near magical experience for her audience. This is what she imagined: Emerging from the darkened hall, concertgoers looked up at the sky. Nearly blinded by the sun, and still under the spell of Bach's music, they were momentarily confused when they caught sight of her. Was she a vision? A miracle? Or the bright embodiment of Bach's resurrected saints?[30]

Moorman specialized in this kind of sweet speculation. But her story is more than pure whimsy. It shows that she at least intuited the deep connections between her work and the baroque sensibility, and it makes possible the reading of *Sky Kiss* proposed in this essay. Following her lead, we might wonder whether in Sydney, for an instant, three centuries of history melted away when *Sky Kiss* and *St. Matthew's Passion* were joined.

Charlotte Moorman performs *Sky Kiss: A Sky Event by Jim McWilliams, Charlotte Moorman, and Otto Piene*, Sky Art Conference '83, Munich, Germany, September 25, 1983. Photographer unknown. Courtesy of Charlotte Moorman Archive, Charles Deering McCormick Library of Special Collections, Northwestern University Library.

Notes

My grateful thanks to Paul Shambroom for his help preparing the image files for the photographs that accompany this essay.

1. "Flying High with Strings Attached," *Sydney Morning Herald*, April 12, 1976.

2. Jim McWilliams quoted in Jeremy Heymsfeld, "Up, Up, and Away Out?" *Philadelphia Inquirer*, March 11, 1968.

3. The event was called *A Balloon Dance for Children*. Event poster in the Charles Deering McCormick Library of Special Collections, Northwestern University Library, Evanston, Ill. (hereafter cited as CMA).

4. McWilliams was forced to cut short his second attempt, on Philadelphia's riverfront, because of rain and high winds on the day of the performance. Jim McWilliams, email message to author, May 13, 2014.

5. Jim McWilliams, email message to author, February 10, 2015.

6. McWilliams did not compose any works for Moorman that involved the fourth classical element, fire. However, during the summer of 1968, he did an event in which he and his students blew up a group of sculptures with dynamite. Jim McWilliams, interview by author, July 18, 2005, San Diego, Calif.

7. Ibid.

8. McWilliams believes he probably did not perform either *Body Color Kiss* or *Street Kiss* because he was preoccupied with getting Moorman off the ground. Ibid.

9. From an undated sheet of notes on *Sky Kiss*, written in Moorman's hand but probably reflective of both her and McWilliams's ideas (CMA); Jim McWilliams, email message to author, April 22, 2014. Thanks to Scott Krafft for alerting me to this important document.

10. Wood and her dance troupe arrived in Little Rock on July 20 and held several public rehearsals before the culminating event on July 26. See "N.Y. Group Will Stage 'Celebration' for Community to Have 'Good Time.'" *Arkansas Gazette*, July 20, 1975.

11. "Aim for High Note Misfires," *Sun* (Baltimore), June 5, 1980; Fred Stern, interview by author, May 16, 2006, Evanston, Ill. Thanks to Barbara Berger for locating the photograph of this performance that is reproduced with this essay.

12. In a telephone interview with the author on June 26, 2014, Piene said that Nam June Paik suggested to Moorman that she contact him. Other sources state that Moorman got the idea to call Piene after seeing his *Flying Girl Sculpture* on the 1969 WGBH-TV program *The Medium Is the Medium*.

13. Lowry Burgess, Elizabeth Goldring, and Otto Piene, "Statement," in Elizabeth Goldring, "*Desert Sun / Desert Moon* and the Sky Art Manifesto," *Leonardo* 20, no. 4 (1987): 346.

14. *Flying Girl Sculpture* was performed and videotaped in fall 1968. It was included in the television program *The Medium Is the Medium*, produced by WGBH-TV in Boston and broadcast in March 1969. For details, see Kathy O'Dell's essay in this volume.

15. On June 25, 1969, *Lift and Equilibrium* was performed at Briggs Athletic Field, MIT, Cambridge, Mass. *Manned Helium Sculpture* took place in Pittsburgh on April 18, 1970, as part of the public art project *Citything Sky Ballet*. See photographs in Ante Glibota, *Otto Piene* (Paris: Delight Edition, 2011), 41, 366, and 368–69, respectively.

16. Otto Piene, *More Sky* (Cambridge, Mass.: MIT Press, 1970), xiv.

17. Ibid., 25.

18. Otto Piene, "Paths to Paradise," in *ZERO* 3 (1961). Reprinted in *ZERO* (Cambridge, Mass.: MIT Press, 1973), 149.

19. Piene, "Paths to Paradise," in *ZERO*, 148.

20. Otto Piene, interview by author, April 15, 2007, Groton, Mass.

21. Otto Piene, remarks made at Charlotte Moorman's memorial service at the Whitney Museum of American Art, February 15, 1992. DVD in the Emily Harvey Foundation Archives, New York. Moorman performed *Sky Kiss* in Linz on September 24, 1982, and in Munich on September 25, 1983.

2. Otto Piene quoted in Vin Grabill, "Otto Piene's Sky Art" (1982), videotape, in CMA. See also Otto Piene, "Charlotte," in *Nam June Paik: Eine DATA Base*, ed. Klaus Bussmann and Florian Matzner (Munich: Hatje Cantz, 1993), 45–46.

3. "Charlotte Moorman als lebende Luftplastik von Otto Piene und als schwebende Cello-Spielerin von Jim McWilliams." *Sky Art Conference '83*, program booklet, 43, in CMA.

4. Although Correggio's *Assumption* was painted during the late Renaissance, it is commonly acknowledged as the inspiration for many of the baroque ceiling decorations made in the late sixteenth and seventeenth centuries.

5. Both the machine and the set design are illustrated in Per Bjurström, *Giacomo Torelli and Baroque Stage Design* (Stockholm: Almqvist and Wiksell, 1961), 141.

6. Charlotte Moorman, "Materials Needed for *Sky Kiss*, a Sky Event by Jim McWilliams, Charlotte Moorman, and Otto Piene," handwritten sheet of notes, ca. 1982, in CMA.

27. Bjurström, *Giacomo Torelli and Baroque Stage Design*, 47.

28. Robert S. Huddleston, "Baroque Space and the Art of the Infinite," in *The Theatrical Baroque*, ed. Larry F. Norman (Chicago: Smart Museum of Art and University of Chicago, 2001), 13.

29. Michael Snodin, "The Baroque Style," in *Baroque: Style in the Age of Magnificence, 1620–1800*, ed. Michael Snodin and Nigel Llewellyn (London: V&A, 2009), 76, 78.

30. See Charlotte Moorman, interview by Vin Grabill (1982) videotape (VHS), in CMA.

Donnerstag in der Aula
der 28.7.1966 20⁰⁰ Uhr

Konzert

Jean Pierre Wilhelm   Introduktion
Charlotte Moorman   (Cello)
Nam June Paik   (Piano)
Joseph Beuys   Phone + Antiphone Objekt

Programm

Entrance Musik   3. Brecht-Tenny   tape
Division the cross   Joseph Beuys
composition 1960 Nr. 5   03 La Monte young
counting Song   1. Emmet Williams count
Electronic Moon   10. Paik-Yalkut   film
Micro Demonstration   Joseph Beuys
Per Arco   11. Guiseppe Chiari celo tape recorder
Synergy 3.   Earl Brown
26 "1.1499" For a Sring Player   John Cage

Shoes of your choice (Intermission)
              Alison Knowles
                           audience
Sensitivo 7   2. Sylvano Bussotti celo and tape
Red Cross-Contergan Joseph Beuys
Durations   5.   Morton Feldmann celo + piano
Instrumental Music 15. Takehisa Kosugi
Celo Sonata 8.   Dick Higgins
Piece for Sari Dienes 5. Jackson Mac Low
Variations on the Theme by Robert Breer, Nam June Paik

Cinema Metaphysic 10. Paik-Yalkut   film
  Publikum   von   Jörg Immendorff
Exit Music   3. Brecht-Tenny   tape

I Love Germany and Germany Loves Me: Charlotte Moorman and the Transatlantic Avant-Garde

Rachel Jans

A photograph of Charlotte Moorman taken at the 1965 happening *24 Hours* (*24 Stunden*) at Galerie Parnass in the West German town of Wuppertal shows the cellist in a full-length concert ball gown beside her collaborator Nam June Paik. It captures the weary and exhilarated-looking pair during a twenty-four-hour happening, the fourth stop of an ambitious tour across West Germany and Europe in the summer of 1965. In the photo, Moorman stands alongside some of the most progressive happenings, Fluxus, and action-based artists in West Germany, including Wolf Vostell, Joseph Beuys, Tomas Schmit, and Bazon Brock. It captures her at the moment she first formed lasting friendships, developing a rich and dynamic network of transatlantic exchange with her fellow participating artists. Writing of her interest in the work of these artists, she remarked in her essay in the collaborative catalog made immediately following the *24 Hours* performances, "Beuys, Brock, Paik, Schmit, Vostell. / All doing quite different things / From America. I want to experience / Your philosophies, hopes and dreams."[1]

Moorman's direct contact with the works of her West German peers prompted her to request their compositions to perform them in the United States. Moorman was constantly on the lookout for new artists and new material to perform, to include in her repertoire, and, most important, to showcase at the large annual avant-garde festivals in New York City that she organized beginning in 1963. Moorman interpreted and performed the works of her international artist peers—most notably works by Wolf Vostell and Joseph Beuys, still largely unknown in the United States—bringing them to the platform of her avant-garde festivals, which served to amplify and disseminate the works to broad and varied audiences in the United States. Her tours in Germany and her performance of German works in the United States reveal the underexplored development of Moorman's political sensitivities during the 1960s. Many of her activities and performances from this time reflect her understandings of violence, war, history, and the upheavals of her time in both Germany and the United States.

In the 1960s, Moorman's tours were a conduit for exchange and a source of artistic material for her repertoire and avant-garde festivals. Her tours with Paik—in Italy, Sweden, Iceland, and Denmark, but especially West Germany—were key to the creation of a comprehensive network of international

OPPOSITE
Jörg Immendorff. Program for Nam June Paik and Charlotte Moorman concert in Düsseldorf, West Germany, 1966. © Estate of Jörg Immendorff. Used by permission of Galerie Michael Werner Märkisch Wilmersdorf, Cologne and New York. Courtesy of Charlotte Moorman Archive, Charles Deering McCormick Library of Special Collections, Northwestern University Library.

135

Artists in *24 Hours*, Galerie Parnass, Wuppertal, West Germany, June 5, 1965. From left to right: Rolf Jährling, Wolf Vostell, Bazon Brock, Eckart Rahn, Joseph Beuys, Tomas Schmit, Charlotte Moorman, Nam June Paik. © Ute Klophaus/bpk, Berlin. Courtesy of AFORK (Archiv künstlerischer Fotografie der rheinischen Kunstszene), Museum Kunstpalast, Düsseldorf, Germany.

artists whose works she encountered in Europe and brought back to the United States. At a time in which few German artists could come to New York—frequently out of financial constraints, including the lack of support from patrons in Germany or the United States—Moorman created a crucial link in broadening the American audience for new German work. Year after year, Moorman fashioned her avant-garde festivals as major platforms where international artists' works were showcased. Since her second festival in 1964, where she offered the American premiere of Karlheinz Stockhausen's experimental opera *Originale*, German culture played an important part in her programming. The following year, during her first 1965 tour to Germany, Moorman expanded her horizons beyond her knowledge of German new music to include more performance-based German art.

Moorman and Paik's tours were a means of widely dispersing the duo's work by traversing Germany's disjointed landscape. This was a cultural and geographic topography with which Paik was familiar, as he lived in Germany from 1956 to 1964 and had collaborated with many of the artists the duo encountered abroad. Through their travels, Moorman and Paik overcame many boundaries, including the cultural and geographic distance between Germany and the United States, as well as Germany's regional landscape, dominated not by one single cultural capital but with distinct cultural scenes spread across various cities. In Aachen, they performed at the Technical University Aachen, where during the infamous Fluxus Festival in 1964 Joseph Beuys received a bloody nose from an audience member. In Cologne, they performed at the well-to-do Galerie Rudolf Zwirner, whose stable that included American pop art made it one of the few venues able to pay them for their performance. And in West Berlin, they performed at Galerie René Block, a hub for some of the most progressive contemporary art in Germany. The infrastructure of their network was fragile and highly contingent. Their tours were built city by city, town by town, through letters and last-minute telegrams and aided by the readiness of their hosts to procure an extensive list of items necessary for their performances. The trail of paper correspondence that traveled slowly over the Atlantic was followed by the burdensome physical movement that included heavy luggage (and no assistants), visa problems (Moorman was stranded in East Germany), missed trains, and even for a while a missing robot, *K-456*, which Paik had brought.[2]

"The Germans love Charlotte, they think she is what American Girl ought to be," Paik once observed in his signature grammar-free style.[3] Indeed, Moorman was not shy about playing the American girl; she exuded a gentility and femininity, cultivated in part by her Arkansas upbringing and conservatory music training. "I love you," is how the bearlike Vostell signed letters to her on more than one occasion, reciprocating her customary signature ♥ Charlotte.[4] But more than anything, Paik and the German artists loved her serious and surprising performances, her willingness to embrace spectacle and risk, and—above all—her interest in their work and eagerness to perform and promote it. As she and Paik were organizing their first German tour, Paik described her to Joseph Beuys as a "very well-known and very progressive-aggressive young and beautiful cellist."[5] It was this combination of talent and tenacity that made her network essential to exchange between Germany and the United States.

The direct exchange that Moorman created represented a crucial reversal in the artistic relations between artists in the United States and Germany. German artists perceived the flow of American art, especially pop art, as dominating their country's market and pushing its art to the margins at home and abroad.[6] If pop art was considered an American import, so was Moorman, at least at first. Paik had been pushed to defend his collaboration and proposed tour with Moorman to Vostell, who helped organize the twenty-four-hour happening at Galerie Parnass. While planning the tour, Vostell wrote to Paik in apprehension about Moorman's participation because of the American nationalism he believed her presence could imply. Paik, in response to Vostell, countered that nationalism was less a concern than class warfare, as it was manifested through the division between uptown and downtown.[7] The implication: uptown is rife with market-based pop while downtown is not. Paik appealed to Vostell to see the internationalism of their project: "Joint appearance with her [Moorman] shall strengthen our alliance, but not prompt short sighted nationalism. As in the labor movement of the 19th century, international cooperation is our strongest means, because it is free from business concerns and big press manipulation."[8] Vostell's objections yielded as Moorman performed at Galerie Parnass. Ultimately, it was not Moorman or her Americanness to which he objected. It was the dominance of the American market, and she offered a direct channel to bypass its powerful flow.

These tensions did not propel Moorman to change her performance program, which dramatized her Americanness. Moorman was certainly aware of this ambivalent view: Paik began his contribution to the *24 Hours* catalog with the phrase "Kill Pop Art!"[9] John Cage's *26'1.1499" for a String Player*, one of the central works in her oeuvre, included the cello and other noise-making elements, such as a gong, a phone call, or sounds from a radio. In her elliptical discussion of *26'1.1499"* she wrote in the *24 Hours* catalog: "My interpretation of Cage's *26'1.1499"* for a String Player / Is very American—a kind of pop music."[10] Moorman's characterization of the work as "a kind of pop music" and her incorporation of props and

Wolf Vostell. Poster for *24 Hours*, Galerie Parnass, Wuppertal, West Germany, 1965. © 2015 Artists Rights Society (ARS), New York/VG Bild-Kunst, Bonn. Courtesy of Charlotte Moorman Archive, Charles Deering McCormick Library of Special Collections, Northwestern University Library.

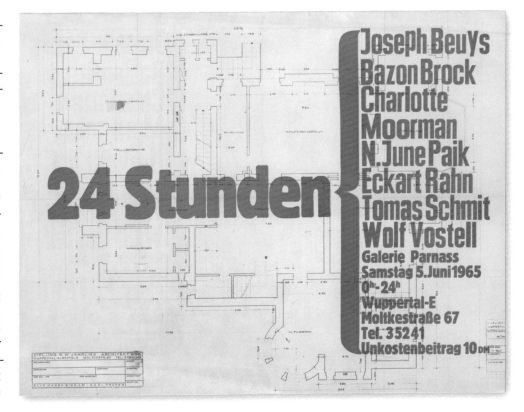

Nam June Paik. *Robot K-456* performs *Robot Opera* at the Brandenburg Gate, West Berlin, June 15, 1965. © Jürgen Müller-Schneck / Archiv Block, Berlin.

noise-making elements that were iconic American commodities branded her performance as undeniably American.[11] In preparation for her concert at each individual tour venue, she would send the host a long, detailed list of her needs, including technical equipment and the goods she required for her works. To Rolf Jährling, the proprietor of Galerie Parnass, she requested, among other items, "1 raw chicken (preferable with head on) / 1 large coke, one eatable (american) hot dog, one package bubble gum / 1 basin filled with water (old metal or plastic wash tub type) / 1 jar katsup."[12]

Moorman's appropriation of pop, within the structure of John Cage's composition, was a provocation, a bawdy joke skillfully aimed at the rigidity and seriousness of some strains of experimental art—including the "chairman" of Fluxus, George Maciunas, as well as the formality of her Juilliard training. It is an example of her radical openness to the art of her time and a sweeping dismissal of artistic and cultural hierarchies. This inclusivity also marked the musical programs she organized and presented with Paik and her avant-garde festivals. It was this same openness and insatiable curiosity that brought the work of her German peers into the fold.

In the other pillar of her program, *Per Arco*, a composition by the contemporary Italian composer Giuseppe Chiari, violence was a predominant theme. *Per Arco* "consisted of five minutes of the recorded sounds of war, one minute and forty seconds of silence, and six minutes of reactions to the noises with a cello and bow."[13] While in the United States, *Per Arco*, as Moorman wrote to Chiari in an unsent letter, was a "very powerful and meaningful piece," she continued the sentence, but crossed out, "especially now with the Viet Nam crisis."[14] While on tour in Germany her political and historical understanding of the work broadened further, so that she reflected on the violence that resulted from U.S. actions at home and abroad and on the violence that had recently shattered Europe:

> i have played Chiari's "Per Arco"
> in many countries but this time
> i have quite a strange feeling because

> i am in the German country
> that is bombing Italy in the tape
> do you recognize your sound[15]

Moorman's performance of *Per Arco* dramatized the larger issues of war and violence, including World War II and the ongoing war in Vietnam. Sharing the details of her performance at *24 Hours*, Moorman wrote to Chiari, "PER ARCO went the best I've ever played it. I've always tried to hold back the tears as I hear the tape, but this time I couldn't hold back."[16] Her reflections, as well as her physical and emotional response to the work displayed during her performance, were surely pivotal to forming a common bond with her fellow artists at Galerie Parnass. This bond was based on a shared commitment to experimental art and reveals her to be fully sensitive to the social and political issues of the time. Vostell, who had initially been so suspicious of Moorman's participation, immediately overcame his objections after her performance and proposed publishing the score for *Per Arco*.[17] Vostell, whose contribution to the event was an environment that mimicked a prison or concentration camp barracks, created the most explicitly political work in the happening.[18] Yet it was not only Vostell and Moorman's shared sensitivity to the issues of their times that reinforced their emerging respect for one another, it was also their commitment to creating transnational outlets for their work and the works of their peers.

Vostell was a crucial agent in the success of the tour, not only inviting Moorman and Paik to participate in *24 Hours* but also connecting them to the young gallerist René Block in West Berlin.[19] The confrontation of boundaries and the overcoming of their limits was the site and subject of their concert in West Berlin, where they performed at the Brandenburg Gate, sealed off by the Berlin Wall. Though the Berlin Wall was a symbol of German division, it was also a symbol of the Cold War, which effectively divided the entire world into two parts. Following Moorman's West Berlin visit, Block distributed a parodic ballot to his mailing list, calling for the election of artists to political office. The ballot listed Moorman as a political candidate alongside other artists, including Stanley Brouwn, Joseph Beuys, Gerhard Richter, Sigmar Polke, Wolf Vostell, and others. In slogans across the flyer, it plainly stated the international implications of division: "The German Problem was an African problem, an Asian problem, an Australian problem, an American problem, and an Antarctic problem."[20] This was a perspective Moorman shared with Block: that a renewed internationalism in the arts could overcome artistic and even political division.

Paik had demonstrated the remote-controlled robot in front of Galerie Parnass during *24 Hours*. But his selection of the Brandenburg Gate fulfilled his desire for a major public platform for *K-456* to perform Paik's *Robot Opera*, as well as a politically charged context.[21] On the afternoon of June 14, 1965, at the East-West border, Moorman played her cello while Paik led *K-456* in fits and starts toward the gate. It might be expected that in 1965 the robot would be an ambassador to a new and technologically advanced future, but this ramshackle and fragile contraption made of metal scraps invoked skepticism of the future and of the stability of political promises. With the

activation of a tape recorder, the robot could also recite speeches by John F. Kennedy.[22] The political context was surely not lost on Paik and Moorman as they performed at the site where John F. Kennedy, just two years before, climbed a viewing platform to peer over the Berlin Wall.

Political and historical circumstances must have been on the minds of both Moorman and Paik as they performed at the Brandenburg Gate, and it must have been particularly poignant for Paik, who was born in Korea, a country militarily divided between North and South. Paik had just written about these tragic historical failures of division in relation to his biography, published by Vostell in the compendium *Happenings, Fluxus, Pop Art, Nouveau Réalisme*. The Brandenburg Gate was located on the Strasse des 17. Juni (Street of June 17), named after the date of the 1953 East German workers' uprising, a failed and fatal protest against the Sovietization of East Germany. Writing of these historical circumstances, Paik linked the failures of World War II to the current disaster of the Cold War. According to Paik, the bloodshed of the workers' uprising and even the Cold War

Program for *Sixth and Seventh Soiree,* Galerie René Block, West Berlin, June 14 and 15, 1965. © Archiv Block, Berlin. Courtesy of Charlotte Moorman Archive, Charles Deering McCormick Library of Special Collections, Northwestern University Library.

Einladung zu den letzten Soireen der Galerie Rene Block Berlin 30 Schöneberg Frobenstr.18 Tel 265418 am 14. und 15. Juni 1965 Charlotte Moorman New York Cello Nam June Paik New York Piano

SECHSTE SOIREE

Montag 14. Juni 1965
17.00 Kurfürstendamm-Gedächtniskirche

ROBOT OPERA

by N. J. Paik

zuvor
15.00 vor dem Brandenburger Tor

Robot: Assignation a l'humanite
Anweisung an die Menschheit
Instruction to humanity

Einladung zu den letzten Soireen der Galerie Rene Block Berlin 30 Schöneberg Frobenstr. 18 Tel 265418 am 14. und 15. Juni 1965 Charlotte Moormann New York Cello Nam June Paik New York Piano

SIEBENTE SOIREE

Montag 14. Juni 1965 21.00
Konzert in der Galerie

Werke von Brecht-Tenney Brock (Uraufführung) Brown Cage Chiari Corner Higgins Ichiyanagi Paik

Dienstag 15. Juni 1965 21.00
Konzert in der Galerie

Werke von Brown Cage Chiari Corner Goldstein Higgins Mac Low Ono Paik Rot Vostell (Uraufführung) Williams

Eintritt durch Erwerb eines Programmes (DM 4) Zur 7. Soiree für Jugendliche unter 21 Jahren kein Einlass.

could have been prevented, he explained, if "the German People had been more against Hitler."[23] In this way, Paik and Moorman's politically resonant performance at the site of the uprising was also a sign of faith in the possibility of public performance to raise political and even historical awareness. It was also their first major outdoor public platform for a performance, a concept that Moorman would build on as she staged her ever-growing and ever-more-public annual avant-garde festivals in New York.

•

When Moorman returned from her European tour, she set out to finalize the details of the 3rd Annual New York Avant Garde Festival, a sprawling multiday event filling Judson Hall in New York City with three evenings in September dedicated to dance, music, and poetry. Reflecting her broadened network, the 1965 festival included works by many of the German artists she had just encountered, including Vostell, Brock, and Ludwig Gosewitz. Among her new compatriots from Germany, Vostell was one of her most frequent correspondents, with whom she traded letters and maintained a friendship throughout her life. In addition to their mutual sensitivity to war and disaster, they exercised the drive and vision to create outlets for happenings and a deft touch for whipping up spectacle.

From West Germany, Vostell eagerly sent Moorman letters and postcards, promising to send works by Kurt Schwitters to present at the festival. "The Schwitters Ur-Sonate— Tape I will send you. Air-Mail the first day of August—also some texts of his Merz-Theater from 1923—it seems to me revolutionary today and much like a happening!"[24] Thus, Moorman's large and inclusive festival offered a genealogy of happenings, including works by the Dada artists Schwitters and Richard Huelsenbeck, who had been in exile in New York since 1936. Though Vostell was genuinely enthusiastic about the work of Schwitters, his eagerness to spread it to the New York avant-garde festival was also an effort to cement the history of happenings as a phenomenon originating in Germany.

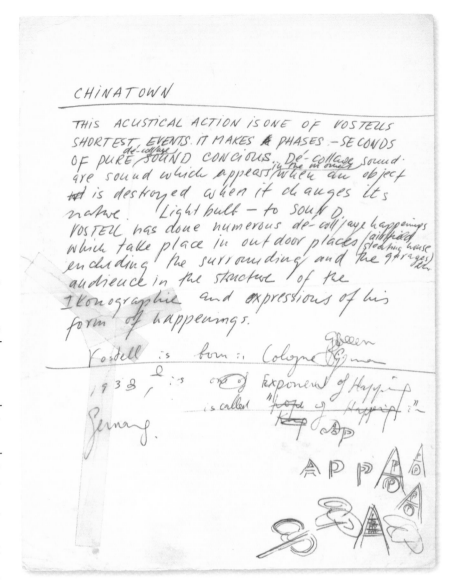

Writing to her in English, Vostell also suggested, "perhaps you could publish something, or read it or perform it. I have confidence in your way to interpret and how you do it is alright!"[25] Vostell's willingness for Moorman to perform his work was unusual, revealing both his confidence in her ability to present his work to a wider audience and his faith in her as a performer. Unlike much Fluxus art, his happenings were generally performed under his direction and grand vision as author. The works Vostell initially sent to Moorman in 1965 were directions for *Kleenex* and *Chinatown*, both examples of his *dé-collage* compositions. He described *dé-collage* as the sound "when an object

Wolf Vostell. Description of *Chinatown*, undated. © 2014 Estate of Wolf Vostell / Artists Rights Society, New York / VG Bild-Kunst, Bonn. Courtesy of Charlotte Moorman Archive, Charles Deering McCormick Library of Special Collections, Northwestern University Library.

is destroyed, when it changes its nature."[26] The principle was not only the basis for his sound works but also for his happenings, paintings, and sculptures, defined by tears, erasures, fragments, and ruins that are the outcome of, or in direct reference to, the destructive and traumatic events of violence and war, which he experienced growing up in wartime Germany.[27] And it is precisely these formative experiences and their post-war aftermath that compelled Vostell to dedicate so much energy to expose these fractures and motivated him to find ways to create international artistic alliances.[28]

After meeting Vostell in Wuppertal, Moorman premiered *Chinatown* during her first performance at Galerie René Block in West Berlin, and she also performed it at her 1965 festival.[29] Reporting to Vostell of the festival, she wrote, it "would be complete if you were here with an evening of your happenings! 'Chinatown' was extremely well received, but it doesn't represent you as the 'Pope of Happenings,'" as she benevolently called him.[30] A few months later, Vostell finally performed *Chinatown* by Moorman's side on March 13,

1966, in Philadelphia, at an offshoot of the avant-garde festival. There, according to the *Evening Bulletin*, Vostell, the "German in dungarees with a walrus mustache" threw "two dozen lightbulbs against a wall."[31] Vostell was not alone in producing loud, disturbing, violent noises. That night not only did Moorman "pluck at her cello. She also smashed the window glass with a hammer and shot off the [blank] pistol."[32]

Moorman's mix of seriousness, humor, and the burlesque strategies in her performances cut a stark contrast with Vostell's absolute earnestness while performing. Nevertheless, violence, chaos, and the sounds of destruction were a shared method for generating sound and making music.[33] This reveals a common thread of Vostell's thinking that intersects with Moorman's description of her performance of Cage's work as pop art—in which she produces sounds with hot dogs and chewing gum, as well as broken glass and a pistol—that he considers pop art to be frozen happenings.[34] This was, perhaps, not only an attempt on Vostell's behalf to further establish the significance of happenings in relation to pop art and is also a revelation of a deep affinity between Moorman's all-embracing and raucous performances that voraciously included the sounds of the world around her and Vostell's own use of found objects in his happenings.

Moorman countered her lack of funding for her festivals through her remarkable ability to generate public spectacle. In this regard, her 1966 festival was a breakthrough, where for the first time the event took place in a major public site, Central Park in and around the pond. Amid a chaotic day of performances and events by many artists, including by Moorman, one of the many feats she achieved was generating broad coverage by the mass media, amplifying the avant-garde, and bringing its coverage to newspapers and television. Moving the festival from Judson Hall to a central public space challenged the boundaries between avant-garde culture and mass culture.

When Moorman performed Vostell's *dé-collage Morning Glory*, at the 1966 avant-garde festival in Central Park, she provoked the media even as she courted it. Surrounded by TV crews and reporters as she carried out the action on a floating stage in the pond, Moorman, enrobed in a ball gown, filled a kitchen blender with pages of the *New York Times*, doused it in perfume, and pureed the mixture into a gray slurry. The following day, the *New York Times* ran an article on the festival, featuring two columns: one covering the daytime events and one covering the evening. In the center of the highly unusual around-the-clock coverage was a photograph of Moorman performing *Morning Glory*.[35] As an action and in its reception, *Morning Glory* came to emblemize the antagonistic yet also dependent relationship between Moorman, the avant-garde, and the masses, including the media and the public. Just as she took apart the hierarchies in her music that ordered classical music, new music, pop, and performance, in her festivals she also dismantled the boundaries between insular experimental art and the mass media. For Vostell, who was always keen to capture the spotlight, not only did his work make the headlines, but the paper also reproduced and disseminated a critique of itself.[36]

In the summer of 1966, before the fourth festival, Moorman and Paik embarked on their second tour through Europe, with a program titled *So langweilig wie möglich* (*As Boring as Possible*), with stops mirroring their earlier circuit of concerts.[37] In their West Berlin concert, the pair performed their regular program, and they made the European debut of Erik Satie's *Vexations*, an eighteen-hour four-hand relay piano performance that Moorman played topless.[38] While in Berlin, the pair also paid a visit to the Dada artist Hannah Höch, extending Moorman's knowledge and interest in her avant-garde predecessors. As Höch wrote of the pair: "very interesting people . . . interested in the artistic work and life of the former Dadasophin."[39] The most significant stop on the 1966 tour, however, was at the Düsseldorf Art Academy. There, in front of an audience of more than five hundred people, Joseph Beuys, the academy's most well-known professor, punctuated their concert with an unexpected performance of his own.[40]

Paik and Moorman's performance in Düsseldorf, as in the other shows on their second tour, was a variety show spanning the serious, sentimental, and even ridiculous. To this visual and aural cacophony, Beuys's action interjected solemnity and silence: from the back of the auditorium Beuys slowly pushed a grand piano to the front of the audience, assisted by his students, Jörg Immendorff, the concert organizer, and Johannes Stüttgen. The piano was shrouded in thick grey felt—Beuys's signature material—both muting and transmuting the instrument into an elephant-like creature. The work, titled *Infiltration Homogen für Konzertflügel, der größte Komponist der Gegenwart ist das Contergankind* (*Infiltration Homogen for Grand Piano: The Greatest Contemporary Composer Is the Contergan Child*), was dedicated to the *Contergankind*, children of mothers who were prescribed the drug thalidomide, under the brand name Contergan, to alleviate morning sickness in the 1950s.[41] The drug, however, caused serious birth defects.

In lieu of playing the instrument, as a part of the performance, Beuys attached to its covering two red pieces of felt, forming a red cross, a multivalent symbol of aid and salvation. Beuys's work often addressed, sometimes obliquely but in this case more explicitly, social and historical trauma. And within Beuys's material repertoire, felt had a warming quality, intended to serve as a critical catalyst for transformation. In the context of his action, it functioned as a symbolic invocation of healing. Accounts of the concert tell of further components of his work, but the covering of the instrument and the pinning of a cross to it were the aspects Moorman held onto when she returned to New York.

Moorman had more time to consider the felt shroud Beuys had created for the piano two days later. The occasion was *Frisches* (*Fresh Things*), an intimate evening of happenings and actions at the Düsseldorf apartment of the artist couple Chris Reinecke and Jörg Immendorff.[42] That night Moorman and Paik performed a joint work, *Bag Piece*, by Yoko Ono, in which they crawled into the sack, so to speak, insinuating copulation.[43] Other artists in attendance, including Beuys, Franz Erhard Walther, Verena Pfisterer, and Christof Kohlhöfer, all either brought a work or performed one. At *Frisches*, Beuys displayed the large felt cover for the piano, which he laid on the floor of the small apartment, where, without the animating form of

Peter Moore. Charlotte Moorman and Takehisa Kosugi perform Joseph Beuys's *Infiltration Homogen for Cello*, 4th Annual New York Avant Garde Festival, Central Park, September 9, 1966. Photograph © Barbara Moore / Licensed by VAGA, NY.

an instrument, it appeared melancholy and lifeless. When she returned to New York, Moorman reinterpreted this work with the blessing of Beuys, making it a central piece of her repertoire.

At the conclusion of her tour, Moorman hauled "nine pieces of luggage that bulged with souvenirs—including a pair of Lederhosen she'd acquired in Düsseldorf—and great quantities of newspapers with reviews of their concerts. Joseph Beuys had to sit on her suitcases so that she could latch them," biographer Joan Rothfuss reports.[44] Among these mementos was the poster Immendorff had made for her performance at the Düsseldorf Art Academy. But more than souvenirs, Moorman returned with ideas and works resulting from her intensified contact with artists in Germany. She incorporated these materials into the program for the fourth avant-garde festival in Central Park, which included her performance of Vostell's *Morning Glory*.

Moorman responded to Beuys's surprise participation in her Düsseldorf concert by taking the unprecedented step of translating his *Infiltration Homogen for Grand Piano* to a work for the cello.[45] She debuted this piece at the 4th Annual New York Avant Garde Festival, and her version was a radical reduction of Beuys's original—in both size and duration.[46] Moorman's version, lasting only minutes, began as Takehisa Kosugi knelt on a platform with the cello resting on his two outstretched arms. Moorman then solemnly approached the instrument, slowly pinned a felt cross onto it, lifted the instrument into her own arms and exited the stage.[47]

In her rendition, the cello, smaller and more intimate than a piano in its relationship to the body, approximates the human form. The act of holding the cello and its fabric cover furthers these bodily and intimate connotations. In this way, she expanded upon the anthropomorphism of Beuys's original work and created a sympathetic relationship to the instrument. Moorman's translation and the performance of the piece was a radical reduction of his original: in the size and type of instrument, through the elimination of the elements Beuys originally

used, as well as his reference to the *Contergankind*. Despite these differences, her interpretation heightened some of the most significant aspects of Beuys's work: the intensity of his physical and mental concentration when carrying out an action, which she developed throughout the years of her performance of the work, and the centrality of material. Not that their collaboration was without misunderstanding—for her debut of the work, Moorman wrapped her cello in soft flannel rather than Beuys's signature felt—which Beuys rapidly corrected.[48]

The importance Beuys placed on Moorman's 1966 New York performance is underscored by his inclusion of it in his *Lebenslauf / Werklauf*, his artistic autobiography.[49] Though Beuys's arrival in the United States is closely linked with his 1974 action, *I Like America and America Likes Me*, in which he was wrapped in felt and transported by ambulance from JFK Airport to the René Block Gallery in New York, Moorman's performances were an antecedent

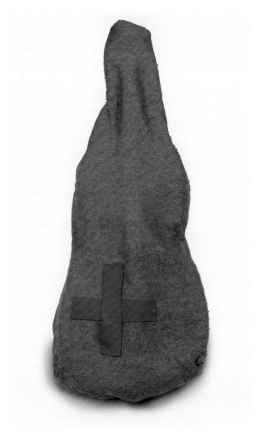

Felt-covered cello with red cross used by Charlotte Moorman in Joseph Beuys's *Infiltration Homogen for Cello*. Cover fabricated in 1975, felt, 52 × 19 × 10½ in. Collection of Deborah Hoyt.

Charlotte Moorman and Nam June Paik perform Joseph Beuys's *Infiltration Homogen for Cello*, Guadalcanal, Solomon Islands, April 21, 1976. Photograph by Frank Pileggi. Courtesy of Charlotte Moorman Archive, Charles Deering McCormick Library of Special Collections, Northwestern University Library.

for his physical entrance into the United States.[50] Beuys had refused to set foot on U.S. soil for the duration of the Vietnam War. Despite his U.S. boycott, Moorman was an early and crucial interpreter and vehicle for the dissemination of Beuys's work to the United States. Through Moorman, Beuys found a way to spread his work and ideas in the United States without going there.[51] Beginning in 1966, *Infiltration Homogen for Cello* became a key part of her repertoire, which she performed throughout her life, in places including Chicago; Ithaca, New York; Lima, Ohio; and beyond. Her performance of *Infiltration Homogen for Cello* coincided with Beuys's first creation of a multiple—a serially produced art object, which Beuys understood as a vehicle for his ideas. "I'm interested in the distribution of physical vehicles in the form of editions because I'm interested in spreading ideas," Beuys later said of his multiples. This statement could also characterize his authorization

of the work Moorman performed.[52] Like *Infiltration Homogen for Cello*, his multiples circulated to New York before Beuys went there himself.

One of her most poignant and politically loaded performances of *Infiltration Homogen for Cello* is captured in Paik's videotape *Guadalcanal Requiem* (1977–79), a joint performance with Paik on the Solomon Islands, one of the Pacific theater battlefields of World War II. Invoking the context of war—both the Vietnam War, which had just drawn to a close, and the World War II battles that had been fought there—Moorman is seen crawling on the shores of the beach performing Paik's *Peace Sonata* with a cello slung over her back like a gun. Soon after, the video shows her at the wreckage of an airplane, where she and Paik perform *Infiltration Homogen for Cello*. Atop these ruins, Paik holds out the felt-wrapped cello as Moorman pins a red cross onto it. The work's siting excavates multiple valances of war, not only because it takes place on an island scarred by war but also because the crashed airplane echoes Beuys's own mythic artistic biography, beginning as he is rescued after a forced plane landing in Crimea in 1942. Moorman's sympathy for Beuys and his work that invoked healing and transformation was a mutual response to the aftershock of war.[53]

Just as Vostell was an important node in Moorman's network, so was Beuys. It was through Beuys that she was introduced to his students at the Düsseldorf Art Academy, including Jörg Immendorff, who organized Moorman and Paik's 1966 concert at the academy and the *Frisches* evening of events. In 1968, Moorman again performed in a concert organized by Immendorff, sponsored by Lidl, the name for Immendorff and Reinecke's socially and politically oriented art activities. At their Lidl concert, Moorman performed the infamous *Opera Sextronique*, for which she had been arrested in New York in 1967 for performing topless. According to a reporter at the Düsseldorf concert, she performed "at first bare-topped, then bare-bottomed, and finally completely nude."[54] [See the photograph in Kristine Stiles's essay in this catalog, page 170.] But sex was not the only provocation of her performance as she also linked it with violence. As a critic reported, she "played a four foot bomb," continuing, "Instead of a bow she used a saw, which she finally broke by smashing it against the metallic 'bomb.'"[55]

For Immendorff, Moorman's performance was further proof of her credibility as an artistic and political ally critical of U.S. involvement in the Vietnam War. It made an impression on Immendorff, who, with his deliberately naive art (including large painted flowers and baby faces), created anti-Vietnam art actions in 1966 and again in 1968.[56] He even included a picture of Moorman's Lidl performance in a photo spread documenting his anti-Vietnam activities in his artist's book *Hier und Jetzt* (*Here and Now*).[57] Finally reciprocating Moorman's Lidl performances in Germany, he sent her a work in 1969 to be included in the 7th Annual New York Avant Garde Festival. As he wrote to her of the work, "It is this letter; please

read it aloud to the audience. It is a greeting to U.S.A."[58] The letter was, in essence, an advertisement for his Lidlraum, a space for meetings and performances, and it used Moorman's festival to broadcast his political agenda of international artistic and political solidarity. As he wrote in the margins of the note: "DIE NORDAMERIKANISCHEN INDI-ANERSTÄMME STEHEN VOLL HINTER LIDL = THE NORTH AMERICAN INDIAN ARE STRONG WITH LIDL."[59] As a piece of mail art to be read at the festival, this unassuming work self-reflexively reciprocated the transatlantic channels of Moorman's German–American network and exploited her avant-garde platform as a place for the dissemination of art and ideas. It also embraced Moorman's "friends" in the United States while still remaining critical of the country.

Immendorff's invocation of the North American Indians fit into a long tradition of German fascination with Native Americans.[60] Their reception and even exaltation of Native Americans allowed them to exercise their interest in the United States while remaining critical of its imperialist history. In the case of Moorman, whose

Charlotte Moorman's event diary for May 1974, noting the days of Joseph Beuys's performance of *I Like America and America Likes Me*, his Pan Am flight number, and his departure time. Courtesy of Charlotte Moorman Archive, Charles Deering McCormick Library of Special Collections, Northwestern University Library.

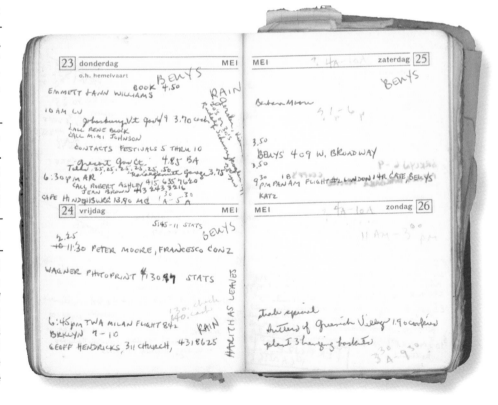

politically aware positions became known to her German colleagues through her performances, she appeared as a natural ally to their causes. Immendorff's letter was not the first time that Moorman herself was the recipient of German works referencing Native Americans. Indeed, as Beuys was preparing his action *I Like America,* Ursula Block, the wife of gallerist René Block, asked Moorman whether the artist knew where she could procure a coyote for the performance.[61] Dieter Roth, the German-born Swiss artist—who spent substantial portions of his itinerant life in Iceland, the United States, Switzerland, and Germany—had composed a piece for Moorman titled *Lullaby for Karl May,* referencing the German author of wildly popular novels about Native Americans. In giving the work to Moorman, Roth, who had a relentless sense of humor, was also spoofing the German fascination with Native Americans. Yet Immendorff's reference was not a joke, nor was it based on symbolism or fantasy. A Native American group had contacted him in an effort to build international solidarity, and his letter to Moorman was to serve as a sign of his strengthening international alliances. The contact materialized a year later, in 1970, when the Native American activist Shirley Keith, on a tour of Europe during which she called on political activists, visited Immendorff's Lidl Academy, his do-it-yourself center for artistic and political activity.[62]

In *I Like America and America Likes Me,* Beuys wore his ambivalence toward the United States on his sleeve, contrasting the coyote, an idealization of what he believed to be Native American values, with a delivery of the *Wall Street Journal* to the gallery, a symbol of what he understood to be the country's current values. Though Beuys only "liked" America, the Germans "loved" Moorman, as Paik had so succinctly put it, and understood her as a sympathetic artist and interpreter of their work, as well as a vehicle for the dissemination of their politically charged work in the United States. When Beuys finally came to New York for his 1974 action at the René Block Gallery, Moorman made notes on her calendar for each day he was in town. On the final day of his action, she met him at JFK airport and had a snapshot taken with him before he embarked on his Pan Am flight back home. It is a remarkable photo summing up a chapter in the history of German–American exchange: of Beuys, who had just thematized his relationship with America in a four-day action in New York, and Moorman, who, eight years before, first brought his work there.

Charlotte Moorman and Joseph Beuys at John F. Kennedy International Airport, New York, after his performance of *I Like America and America Likes Me*, May 1974. Photograph by Francesco Conz. Courtesy of Charlotte Moorman Archive, Charles Deering McCormick Library of Special Collections, Northwestern University Library.

Notes

I am grateful for the comments of Ann Patnaude, Iva Olah, Michael Tymkiw, and Nancy Lin. Thanks goes to Kate Hers Rhee for her research assistance; Scott Krafft and Sigrid Pohl Perry for facilitating my research in the Charlotte Moorman Archives at Northwestern; Lisa G. Corrin and Corinne Granof for inviting me to participate in the Charlotte Moorman study day. I would like to thank Joan Rothfuss for generously sharing a chapter from her biography on Charlotte Moorman before its publication. Because the book was released when this essay was written, I was unfortunately not able to build on its groundbreaking research.

1. The production of the catalog immediately followed the *24 Hours* happening, which Moorman called a "48 Hour Happening." Charlotte Moorman to Giuseppe Chiari, June 19, 1965, Charlotte Moorman Archive, Charles Deering McCormick Library of Special Collections, Northwestern University Library (hereafter cited as CMA). During the happenings, the photographer, Ute Klophaus, who captured the activities on film, rushed to a studio to process the film and returned to the gallery with the photographs. Upon her return, the artists set to work creating a joint catalog that included the Klophaus photos, and Moorman penned her immediate reactions to the event. For an account of the event and Wolf Vostell's contribution to it, see Mercedes Vostell, *Vostell—Ein Leben lang: eine Werkbiographie* (Berlin: B und S Siebenhaar, 2012), 85–87.

2. Moorman described her visa problems to Chiari in a letter dated June 19, 1965. For *K-456*'s mysterious disappearance, see Howard Klein, "Lost and Found," *New York Times*, June 13, 1965.

3. Nam June Paik, cited in Calvin Tomkins, "Profiles: Video Visionary," *New Yorker*, May 5, 1975, 61.

4. Wolf Vostell to Charlotte Moorman, December 12, 1973, CMA.

5. Undated letter from Nam June Paik to Joseph Beuys, sent in advance of their 1965 German tour, CMA.

6. On the reception of American pop art in West Germany, see Catherine Dossin, "Pop begeistert: American Pop Art and the German People," *American Art* 25, no. 3 (Fall 2011): 100–111.

7. Nam June Paik to Wolf Vostell, undated letter, 1964. Happening Archive Vostell.

8. Ibid.

9. Nam June Paik, "Pensée 1965," in *24 Stunden* (Itzehoe-Vosskate: Hansen and Hansen, 1965).

10. Charlotte Moorman, "Cello," in *24 Stunden*.

11. Benjamin Piekut offers a detailed account of Moorman's development and interpretation of *26′1.1499″ for a String Player* in "Murder by Cello: Charlotte Moorman Meets John Cage," in *Experimentalism Otherwise: The New York Avant-Garde and Its Limits* (Berkeley: University of California Press, 2011), 140–76.

12. Charlotte Moorman to Rolf Jährling, May 31, 1965, CMA.

13. Moorman, "Cello."

14. Unsent letter draft from Charlotte Moorman to Giuseppe Chiari, April 2, 1965, CMA. In her draft, Moorman crossed out "Viet Nam crisis," perhaps thinking the language too strong.

15. Moorman, "Cello."

16. Charlotte Moorman to Giuseppe Chiari, June 19, 1965, CMA.

17. Ibid.

18. Mercedes Vostell describes Wolf Vostell's work *Die Folgen der Notstandgesetze* (*The Consequences of the Emergency Laws*), in *Vostell: Ein Leben lang*, 85.

19. Wolf Vostell introduced Paik and Moorman to René Block, who had just opened up a gallery in West Berlin in the fall of 1964. Wolf Vostell to René Block, April 3, 1965, Happening Archive Vostell. For a history of Galerie René Block, including a discussion of Paik and Moorman's 1965 performance in West Berlin, see: Rachel Jans, "Art on the Border: Galerie René Block and Cold War Berlin" (PhD diss., University of Chicago, 2014).

20. Galerie René Block, *Wahlaufruf*, 1965. Translation by author.

21. According to René Block, Paik wanted to perform the *Robot Opera* on the West German side of the Brandenburg Gate. During their performance they were confronted by the British Military Police as the robot approached the nearby Soviet Memorial. It was Block's suggestion for Paik, Moorman, and *K-456* to also perform near the bombed-out Kaiser-Wilhelm Memorial Church, on Kurfürstendamm, where the performance lasted a few minutes. René Block, email to author, September 3, 2014.

22. John G. Hanhardt, "The Seoul of Fluxus," in exhibition catalog *The Worlds of Nam June Paik* (New York: Guggenheim Museum, 2000), 37.

23. Nam June Paik, "Nam June Paik," in *Happenings, Fluxus, Pop Art, Nouveau Réalisme*, ed. Jürgen Becker and Wolf Vostell (Hamburg: Rowohlt, 1965), 444.

24. Wolf Vostell to Charlotte Moorman, July 13, 1965, CMA. During a 1964 visit, Vostell and the Fluxus artist Al Hansen performed a *dé-collage* happening in the apartment of Richard Huelsenbeck as a part of service they called *Happenings in Your Home*. See Grace Glueck, "Art Notes," *New York Times*, April 12, 1964.

25. Vostell to Moorman, July 13, 1965.

26. Grammar altered by author of this article for legibility. See Vostell's description of *Chinatown* in the program for *The Avant-Garde in Philadelphia*, March 13, 1966, CMA.

27. Perhaps Vostell's most well known *dé-collage* happening to engage city space and ruins was *Cityrama (1 & 2)*, which took place in Cologne in 1961. For a discussion of this happening, see Claudia Mesch, "Vostell's Ruins: dé-collage and the mnemotechnic space of the postwar city," *Art History* 23 (2000): 88–115.

28. Like Moorman, Vostell was deeply committed to creating open channels for the transatlantic transfer of contemporary art. One of Vostell's major outlets was his journal, *dé-coll/age* (1962–1969), in which he published German, European, and American scores, documentation, and information. In New York in the 1960s, Dick Higgins contributed greatly to transatlantic exchange through the publication of many European scores, including Vostell's, through Something Else Press.

29. Program for the 3rd Annual New York Avant Garde Festival, CMA. A *New York Times* review of the festival mentions that a composition by Vostell was included but does not name it. Richard D. Freed, "Variety Provided by Avant-Garde, 14 Works Employ Silence, Recordings and Paper," *New York Times*, August 30, 1965.

30. Charlotte Moorman to Wolf Vostell, September 3, 1965, CMA.

31. "200 Hear 'New Music' with Duck Calls, Sirens," *Evening Bulletin*, Philadelphia, March 14, 1966.

32. Ibid.

33. Ibid.

34. Wolf Vostell, "Happening in New York," *Kunst*, June/July, 1964, 17, 16–18.

35. In 1963 Vostell performed the *dé-collage Morning Glory* at the Third Rail Gallery in Lower Manhattan, gaining little attention. A copy of the score is published in Wolf Vostell, *TV-De-coll/age—Morning Glory* (New York: Smolin Gallery, 1963). For a discussion of Vostell and his use of television, see John Alan Farmer, "Art into Television, 1960–65," (Ph.D. diss., Columbia University, 1998).

36. Dan Sullivan, "Avant-Garde Day in Park Goes On and On," *New York Times*, September 10, 1966.

37. Based on my research, the concert dates for the German leg of their 1966 tour are as follows: July 13, Galerie Rudolf Zwirner, Cologne; July 15, Forum Theater/Galerie René Block, West Berlin; July 16, Satie's *Vexations*, Forum Theater/Galerie René Block, West Berlin; July 25, Galerie Aachen; July 26, J. W. Goethe Universität, Frankfurt am Main; July 28, Kunstakademie Düsseldorf; July 30, *Frisches*, Düsseldorf.

38. She performed with the German concert pianist Lissa Bauer, the Berlin-based artist Ludwig Gosewitz, Austrian artist and composer Gerhard Rühm, British artist David Llewlyn, and Paik. See Paul Moor, "Musik, die immer mehr in die Nähe von Theater rückt," *Die Zeit*, July 22, 1966; "Große Nachtmusik," *Der Spiegel*, July 25, 1966.

39. Höch's diary entry detailing Moorman and Paik's visit to her home is reproduced in Ralf Burmeister, "Fluxus besucht Heiligensee," in *Hannah Höch–Eine Lebenscollage Band III 1946–1978 1. Abteilung I* (Berlin: Künstler-Archiven der Berlinischen Galerie, 2001), 132–33.

40. Competition grew between Beuys and Vostell as Paik and Moorman were planning their first German tour. Vostell had invited the pair to perform at *24 Hours*, but Beuys wanted them to perform at the Düsseldorf Art Academy in 1965, on the condition that they perform first in Düsseldorf. As a result of their decision to participate in *24 Hours*, Paik and Moorman did not perform in Düsseldorf until their second tour in 1966. See Joseph Beuys to Nam June Paik, undated, CMA. René Block discusses the tension between Vostell and Beuys in "Fluxus and Fluxism in Berlin 1964–1976," in *Berlinart 1961–1987*, ed. Kynaston McShine (New York: Museum of Modern Art, 1987), 68, 75–76.

41. For accounts of the 1966 Kunstakademie Düsseldorf concert, see Uwe M. Schneede, "*Infiltration homogen für Konzertflügel, der größte Komponist der Gegenwart ist das Contergankind,*" in *Joseph Beuys: Die Aktionen Kommentiertes Werkverzeichnis mit fotografischen Dokumentation* (Ostfildern: Hatje-Cantz, 1994), 112–15; Johannes Stüttgen, "Konzert mit Charlotte Moorman und Nam June Paik und Joseph Beuys," in *Der Ganze Riemen: Der Auftritt von Joseph Beuys als Lehrer die Chronologie der Ereignisse der Staatlichen Kunstakademie Düsseldorf 1966—1972* (Cologne: Walther König, 2008), 28–32; and Mario Kramer, *Klang und Skulptur: Der musikalische Aspekt im Werk von Joseph Beuys* (Darmstadt: Jürgen Hüsser, 1995), 48–69. Reviews of the concert include Reinhard Oehlenschlägel, "Budenzauber für Intellektuelle: Nam June Paiks Unterhaltung durch Langeweile," *Frankfurter Allgemeine Zeitung*, July 30, 1966; and Wolfgang Breuer, "Striptease, Rühreier und ein Happening," *Neue Ruhr/Rhein Zeitung*, July 30, 1966.

2. For photo documentation of *Frisches*, see *Reiner Ruthenbeck Fotografie, 1956–1976*, ed. Brigitte Wontorra (Stuttgart: Cantz, 1999), 136–47. In addition to the artists mentioned, those present reportedly included the gallerist Jean Pierre Williams, René Block, Professor Karl Otto Götz, Gerd Vorhoff of Galerie Aachen, and Valdis Abolins, though accounts vary. Immendorff discusses *Frisches*, and the attending guests, in Pamela Kort, *Jörg Immendorff im Gespräch mit Pamela Kort* (Cologne: Kiepenheuer und Witsch, 1993), 31–32.

43. Joan Rothfuss, *Topless Cellist: The Improbable Life of Charlotte Moorman* (Cambridge, Mass.: MIT Press, 2014), 161.

44. Ibid., 163.

45. These performances are captured in *4th Annual New York Avant Garde Festival*, directed by Jud Yalkut (New York: Electronic Arts Intermix, 1966–1972), DVD.

46. The name of this work varied throughout the years. Moorman sometimes referred to it as *Cello Sonata by Joseph Beuys* or simply as *Cello Sonata,* as well as *Infiltration Homogen for Cello.*

47. Yalkut, *4th Festival*.

48. Kramer, *Klang und Skulptur*, 89, 154n407–9. My thanks to Joan Rothfuss for sharing this source with me.

49. Joseph Beuys, "Joseph Beuys: Life and Works," ed. Goetz Adriani, Winfried Konnertz, and Karin Thomas, trans. Patricia Lech (New York: Barron's, 1979), 138. Here, the work is titled *Infiltration Homogen for Cello (felt)*.

50. Five months before *I Like America and America Likes Me*, Beuys had a ten-day lecture tour in New York, Chicago, and Minneapolis. For an account of Beuys's reception in the United States, including his January 1974 visit, see Joan Rothfuss, "Joseph Beuys: Echoes in America," in *Joseph Beuys: Mapping the Legacy,* ed. Gene Ray (Sarasota, Fl.: John and Mable Ringling Museum of Art, 2001), 37–53. See also Carin Kuoni, ed., *Joseph Beuys in America: Energy Plan for the Western Man* (New York: Four Walls Eight Windows, 1990).

51. Beuys had similarly tried to link his work to the United States through a proposed simultaneous performance of *Der Chef / The Chief* in New York by Robert Morris, who had performed at the Düsseldorf Art Academy with Yvonne Rainer on October 25, 1964. See Dirk Luckow's chapter on the relationship between Robert Morris and Joseph Beuys, "Robert Morris und Beuys: Ein Verhältnis mit vielen Differenzen," in *Joseph Beuys und die amerikanische Anti Form-Kunst: Einfluss und Wechselwirkung zwischen Beuys und Morris, Hesse, Nauman, Serra* (Berlin: Gebr. Mann Verlag, 1998), 31–108.

52. Joseph Beuys, "Klüser, Schellmann: Fragen an Joseph Beuys," in *Multiples: Ein Versuch die Entwicklung des Auflagenobjektes darzustellen*, ed. René Block (Berlin: Neue Berliner Kunstverein, 1974), 91.

53. See Edith Decker-Phillips, *Paik Video* (Cologne: Dumont, 1988), 164–66.

54. Ralph Blumenthal, "Naked Cellist Completes Her Concert in Germany," *New York Times*, October 9, 1968.

55. Ibid.

56. See "Jörg Immendorff Vietnam 23.4.1966," in Adam C. Oellers and Neuer Aachener Kunstverein, eds., *"Wollt Ihr das Totale Leben?": Fluxus und Agit-Pop der 60er Jahre in Aachen* (Aachen: Neuer Aachener Kunstverein, 1995), 101–5.

57. Jörg Immendorff, *Hier und Jetzt: Das tun, was zu tun ist* (Cologne: Walther König, 1973), 43–58, at 58.

58. Jörg Immendorff to Charlotte Moorman, September 10, 1969, CMA.

59. Ibid.

60. Pamela Kort explores the history of German artists' fascination with the American Indian in "The Unmastered Past of the Indian's Murder," in *I Like America: Fictions of the Wild West*, ed. Pamela Kort and Max Hollein (Munich: Prestel, 2007), 44–67.

61. Urusla Block to Charlotte Moorman, undated letter, CMA.

62. Harald Szeemann chronicles Lidl's activities in the 1960s and Shirley Keith's visit in "ostwest: ste(h)st wo?: Zur Ausstellung," in *Immendorff*, ed. Johannes Gachnang et al. (Zurich: Kunsthaus Zurich), 30.

Bomb-Paper-Ice: Charlotte Moorman and the Metaphysics of Extension

Kathy O'Dell

At last she lifts off the bow and sits back.
Her face shines with the unselfconsciousness of a cat
screaming at night and the teary radiance of one
who gives everything no matter what has been given.

—Galway Kinnell, "The Cellist," 1994

Galway Kinnell, Pulitzer prize-winning poet, might have been writing about Charlotte Moorman in his 1994 poem, as excerpts from "The Cellist" punctuating this essay will show. He did not know Moorman. Nor did I. But thanks to the testimony and documentation from those who did, and to the interpretations of rigorous thinkers and interpreters of textual, photographic, and video accounts, a clear portrait of the artist's persona and production takes shape. From this foundation in fact and analysis, interlaced with poetry, I argue that Moorman came to understand her cello as an extension of her body, not an entity with which she "became one," and I explore how the materials used to fabricate her many unconventional cellos serve as metaphors for concerns of the body central to later feminist discourses.[1]

The Sensorium of Traditional Materials

Spruce. Maple. Poplar. Sometimes pine or willow. Smooth, ineffably smooth, like the feel of bathwater when moving one's fingertips slowly across its surface. Not warm, although it might give the allusion thereof, especially the sides, to which just the right amount of heat was applied to coerce them into properly bent curves. Then there's the purfling. So lovely with its strip of light-hued wood sandwiched between two darker ones, yet so requisite. For without this decorative inlay along the edge of the top and back plates, the wood is at risk of cracking upon the slightest smack of the instrument against table edges or car doors, or after too many hours on the road, or in response to the punishments of weather.[2]

The cello, like most string instruments, can be easily romanticized. It is, after all, an exquisite object, the result of hundreds of hours of skilled artisanal focus. Consistently since the late sixteenth century,[3] the angle of this and that part of the cello has been altered to enhance its contribution to the sounds of the symphony orchestra. The size of the cello, however, was not standardized until the mid-eighteenth century, and only in the mid-nineteenth century was the endpin introduced, relieving the cellist from having to focus on forcefully squeezing the instrument between the calves or balancing it on a stool. The innovation of the endpin, or spike, which the notable cellist Adrien-François Servais invented to provide more room for his ever-expanding girth, also allowed more women to play the cello, "since no lady would dare to straddle her legs around an instrument in the same way as men."[4] Previously, women had to

OPPOSITE
Peter Moore. Charlotte Moorman and Nam June Paik perform Human Cello variation as part of John Cage's *26'1.1499" for a String Player* at Café au Go Go, New York City, October 4, 1965. Photograph © Barbara Moore/Licensed by VAGA, NY.

153

play from a sidesaddle position, which made it challenging for them to play as expertly as men, who could sit astride the instrument.

The bow, usually made of the heartwood of a species of *Caesalpinia echinata* that is especially viscous and supple, is traditionally strung with horsehair. Players rub the horsehairs with rosin to make them tacky enough to create the desired amount of friction to elicit, in turn, the preferred acoustic dynamics.[5] Though the core of cello strings originally comprised catgut (the fibrous membrane of sheep or goat intestines, not of cats), the construction of strings today involves a variety of metals, ranging from titanium to aluminum, each metallic material yielding a slightly different tone.

> Now she raises the bow—its flat
>   bundle of hair
> harvested from the rear ends of
>   horses—like a whetted
> scimitar she is about to draw across
>   a throat,
> and attacks. In a back alley a cat
>   opens
> her pink-ceilinged mouth, gets netted
> in full yowl, clubbed, bagged, bicy-
>   cled off, haggled open,
> gutted, the gut squeezed down to its
>   highest pitch,
> washed, sliced into cello strings,
>   which bring
> an ancient screaming into this duet of
>   hair and gut.

The Quotidian Turn

"Somewhere in New Jersey" in 1962, as art historian Joan Rothfuss recounts in her robustly detailed biography of Moorman, the Juilliard-trained cellist lost track of what she was doing with her instrument for a moment.[6] While "playing the Kabalevsky cello concerto . . . for the thirty-fifth time," Moorman reflected two decades later, she began to question whether she had "turned off the gas" at home. She caught herself and pondered: "Holy shit—if my mind can wander like this, so can the audience's."[7]

Rothfuss points out that Moorman "was a chronic storyteller with an entertaining collection of tales about her life, many of them repeated so many times that they were rubbed as smooth as lucky stones."[8] So it is unknown whether this story occurred exactly as told or whether it was fabricated to rationalize the distractions Moorman started feeling one year earlier, in 1961, when she frequented performances by experimental artists Toshi Ichiyanagi, Yoko Ono, Kenji Kobayashi, David Tudor, Simone Forti, and others at downtown New York City venues.[9] But that she had concern enough about her own and the audience's lack of attentiveness reveals a change in her relationship to the instrument to which she had been attached literally and figuratively: literally throughout her training and figuratively in terms of staking her hopes of making a career and a living.[10]

Another distraction, also dating to 1961, was Moorman's desire to organize a concert for fellow Juilliard-trained Kobayashi at Town Hall in midtown New York, for which Ichiyanagi served as accompanist on a piece he had composed for Kobayashi that involved "thousands of tiny plastic beads" dropped onto piano strings.[11] To accomplish her administrative feat, Moorman had worked alongside the prolific producer Norman Seaman, who "singlehandedly staged 115 events during the 1960–1961 season."[12] But it was she who creatively raised the $900, today the equivalent of about $7,000, to stage it.[13] Moorman continued working with Seaman for the next year and a half, mounting solo concerts for Ono, La Monte Young, Richard Maxfield, and Joseph Byrd. She was fast becoming as much an impresario as a performer, parallel career tracks she sustained for much of the remainder of her professional life, with her event organizing waning only after her cancer diagnosis in March 1979.

It was in these moments of distraction in 1961, I believe, that Moorman ceased being one with her instrument, however sensuous an experience one might imagine that to be, and lured as she was by the avant-garde's lack of convention and by the personal satisfaction of organizing other artists' and her own performances on a grand scale. In the latter category, her rightful claim to fame

Nam June Paik. Film still from *A Tribute to John Cage*, 1973, reedited 1976. Courtesy of Electronic Arts Intermix (EAI), New York.

came with mounting fifteen avant-garde festivals between 1963 and 1980. Her tale of wondering about the gas spigot at home, a wandering of the mind toward quotidian concerns, may indeed have been her lucky stone, one she rubbed smoother and smoother as she explored how the cello could better serve her interests as an extension of her body.

> Now she is flying—tossing back the goblets
> of Saint-Amour standing empty,
> half-empty, or full on the tablecloth-
> like sheet music. Her knees tighten
> and loosen around the big-hipped creature
> wailing and groaning between them
> as if in elemental amplexus.

The Metaphysics of Extension

What does it mean for an object to be considered an extension of the body? What does such an annexation look like? What is at stake philosophically and conceptually in such a transformation? And if that object happens to be a cello in the performance arena, what difference does it make in viewers' interpretations of what they see, hear, and feel for the instrument to be an extension of the player's body? Moreover, what happens when the cello is no longer made of fine-grained wood with proper purfling? What if it is a bomb? Or a delicate piece of tissue paper, cut in the shape of the instrument? Or ice cubes molded into a vague semblance of a cello?

In a recent study, cognitive brain researchers found that more than 51 percent of musicians surveyed "felt united with" or "one with their instrument," in contrast to those who deemed it "an obstacle to overcome" (2 percent) or something to hide behind (11 percent). Another 28 percent viewed their instrument as secondary and perceived themselves as first and foremost when performing before an audience.[14] Moorman, to my mind, landed in this last category.

Coming to view her cello as an extension of herself, she saw it as something linked to, but very much distinct from, her own persona, which flourished only when she considered herself the primary focus of the audience's attention. The early 1960s moments of distraction that helped shape this self-perception simultaneously allowed her to do with her instrument whatever she wished. As her self-identity became increasingly fixed and unified (avant-garde artist and impresario), the identity of her cello became increasingly diffuse and multiple (bomb, paper, ice). But extension was at play in Moorman's work in a more metaphysical sense as well.

Extension became a topic of interest in intellectual circles in the seventeenth century, the same era in which the cello came into its own. As the cello was assigned a standard role in the orchestra's string quartet in the first half of the 1600s,[15] René Descartes (1596–1650) was igniting what would become a century-long discussion of extension among philosophers, mathematicians, physicists, linguists, and other scholars. In brief, Descartes saw extension in strictly spatial terms as the basic quality of matter, apart from thought, that allows substance to exist in multiple dimensions. Benedict Spinoza (1632–1677) agreed with the concept of multiple dimensions but argued that extension in the physical realm cannot be separated from idea in the conceptual realm; both body and mind hold the capacity for extension ad infinitum. The latter triggered exploration by Gottfried Wilhelm Leibniz (1646–1716) of infinite divisibility, the principle that any entity can be divided, its parts divided again, and on and on in perpetuity without ever disappearing, without reaching zero.[16]

Two centuries later, the principle of infinite divisibility would become foundational to the development of quantum physics by Max Planck (1858–1947) and his identification of the smallest measurable length, now called the Planck length, which can be visualized as the size of a dot after first replicating and extending it to the size of the universe, then measuring the size of the original dot.[17] Also in the twentieth century, Rudolf Carnap (1891–1970) developed the notions of extension and intension, which comprised the foundation for a new linguistic methodology. Extension, as he saw it, aligns with denotation, which places emphasis on the referent, or the thing in the world to which a word or sign refers; in contrast, intension is linked with connotation, with its focus on the signified, or the concepts that a thing evokes.[18] So how do these aspects of extension figure in Moorman's work?

> The music seems to rise from the
>   crater left
> when heaven was torn up and taken
>   off the earth . . .

Bombs

Moorman's use of bombs instead of cellos was frequent. In her 1968 performance of Nam June Paik's *Opera Sextronique* in Düsseldorf, Moorman straddled a "four-foot bomb," according to the *New York Times*'s West Germany correspondent Ralph Blumenthal.[19] Thomas Tilly's photograph of this portion of the performance, Aria 4, shows a naked Moorman with a bomb-like object resting against her left arm, her right arm raised and holding a conventional bow about to strike or stroke the "instrument," which appears to be wired with a microphone. [See the photograph in Kristine Stiles's essay that appears in this catalog, page 170.] Musicologist and historian Benjamin Piekut also cites Moorman's use of a "four-foot-long bomb that Paik had enhanced with a contact mic" in her performance of John Cage's *26'1.1499" for a String Player* in London in 1968.[20] When performing the same Cage composition on the *Mike Douglas Show* in November 1969, she played "a World War II–era surplus practice bomb," according to Rothfuss, using a "bunch of plastic flowers" as a bow.[21]

World War II "practice bombs" came in numerous lengths and widths, though they were typically made of sheet metal and had fins and curved or pointed noses. The cylindrical shafts were filled with sand and "spotting charge," an incendiary that would "produce a flash and smoke when detonated . . . to give observers or spotters a visual reference of ordnance impact."[22] It is unclear what type of bomb Paik and

Moorman used in the Düsseldorf performance, and it is even possible that it was fabricated from sheet metal to look like a bomb. But from comparisons to World War II photographs, the object appears similar to an M38A2 practice bomb used in military training to improve bombardiers' accuracy in hitting targets.[23]

Photographs and descriptions of the bomb-instruments used in Düsseldorf, London, and on the *Mike Douglas Show* indicate that the bomb was not the same type that Moorman used in an edition of ten *Bomb Cellos* she created for the Carl Solway Gallery in 1984 to sell as sculptures priced at $4,500 each,[24] the equivalent of more than $10,000 in 2015 dollars. For *Bomb Cellos*, it would appear she used bombs from the Mk-80 series, a Low Drag General Purpose (LDGP) line of bombs developed in the 1950s to achieve less aerodynamic drag than earlier models to "ensure reliability and produce effects of blast, cratering, or fragmentation."[25]

From our perspective in the second decade of the twenty-first century, an era of heightened sensitivity to incendiary devices and the laws regulating their distribution, it may be hard to imagine how a private citizen like Moorman could come into possession of a bomb to use in art making. But the fact is that today, if I wished to place a bid on a "Vintage WW2 M38A2 Practice Dummy Inert Bomb US Army Navy Air Force 1952," estimated at $140 on eBay,[26] I could do so. This suggests that in the less regulated era of the 1960s, it was not so difficult to acquire such an object. Nor is it difficult to imagine how viewers might have responded to Moorman's performances with bombs in lieu of cellos, be it October 7, 1968, in Düsseldorf, or February 24, 1990, in New York, where she played one of her 1984 *Bomb Cellos* at the opening of her retrospective at the Emily Harvey Gallery.[27] For in these performances, I would argue, the cello functioned as an extension of her body in the linguistic context of the referent. The bomb, in other words, was the thing in the world to which Moorman's body referred. Whether naked or clothed, her body became that with which viewers related physically, leaving the bomb

as the thing with which audience members had to grapple intellectually.

Not least among the associations viewers would have made to the bomb was its spinoff "bombshell." Technically, a bombshell is the cylindrical canister into which the bomb is placed in preparation for its use as a weapon, but by the 1960s, it was a term commonly used to refer, however crudely, to voluptuous women. The term's etymological roots date to at least 1931, when Jean Harlow was dubbed the "blonde bombshell" for her performance in Columbia Pictures' *Platinum Blonde*, which led to the same studio's production of *Bombshell*, also starring Harlow, in 1933.[28] Thereafter, the decorating of military aircraft noses with this pinup stereotype became common, even as the code names for bombs

Charlotte Moorman performs with one of her *Bomb Cellos* (1984) at the opening of *Child of the Cello*, Emily Harvey Gallery, New York City, February 24, 1990. Photograph courtesy of Christian Xatrec.

Charlotte Moorman performs Nam June Paik's *Tele Paik Tele Moorman*, Sky Art Conference '82, Linz, Austria, September 26, 1982. Photograph by Vin Grabill. © Vin Grabill.

themselves were typically male, "Little Boy" and "Fat Man" perhaps being the most well-known examples for the nuclear atrocity the United States caused by dropping them over Hiroshima and Nagasaki, respectively, in August 1945, the beginning of the end of World War II in September 1945. While these bombs were a far cry from the M38A2 practice-type bomb Moorman used in Düsseldorf in 1968 or from the Mk-80 she used in creating the Solway series in 1984 and played at her retrospective in 1990, each time she performed with her bombs, their status as meaning-loaded objects—their objecthood—was reinforced above and beyond her own.

It could be said that by taking off her clothes and performing naked, Moorman foregrounded her body as object. But by making the decision to strip naked, she made it clear she was a subject first and foremost, a subject with agency in person-to-person interactions between audience and performer. What remained for the audience to deal with conceptually, then, was the object, in this case a bomb so "loaded" with historical, political, and cultural meaning that there is no way for it to be seen as a neutral object but rather as a complex thing invented and used for purposes of human obliteration—for "blast, cratering, or fragmentation."

"Break a leg!" somebody tells her.
Back in my seat, I can see she is
    nervous
when she comes out; her hand
    shakes as she
re-dog-ears the top corners of the
    big pages
that look about to flop over on
    their own.

Paper and Ice

Moorman, sometimes in collaboration with Paik, used a variety of materials to make cellos: Paik's own back; television monitors encased in Plexiglas boxes; neon tubing bent into the outline of the instrument; and cello-shaped sheets of Plexiglas onto which Moorman glued syringes that had been used to administer morphine to ease her cancer-induced pain in the latter years of her life. But no materials stand in greater contrast to the bomb than paper and ice. Among those made of paper are hundreds of small cello-shaped cutouts, fashioned out of gift-wrapping paper embellished with autumn leaves, tiny hearts, and abstract designs. Only seven inches long, each cutout fits in the palm of one's hand, resting there almost weightlessly. Even more ephemeral is a much larger, almost five-foot-long cello cut

out of tissue paper. This piece cannot stand on its own, of course; it can only be viewed in full if flattened and held in place against a horizontal or vertical surface. If held by fingertips at the top, it will fold in on itself, draping like the crimson, teal, or black skirts of the orchestra-style garments that Moorman sometimes wore when performing.

Moorman's performances of *Ice Music*, which collaborator Jim McWilliams wrote for her in 1972, entailed playing a cello-shaped block of ice until it was destroyed, according to Rothfuss, with the "dripping sounds" and "chipping noises made by her plastic bow" comprising the audio component of the work.[29] Moorman performed the piece seven times in the 1970s, and in all cases but the first, she "hired professional ice sculptors to carve a more naturalistic instrument" than the inaugural one, which was made by

Charlotte Moorman. Paper cellos, undated. Courtesy of Charlotte Moorman Archive, Charles Deering McCormick Library of Special Collections, Northwestern University Library.

stuffing a soft cello bag full of ice cubes and leaving it in a freezer of an ice-cream factory near the site of the International Carnival of Experimental Sound in London.[30] There in 1972 at ICES (the festival's acronym, which perhaps inspired McWilliams to write the composition), Moorman performed *Ice Music for London* naked, except for protective pads she had taped onto her left hand and the inside of her knees. The pain entailed in exposing her naked flesh to ice must have been heightened in London by the fact that Moorman had only weeks earlier undergone gall-bladder surgery.[31] An eight-inch-long vertical scar appears in at least one photograph of the performance.[32]

Paper so sheer it can take on the shape of the palm of your hand. Thinner still, it dangles and folds in on itself. Ice melting into water. Growing less and less stable, it evaporates into thin air. These metaphors of infinite divisibility ensure, once again, that our attention stays focused on their function as extensions of the performer's body and, by association, our own, as objects to be examined for their ephemerality, yes, but also their vulnerability to invisibility. But embedded even in the term, if not the theory, of infinite divisibility is just that—the infinite. No matter how thin the paper is sliced, it will still exist. And like Planck length, water from melting ice may contract to the size of a drop but is then, both in theory and in reality, the dot that Planck envisioned: a droplet, expanded to the magnitude of the universe, can still be considered the size of the original drop of water left on the floor of the performance venue where Moorman last played.

Feminism's Objects

For all the traditional feminist implications of the theoretical contexts in which I have been discussing Moorman and her work—that is, how she preserved her subjecthood while ceding her objecthood, by means of extension, to her cellolike objects made of bombs, paper, ice, and other materials—another interpretation is possible.[33] After all, Moorman undeniably appeared as an object before her audience—the object of their gaze. Moorman may have grown to understand her cello as secondary to her own presence before viewers, rather than becoming one with her instrument, but this does not mean that she automatically retained in toto her identity as a subject, to be privileged over that of an object. To some contemporary feminist thinkers, the retention of objecthood can be not only positive but also a form of survival. For scholars such as Martha Nussbaum and Leslie Green, it comes down to parsing types of objectification. Nussbaum has built a systematic typology,[34] and Green assesses levels of instrumentality. Green asserts: "We must treat others as instruments, for we need their skills, their company, and their bodies—in fact, there is little that we social creatures can do on our own." This realization can enhance understanding of the elderly, the disenfranchised, the ill and disabled, she argues, those who "miss not only their diminished agency, but also their diminished objectivity," as "they become . . . *subjectified*" [Green's emphasis].[35]

Given Moorman's struggles with her health,[36] it may be just as tenable to look at her identity as a subject and an object as shifting over the course of her career as it is to view her subjecthood as more favorable than her objecthood, or vice versa. Especially in the last seven years of her life, when her cancer was metastasizing, her objectification by the medical world was essential to her survival. Equally important was her work, which Moorman managed to sustain beyond the capacity of many to understand—except, perhaps, her husband and close artist friends, who bolstered her efforts.

> At intermission I find her backstage
> still practicing the piece coming up
>   next.
> She calls it the "solo in high dreary."
> Her bow niggles at the string like a
>   hand
> stroking skin it never wanted to touch.
> Probably under her scorn she is sick
> that she can't do better by it. . . .

With a Little Help from Her Friends

Among those who helped to keep Moorman's work—and, thus, Moorman—going was Otto Piene, cofounder in 1957 of the group ZERO, and as of 1968 associated with MIT's progressive Center for Advanced Visual Studies (CAVS) in Cambridge, Mass., first as its inaugural fellow (1968–1971) and then as its director (1974–1993). In the latter role, he brought scores of artists who were experimenting with media, including Moorman, to conduct research and perform at CAVS. His and Moorman's "fondness for each other," he recalls, increased after 1969, when Moorman "heard about and saw" his contribution to Boston public television station WGBH's legendary *Medium Is the Medium* broadcast in March of that year.[37] Piene's contribution to this project featured one of his "helium sculptures" lifting a young woman some forty feet off the ground with the aid of eight hundred feet of polyethylene tubing and twenty-two tanks of helium.[38] The piece was performed and videotaped in fall 1968,[39] coinciding with Moorman's premiere of Jim McWilliams's *Sky Kiss* on September 14, 1968, at the 6th Annual New York Avant Garde Festival. McWilliams's piece also involved helium in the form of a huge cluster of balloons designed to lift Moorman off the ground as she played a standard cello. Since the debut performance of *Sky Kiss* was "not a success, either technically or artistically" (McWilliams misjudged the amount of helium needed, someone popped one of the balloons, and Moorman had to keep pushing off to get any distance from the ground),[40] and even though her elevation was greater in subsequent iterations of the piece (some fifteen feet in Sydney, Australia, a "spectacular" setting in which she felt "voluptuously buoyant, almost weightless"),[41] it is not surprising that Piene's highly successful and broadly televised piece attracted her to him and to CAVS. (For further detail on Moorman's performances of *Sky Kiss*, see the Rothfuss-authored essay in this volume.)

Moorman first visited CAVS in 1975 to perform *TV Cello* at a conference called "Arttransition" that Piene and others had organized.[42] She last visited in April 1988 to participate in CAVS' twentieth-anniversary celebration when she performed Mieko Shiomi's *Cello Sonata*. Sitting atop the building that housed CAVS, she held a pole from which a standard cello dangled. Piene's colossal inflatable titled *Berlin Star* (1984) loomed high behind her against a dark night

Charlotte Moorman performs Mieko Shiomi's *Cello Sonata,* Center for Advanced Visual Studies (CAVS), MIT, Cambridge, Massachusetts, April 30, 1988. Video still by Vin Grabill. © Vin Grabill.

sky. By this time in Moorman's life, her long battle with cancer had left her quite frail, and Piene sat next to her for part of the performance, probably to ensure that she did not fall but also to celebrate their thirteen years of artistic interactions. Among these had been numerous collaborations on the production of *Sky Kiss,* one of them at the "2nd Sky Art Conference," an event Piene organized and presented at Ars Electronica in Linz, Austria, in September 1982.[43] Moorman "brought the title [*Sky Kiss*] into the collaboration," Piene recalls, "and I brought the history, skill, record, and know-how to actually make her rise high."[44] And she did, some forty feet at Linz, although in other iterations with Piene—in a windy environment in the California desert in 1986, for example—the result was not unlike the 1968 avant-garde festival, where she had to keep pushing off the pavement to stay afloat. In the 1986 desert attempt, she managed from time to time to rise as high as thirty feet but because of wind gusts had trouble staying

there for long, and at one point she was held aloft by the palm of husband Frank Pileggi's hand.[45]

To prepare for the Linz collaboration, Piene asked one of his former graduate students, Vin Grabill, to interview Moorman.[46] Grabill conducted the video interview on the roof of Moorman's Pearl Street loft in New York City on July 30, 1982. She appears as her usual ebullient, charming, charismatic self, talking enthusiastically about having helped Paik mount his retrospective at the Guggenheim Museum in the previous months, during which she also performed several times at the museum. She is excited about performing in Linz and eager also to perform for Grabill, right then and there. There are many important informational details in this video, but perhaps the most stunning moment is in the unedited version.[47] As Moorman unpacks the case in which she stored all the accouterments for *TV Bra for Living Sculpture* (1969), which she is about to assemble, don, and play on camera, she pauses for a moment, places her right hand on her left breast, looks over at the videographer, and says, "I'm having trouble with my breast." Grabill's battery pack died at precisely the end of her sentence. He changed to his still camera to photograph her wearing her crimson gown, pulled down to her waist to accommodate the apparatus for *TV Bra for Living Sculpture* as she performed.

That the video stopped with this sentence seems an uncanny forecast of significant changes that would soon occur in the trajectory of Moorman's health. For within the next few weeks, she underwent a biopsy of a lump in her right breast that she had put off for nine months (while preparing for and performing during Paik's retrospective).[48] Though the biopsy was clear, her cancer had spread, and her remaining years became increasingly challenged. It may seem even more startling that she referred to "having trouble" with her left breast, since it was that breast that had been removed by mastectomy following her first cancer diagnosis in 1979. But both "non-painful phantom breast sensation" (the feeling that a removed breast still remains) and "phantom breast pain" (the feeling of pain in the area where a breast once existed) are not uncommon.[49] To imagine an extension of the body, in other words, is not unusual.

As a member of a family with three times more incidence of cancer than the national average, I am especially fascinated by the part of Moorman's life story that entails management of her cancer.[50] My thoughts about the disease are both abundantly informed and forever inchoate. In all its varieties, permutations, inconsistencies, and slipperiness, the disease is infuriating, humbling, and above all, baffling. But one thing is certain: venerating the body's objecthood is intermittently invaluable. When Elizabeth Goldring, Otto Piene's artist-poet wife, administered morphine injections to her friend Charlotte Moorman to give Frank a break, I believe it was only by being able to imagine her friend's body as an object in the moments immediately before, during, and after giving Moorman the shot that Goldring was able to carry out the act, even as the capacity to do

Charlotte Moorman performs *Sky Kiss: A Sky Event by Jim McWilliams, Charlotte Moorman, and Otto Piene*, Sky Art Conference '82, Linz, Austria, September 25, 1982. © Estate of Manfred Leve. Courtesy of Charlotte Moorman Archive, Charles Deering McCormick Library of Special Collections, Northwestern University Library.

so was likely driven by the shared subjective experiences of the two women.[51]

The concept of extension may be another potentially helpful theoretical construct in which to conceive of the management of cancer—namely, something that may be of and in the body but also, if managed effectively, apart from it. In a literal sense, Moorman's first mastectomy put cancer at a distance for a while. In the figurative sense, Moorman imagined a phantom breast. Similarly understanding her cello as an extension

Charlotte Moorman performs
Nam June Paik's *TV Bra for Living
Sculpture* on the roof of her loft, 62
Pearl Street, New York City, July 30,
1982. Photograph by Vin Grabill.
© Vin Grabill.

of her body allowed Moorman to remain first and foremost before her audience and to do with her instrument whatever she wished. As such, she left the cello for us, as viewers, to contend with its meanings, which change over time—from "bombshell," to infinitely divisible tissue paper, to droplets of water in a universe that assures its measurement, and so many more. And sometimes, in traditional orchestral attire, sitting atop a building, she let the cello be just a cello, dangling from a pole over a sidewalk filled with celebrants. Despite any other elements in the scenario—Piene's *Berlin Star*, the chatter of dozens of people below, photographers snapping just the right angles for their documentation—Moorman was, as always, front and center.

The music seems to rise from the
    crater left
when heaven was torn up and taken
    off the earth;
more likely it comes up through her
    priest's dress,
up from that clump of hair which
    by now
may be so wet with its waters, like
    the waters
the fishes multiplied in at Galilee, that
each wick draws a portion all the
    way out
to its tip and fattens a droplet on
    the bush
of half notes now glittering in
    that dark.

Notes

The epigraph is from Galway Kinnell, "The Cellist," *Atlantic Monthly* 274, no. 4 (October 1994): 100.

A recent study shows that more than half the professional musicians surveyed felt "one with their instrument." Other findings from this study will be discussed later in this essay. Veerle L. Simoens and Mari Tervaniemi, "Musician–Instrument Relationship as a Candidate Index for Professional Well-Being in Musicians," *Psychology of Aesthetics, Creativity, and the Arts* 7, no. 2 (2013): 178.

2. John Dilworth, "The Cello: Origins and Evolution," in *The Cambridge Companion to the Cello*, ed. Robin Stowell (Cambridge: Cambridge University Press, 1999), 5.

3. The "earliest surviving cello" dates to 1572. Tony Faber, *Stradivari's Genius: Five Violins, One Cello, and Three Centuries of Enduring Perfection* (New York: Random House, 2006), 234.

4. Margaret Campbell, "Nineteenth-Century Virtuosi," in Stowell, *Cambridge Companion to the Cello*, 64.

5. Bernard Richardson, "Cello Acoustics," in Stowell, *Cambridge Companion to the Cello*, 38–39.

6. Joan Rothfuss, *Topless Cellist: The Improbable Life of Charlotte Moorman* (Cambridge, Mass.: MIT Press, 2014), 58. I am indebted to Rothfuss's extraordinary research and writing, from which I have borrowed extensively.

7. Ibid. Moorman told this story to interviewers preparing a retrospective of the work of her collaborator Nam June Paik at the Whitney Museum of American Art, April 30–June 27, 1982 (386n9; also see related note on page 380), an exhibition at which she performed numerous times.

8. Rothfuss, *Topless Cellist*, 58.

9. Ibid., 48.

10. Rothfuss explains how Moorman continued at least through 1963 to take on classical music performance gigs for income. Ibid., 55–58.

11. Ibid., 46.

12. Ibid., 44.

13. Today's dollar value was computed using the U.S. Department of Labor's Bureau of Labor Statistics online Consumer Price Index (CPI) Inflation Calculator, accessed June 4, 2015, http://www.bls.gov/data/inflation_calculator.htm. For other details concerning Moorman's work with Seaman cited in this section, see Rothfuss, *Topless Cellist*, 43–51.

14. Simoens and Tervaniemi, "Musician–Instrument Relationship," 178.

15. Claudio Monteverdi, "the most prominent musical figure of his time . . . was the first composer to specify the use of violins and cellos in his compositions," specifically in his 1607 opera *Orfeo*, following which Venetian opera started standardizing the orchestra's inclusion of a string quartet comprising two violins, one viola, and one cello. Carlos Prieto, *The Adventures of a Cello*, trans. Elena C. Murray (Austin: University of Texas Press, 2006), 16–17. (Original publication in Italian, 1998.)

16. For discussion of these three philosophers' views of extension, see R. S. Woolhouse, *Descartes, Spinoza, Leibniz: The Concept of Substance in Seventeenth Century Metaphysics* (London: Routledge, 1993).

17. Rhodri Evans, *The Cosmic Microwave Background: How It Changed Our Understanding of the Universe* (Cham, Switzerland: Springer International Publishing, 2015), 195–96.

18. Rudolf Carnap, *Meaning and Necessity: A Study in Semantics and Modal Logic* (Chicago: University of Chicago Press, 1947), 1–65.

19. Ralph Blumenthal, "Naked Cellist Completes Her Concert in Germany," *New York Times,* October 9, 1968, as quoted in Rothfuss, *Topless Cellist*, 238.

20. Benjamin Piekut, *Experimentalism Otherwise: The New York Avant-Garde and Its Limits* (Berkeley: University of California Press, 2011), 162.

21. Rothfuss, *Topless Cellist*, 1.

22. "Ordnance Fillers," UXOINFO.com, accessed June 4, 2015, http://www.uxoinfo.com/uxoinfo/ordfillers.cfm.

23. The M38A2 100-lb practice bomb "simulate[d] a General Purpose bomb of the same size," 472 inches long and 8 inches in diameter (smaller than the one in Tilly's photo) and made of rolled sheet metal. See excerpt from *Ammunition Inspection Guide*, March 1944; NAVSEA OP 1664 Volume 2, U.S. Explosive Ordnance, February 1954; Complete Round Chart #5981, October 1944, accessed June 4, 2015, http://www.swf.usace.army.mil/portals/47/docs/environmental/fuds/5points/specs/100practice.PDF.

24. "Digging in the Archives: Charlotte Moorman," *Carl Solway Gallery* (blog), August 1, 2014, http://blog.solwaygallery.com/2014/08/digging-in-archives-charlotte-moorman.html.

25. "Mk82 General Purpose Bomb," FAS Military Analysis Network, accessed June 4, 2015, http://fas.org/man/dod-101/sys/dumb/mk82.htm.

26. Post on eBay, accessed December 27, 2014, http://www.ebay.com/itm/Vintage-WW2-M38A2-100lb-Practice-Dummy-Inert-Bomb-US-Army-Navy-Air-Force-1952-/391011425369?pt=LH_DefaultDomain_0&hash=item5b0a18dc59.

27. "February 24, 1990—Charlotte Moorman, Child of the Cello," Emily Harvey Foundation, accessed June 4, 2015, http://www.emilyharveyfoundation.org/ehg_49.html.

28. See Darrell Rooney, *Harlow in Hollywood: The Blonde Bombshell in the Glamour Capital, 1928–1937* (Los Angeles: Angel City Press, 2011); and Stephanie Ann Smith, *Household Words: Bloomers, Sucker, Bombshell, Scab, Nigger, Cyber* (Minneapolis: University of Minnesota Press, 2006).

29. Rothfuss, *Topless Cellist*, 281.

30. Ibid., 277–79. The version of *Ice Music* always bore the name of the city in which it was played. The only time the title changed beyond that configuration, as Rothfuss reports, was *Yellow Ice Music for Washington*, when the ice was dyed yellow (411n11).

31. Ibid., 277–79.

32. Photograph viewable on unidentified website, accessed June 4, 2015, http://media-cache-ak0.pinimg.com/originals/81/86/f8/8186f89aec25bbe1a6da2c9f03f8b055.jpg.

33. For a superbly comprehensive overview of subjecthood and objecthood in the context of feminist thought, see Evangelia (Lina) Papadaki, "Feminist Perspectives on Objectification," *Stanford Encyclopedia of Philosophy*, ed. Edward N. Zalta, March 10, 2010, revised June 6, 2014, accessed June 4, 2015, http://plato.stanford.edu/entries/feminism-objectification/#PosPosObj.

34. Martha Nussbaum, "Objectification," *Philosophy and Public Affairs* 24, no. 4 (1995): 257; cited in Papadaki, "Feminist Perspectives on Objectification."

35. Leslie Green, "Pornographies," *Journal of Political Philosophy* 8, no. 1 (2000): 45–46; cited in Papadaki, "Feminist Perspectives on Objectification."

36. Her struggles were increasingly acute after March 1979, when she was diagnosed with cancer in her left breast and underwent a mastectomy. Then in November 1981, she discovered a lump in her

right breast, and in August 1982 she finally had the lump biopsied; the lump was benign, but her cancer had spread. By 1984, it had metastasized to the bone and continued to spread until her death in November 1991. See Rothfuss, *Topless Cellist*, 335–37, 341, 345, 354.

7. Otto Piene, video interview by Vin Grabill, in "Charlotte Moorman at CAVS/MIT, 1982–1988," produced by Vin Grabill (Cambridge, Mass.: MIT Center for Advanced Visual Studies, 2007), DVD, disc 2.

8. James A. Nadeau, "The Convergence of Video Art and Television at WGBH (1969)" (master's thesis, Tufts University, 2006), 63, http://dspace.mit.edu/bitstream/handle/1721.1/39146/123349020.pdf. The other five artists featured in *Medium Is the Medium* were Allan Kaprow, Thomas Tadlock, Nam June Paik, James Seawright, and Aldo Tambellini.

9. Ibid., 52.

0. Rothfuss, *Topless Cellist*, 229.

1. Ibid., 317.

2. Ibid., 289.

3. The performance took place on September 24, 1982. See Ars Electronica Archive for full schedule: http://90.146.8.18/en/archives/festival_archive/festival_catalogs/festival_artikel.asp?iProjectID=9375.

4. Piene, Grabill interview.

45. "Sky Kiss," Desert Sun/Desert Moon, 1986," in "Charlotte Moorman at CAVS/MIT, 1982–1988," disc 1.

46. Vin Grabill received his M.S. in Visual Studies from MIT in 1981 and has worked and taught as a video artist at the University of Maryland, Baltimore County (UMBC) since 1988, where I have been employed since 1992. All details in this section of the essay are from my conversations with Grabill through the month of December 2014 and screenings of his video and DVD cited above, as well as uncut versions he generously provided. For more on Grabill, see "Vin Grabill, Video Artist," http://www.vingrabill.com/pages/about.html.

47. Many thanks to Vin Grabill for providing access to this footage and for his personal reflections on interactions with Moorman at CAVS and at CAVS-related events.

48. According to Rothfuss, "On November 16, 1981, Moorman discovered a lump in her right breast. She did not have it biopsied until nine months later because she feared she might need another surgery that would interfere with her work schedule" (*Topless Cellist*, 341). Nine months from November 16, 1981, would have been mid-August 1982, a few weeks following Grabill's video interview on July 30, 1982.

49. Beth F. Jung, Gretchen M. Ahrendt, Anne Louise Oaklander, and Robert H. Dworkin, "Neuropathic Pain Following Breast Cancer Surgery," *Pain* 104 (2003): 3–4.

50. Many thanks to Kristine Stiles, who encouraged me to provide a personal health context for this essay.

51. Elizabeth Goldring, video interview by Vin Grabill, in "Charlotte Moorman at CAVS/MIT, 1982–1988," disc 2. Grabill noted to me in an email dated January 7, 2015, that "Elizabeth had been administering her own insulin injections for years due to her diabetes," a practice that may have made it somewhat easier for her to administer morphine to Moorman. That said, it is quite different to self-administer a medication than to administer a medication, especially something as powerful as morphine, to another individual.

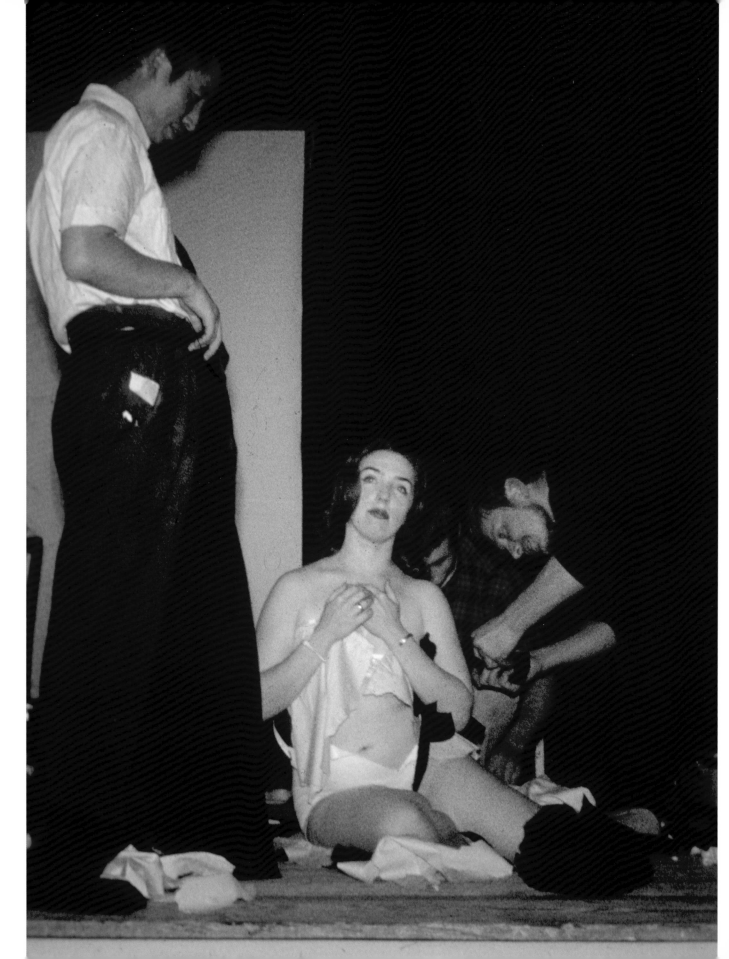

"Necessity's Other": Charlotte Moorman and the Plasticity of Denial and Consent

Kristine Stiles

Naked Up There

Charlotte Moorman began taking her clothes off in the name of art in September 1964. The debut of her unveiling occurred in one of the performances of German composer Karlheinz Stockhausen's *Originale* (1961), which she presented in the 2nd Annual New York Avant Garde Festival and in which she appeared as the "String Player." According to *The Nation* critic Faubion Bowers, after several "offstage costume changes," Moorman was hoisted over the audience wrapped in gauze, "underneath which she was 'startlingly nude.'"[1] Apparently the semitransparent costume was a compromise owing its inception to a conversation that Moorman had had with Carolee Schneemann, who was assisting during a dress rehearsal. When Moorman complained about the interference of her gown in the section of *Originale* that called for her to rise above the audience while playing the cello, Schneemann suggested wrapping her in "a sheet," which would make her "look like a flying angel." Fearing that the cloth, would "fly open" to reveal her as "too fat," Moorman exclaimed, "I don't want to be naked up there."[2]

Being up there naked is precisely what Moorman wanted to do. Her temporary denial merely facilitated screening from her psyche her consent to the act of exposing the image of her zaftig figure to public view. Moorman dissociated from the suggestion, donned the convenient gauze cover (less concealment than refuge), and got on with the business at hand: provocation at all costs. This essay is about that business, as well as Moorman's repeated disavowal of the impact of her nudity, denial with roots at least as far back as college, where she was the "opposite of discreet," Joan Rothfuss observed in her biography of the artist, before recounting the following story: "The dean of the music school had a studio directly under the student practice room," where he could hear Moorman regularly engage in sex with her boyfriend, and insisted, "This screwing has got to stop!"[3] This essay is also about Moorman's erotic identity as an avant-garde artist.

To wit, a little over a month after her sensational appearance in *Originale*, "a nervous security guard" intervened at the Philadelphia College of Art to halt Moorman from a striptease during a section of *Pop Sonata*, the first piece that Nam June Paik composed explicitly for her.[4] Its score reads: "Play a few measures of J. S. Bach's Suite no. 3 in C Major for solo cello. Remove an item

OPPOSITE
Charlotte Moorman performs Yoko Ono's *Cut Piece*, Aachen, West Germany, July 25, 1966. Photograph by Kenneth Werner. Courtesy of Charlotte Moorman Archive, Charles Deering McCormick Library of Special Collections, Northwestern University Library.

169

of clothing. Repeat."[5] Three months later, in January 1965, no one prevented Moorman from disrobing when she again performed the composition at the New School for Social Research in New York City. After undressing to bra and panties, she exaggerated the sexuality of her action by lying down "on the floor . . . her cello atop her like a lover."[6] Soon thereafter, Paik revised *Pop Sonata*, having Moorman "perform

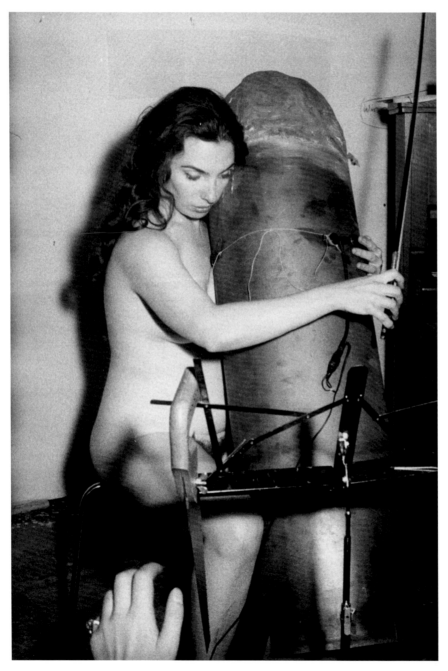

behind a gauze curtain, backlit by a spotlight [that] transformed her into a silhouette and made the viewing experience one of clandestine voyeurism."[7] Paik also retitled the work *Sonata for Adults Only*. The pretense of the flimsy covering in *Originale* would again serve to indulge Moorman's consent to progressive corporeal exposure while simultaneously permitting her to avoid direct confrontation with its cultural import.

Moorman's erotic appearances epitomize the intoxicating drive toward sexual liberation of the times, as much as they wed the period's heightened sexuality to its tumultuous upheaval in national, social, and cultural revolutions, wars, assassinations, and destruction. In 1968, she captured the aura of this spectrum in Aria 4 of Paik's *Opera Sextronique* in Düsseldorf. Tenderly embracing a military "practice bomb,"[8] the naked artist rested her head against the object that resembled an engorged, erect penis, nearly the height of her body. Moorman was a picture of sensuality with dark flowing tresses, elegant eyebrows, long lashes, aquiline nose, and voluptuous lips. The angle of Moorman's head conjured fellatio while her bodily position suggested intercourse, legs wrapped around the sexualized object to reveal her belly, pubis, and pubic hair. Only her arm covered her breast's curve as she grasped the bow, insinuating that the bomb was a cello and animating the erotic connection with music, despite the cello's lack of "equipment" for sex.[9]

Moorman's gestures deactivated the bomb as a lethal instrument and reactivated it as an object of pleasure, a "Thing" to be played and played with. Mario Vrančić, writing in another context, explains that "both rocket and phallus" fuse "scientific Newtonian associations with the Freudian death drive,"[10] and that for Jacques Lacan, "this rocket-phallus is the Thing of steel and mathematics as well as of human flesh . . . that 'quilts' the whole system [and] is the seat of fundamental antagonisms in society."[11] This essay is equally about the nexus in which Moorman's sensuality intertwined with violence, or what the Greeks identified as Eros and Thanatos: the interstice of life, sexual vitality, and reproduction in the cycle of destruction and death.

"Oh, No!"

The psychological detachment that Moorman permitted herself when performing in *Originale* had evaporated by May 21, 1965, when she appeared nude, albeit covered by a roll of transparent plastic, to perform *Variations on a Theme by Saint Saëns* at the American Center in Paris. Moorman would repeat the plastic covering when she performed the piece in Wuppertal a few weeks later in June at *24 Hours* (*24 Stunden*), a twenty-four-hour performance involving six artists, including Joseph Beuys, Wolf Vostell, Tomas Schmit, Bazon Brock, and Eckart Rahn. According to Paik, he was the agent who inspired her disrobing. The idea came to him, he recalled, some thirty minutes before their performance was due to begin when Moorman announced that she had left her black formal gown at their hotel and was returning to retrieve it. Paik realized that this trip would make her late for their scheduled performance, and, spotting a "huge roll of clear plastic drop cloth," asked: "How about that?"

"'Oh, no!'" Moorman exclaimed, seeming "quite perplexed," Paik remembered. Then he described what happened next:

> I noticed a very quick change of her expression—in a split second I sensed something was clicking in her mind. . . . Her vacillation went up and down in waves in a very short time. . . . It was not easy but she crossed the Rubicon. In order to hide her shyness she drank straight scotch. When she stepped out there was a roar of applause, so she drank more, played some more, drank more, got more applause. She fell backward on the makeshift stage. On that day she got enlightened. She had been a rather stiff performer, self-conscious with a great amount of stage fright. But this baptism of nudity, uproar, and straight scotch opened a new nerve center, which made her a sensitive and inspiring performer.[12]

He also recalled: "Many years later, I analyzed Greta Garbo's facial complexion and found that she can become a virgin then a whore, then a saint, and back to a virgin many times in a split second. I sensed that that kind of tension was passing through [Charlotte's] mind in this fateful second—after all it was 1965."[13]

While it is tempting to consider Paik's story the sum of the situation, he did not stipulate that Moorman should appear naked underneath the plastic and, given that she had stripped to bra and panties only four months earlier, he might well have assumed

Charlotte Moorman performs Nam June Paik's *Variations on a Theme by Saint-Saëns* at *24 Hours,* Galerie Parnass, Wuppertal, West Germany, June 5, 1965. © Ute Klophaus/bpk, Berlin. Courtesy of Charlotte Moorman Archive, Charles Deering McCormick Library of Special Collections, Northwestern University Library.

that she would remain in her underwear. In addition, hardly a spur-of-the-moment proposal, Paik's suggestion was rooted in the impact of Moorman's former bodily displays. Capitalizing on her sensational appearance in the transparent materials and hoping to use that drama to their advantage in Paris, Paik's instigation served their shared interest in public spectacle. But the "cellophane," as Moorman called it, was as transparent as her alleged split-second decision to perform nude. It is more likely that she had been calculating the right moment to do so for some time. The gossamer cloth in *Originale* (and later in *Sonata for Adults Only*) had proved that her unclothed body had a commanding effect and, henceforth, there would be no stopping Moorman.

Eager to be accepted among the avant-garde, not only as the impresario of her festivals but also as an artist in her own right, not just an interpreter or prop for Paik's work, she dispensed with conventional mores and secured her position in the ranks of the counterculture. Paul O'Neil, a veteran writer and reporter with Time Inc., ratified her position in "Nudity," a widely read article published in *Life* magazine in October 1967, by awarding Moorman the "crown" as "queen of artistic-intellectual-avant-garde (as opposed to vulgar-money-grubbing lubricious) nakedness."[14]

Paths to the Rubicon
The circumstances preceding this crowning of Moorman must be taken into account. Moorman matured in the milieu of the liberation politics promoted by many thinkers of the time and encapsulated in Herbert Marcuse's *Eros and Civilization: A Philosophical Inquiry into Freud* (1955) and Norman O. Brown's *Life against Death: The Psychoanalytical Meaning of History* (1959). Aiming to free individuals from the destructive conditions of capitalism (Marcuse) and seeking psychoanalytic alternatives to repression identified in the metaphysics of Freud (Marcuse and Brown), both critiqued the extremes of Wilhelm Reich, such as the pseudoscience of his theory of orgone energy, or universal life force, for which he designed "orgone accumulators"

for collecting and storing orgone energy. Brown would soon repudiate his own *Life against Death* as "immature" and, in *Love's Body* (1966), affirm Eros in the historical struggle for "civilization."[15] Paul Goodman and Betty Friedan, among others, must be added to these authors, as Todd Gitlin has insisted, for how they "set the tone for rebellion when rebels came up from the underground streams, looked around, and decided to make history."[16]

Moorman belonged to that next generation and was her own kind of rebel. But that she "crossed the Rubicon" in Paris, reaching the point of nudity, requires closer examination. For Moorman and Paik were in Paris in 1965, "after all," to perform in the second Festival de la Libre Expression (Festival of Free Expression), organized by the legendary French artist Jean-Jacques Lebel. Poet, painter, theorist, organizer, and political activist, Lebel had been raised in the circle of André Breton, Marcel Duchamp, Man Ray, and Francis Picabia; had roots in and associations with the Situationist International, the Living Theatre, the American beat poets, and figures in the activist political underground; had authored the first book in France on happenings; would become central to the revolutionary events in France in May 1968; and would tutor the philosopher Gilles Deleuze (whom he met in 1955) and the psychoanalyst Félix Guattari (whom he met in 1965) on art and culture.[17]

Lebel's happenings during his festivals were notorious, and for this second festival in which Moorman and Paik would perform, attendance reached two thousand with Duchamp, Man Ray, Jean-Luc Godard, and Peter Brook in attendance. On the first night, Lebel staged *Déchirex* (meaning to tear or rip), a happening that suggested "ripping away of the blinders of everyday life."[18] The climax of *Déchirex* occurred when

a nude woman on a motorcycle roared into the auditorium . . . chased through the crowd until the lights suddenly went off. A spotlight focused on an old car that was being demolished [by men] with axes and hammers. A woman with a death mask kneeled on the crushed roof and a young man covered her body with spaghetti, which she then hurled into the jeering crowd. All the while one could hear a tape of Mayakovsky reading some of his poems, the noise of heavy gunfire and of screaming fire brigades, and finally a political speech by Fidel Castro.[19]

Given the wild scene of sex and destruction, Moorman chose to participate in the efforts of her generation to tear away the pseudomodesty of normative mores and appear nude, dramatically wrapped in transparent cellophane.

Moorman knew well that Schneemann had performed her kinetic theater piece *Meat Joy* in Lebel's first Festival of Free Expression in May 1964. Schneemann gained international acclaim for *Meat Joy*, which became synonymous with the '60s as a period of "sex, drugs, and rock 'n' roll," for how she and her male and female cast stripped each other to scanty bikinis and formfitting Speedo swimsuits before reveling to rock music in a celebration of the eroticism of flesh and meat. Five months earlier, in late December 1963, Schneemann had also posed in her studio for photographs taken by the Icelandic artist Erró. "Charlotte knew those photographs," Schneemann remembered.[20] The suite, titled *Eye Body*, depicts a nude Schneemann, often with her body and face overpainted as an extension of the environment of her assemblages, which feature partially destroyed found objects and shattered glass, materials suggestive of the merger of sex and violence. Moorman also knew of Schneemann and Robert Morris's performance *Site* at Surplus Dance Theater in New York City in March 1964. Morris, masked and wearing a T-shirt and slacks, undertook minimalist actions with a large sheet of plywood, as Schneemann reclined nude, posing in the role of "Olympia" in Édouard Manet's famous 1865 painting of the same name.[21] In chronological order, *Eye Body, Site*, and *Meat Joy* are antecedents for Moorman's nude appearances in *Originale* in September 1964 and *Variations on a Theme by Saint Saëns* in May 1965.

The exploration of both eroticism and violence in Schneemann's and Lebel's work also characterized Paik's approach to his early performances. Already in October 1960, in a joint concert with John Cage, Paik famously cut off Cage's tie while performing his own *Etude for Piano*. In *One for Violin Solo*, in June 1962 at the exhibition "Neo-Dada in der Musik" in Düsseldorf, Paik secured his reputation as the ferocious performer of new music. Standing before a wooden table and holding a violin by the neck, Paik slowly raised the instrument above his head before bringing it smashing down on the table with great force. For dramatic effect, he instructed that the stage lights be turned off at the instant the violin shattered. That year, Paik also wrote *Serenade for Alison*, a semistriptease that had Alison Knowles successively remove a series of panties described in Paik's score as "yellow . . . white-lace . . . red . . . light-blue . . . violet . . . nylon . . . black-lace . . . blood-stained . . . and green."[22]

Once Paik began to work with Moorman, he recognized a willing partner in the sexual emancipation of music. John Cage, too, incited Moorman's nudity by betting her that she would not perform Erik Satie's piano piece *Vexations* partially nude during her European performance tour with Paik. Taking the bet, she performed the piece topless in West Berlin. Rothfuss classifies this event as a "stunt," crediting Paik (rather than Cage or Moorman) "most certainly" with its "conception," and identifies this moment as "the kernel of an idea" that would prompt Paik to write *Opera Sextronique*.[23] Clearly, the image of Moorman topless playing the piano was astonishing and fueled Paik's imagination. But rather than as a stunt, I think Moorman took Cage's dare as much for fun as for money, and as much in the spirit of her competitive nature as her ambition to best Cage in a competition of wills. She even bragged to a German journalist, "Now he [Cage] owes me a hundred dollars."[24] In this anecdote, Moorman may be seen frankly admitting, albeit through winning a bet instigated by Cage, that she practiced her own style of agency.

Charlotte Moorman reenacts her performance of Erik Satie's *Vexations* for the magazine *Der Spiegel*, Cologne, West Germany, July 6, 1966. © Ute Klophaus/bpk, Berlin. Courtesy of Charlotte Moorman Archive, Charles Deering McCormick Library of Special Collections, Northwestern University Library.

As If

What I am suggesting is that behind the mid-twentieth-century southern girl's coy facade, Moorman always knew exactly what she was doing and why, and she loved every minute of it. But, more often than not, she offered exaggerated, artificial excuses for not understanding why the public might be shocked or why she might run afoul of the law. It was convenient for Moorman to let Paik, Schneemann, or even Cage instigate her titillating actions, as that credit relieved her of accountability. Hedging also permitted her to pretend that she "simply cannot understand why everyone was so noisy and difficult about it all," as Paul O'Neil reported her reference to performing topless in *Opera Sextronique* in his article "Nudity."[25]

The extremes to which Moorman could, and did, deny culpability for her actions is exemplified in her unpublished text, "An Artist in the Courtroom (People vs. Moorman)," the implausible defense she made for her arrest.[26] "I could not then, and still cannot, believe," she exclaims, "that such a thing is possible." She finds it incredible that her reputation as one who has "performed and been applauded for in newspapers and books throughout the world" would not save her from legal scrutiny. She equally claims Paik's arrest to be "Unbelievable!"

recounting his degrees and international renown *as if* they could protect him from being culpable for breaking the law. She charges that "an army of <u>uninvited</u> policemen" (Moorman's emphasis) had "abruptly interrupted and raided the performance," *as if* the police needed to be invited to do their duty. "How and why these plainclothesmen came I'll never know," she pretends. Moorman betrayed her bogus innocence when she also explained that she had consulted her attorney prior to the performance, assuming that it might be raided. As Rothfuss put it, "Moorman professed to be baffled by the events [but was] herself . . . probably responsible for the leak."[27]

In her text Moorman also recounts reactions by friends, including whining about— but obviously enjoying—the attention that "certain 'friends' were so so sick that they were actually <u>jealous</u> of the scandalous, sensational publicity" (Moorman's emphasis). Continuing with an air of disdain, she states that "a lot of the 'wrong' people were attracted to my avant garde [*sic*] work for all the wrong reasons, and unsuitable offers came in by the carloads." Moorman's most insincere comments come when she presents herself *as if* she were a vulnerable child. "Not since my daddy died when I was 12 years old," she pouts, "had I been so shocked." Later she adds, "If only I could have reached my mother and grandmother before they read that their only child had been arrested. Imagine their shock and pain!" Rothfuss reports, "In truth, she had had plenty of time to warn her family [as Moorman's] arrest was not reported in the Little Rock newspapers until . . . thirty-six hours after the fact."[28] In a particularly hyperbolic comment, Moorman expresses fear that she will "never get out of jail" and disingenuously asks, "Was I being prosecuted for having the courage to carry out a vital, new artistic experiment . . . because of my partial nudity?"

Toward the end of her text, Moorman contradicts herself. On the one hand, she claims to be "amazed at how little of my performance [the court] had absorbed and how its meaning seemed to have totally gone above their heads. Their knowledge of the new art forms was even more limited than mine of the Law." On the other hand, her so-called superior knowledge of law, compared to the court's lack of knowledge of art, dissolves into vulnerability, as "frustration" at being obliged to answer "yes" or "no" to complex legal queries caused her "to break down in tears," requiring the court to recess. The report ends with a long account of the judge's verdict. The level of Moorman's pretense to naïveté, contrived surprise, and emotional dishonesty throughout the document is palpable.[29]

Destruction's Cut

After her trial, Moorman became increasingly involved in the intersection of eroticism and destruction. So, too, had one of her closest friends, Yoko Ono, early in her career used destruction as a creative device. Moorman knew that Ono had premiered her performance *Cut Piece* in Kyoto in July 1964 and had seen Ono perform it again at Carnegie Recital Hall in New York in March 1965. Sitting motionless after inviting the audience to come to the stage and cut away her clothing, and with the stoicism of a rock, Ono displayed no emotion, conveying something of the "psychic experiences and intimate sensations" she alluded to in her "Statement" in the *Village Voice* some years later:

People went on cutting the parts they do not like of me finally there was only the stone remained of me that was in me but they were still not satisfied and wanted to know what it's like in the stone.[30]

Moorman carefully scrutinized Ono's performance and described "the elegance, the drama, and the seriousness" of the work.[31] Moorman would perform the piece throughout her life.

Ono presented *Cut Piece* again at the Destruction in Art Symposium (DIAS) in London in September 1966, the same year that, while on tour in Europe, Moorman first performed *Cut Piece*. But unlike Ono, Moorman "claimed that she 'could be raped onstage,'" a comment that Rothfuss describes as "melodramatic" and that I would label as nonsense.[32] Rothfuss interprets Moorman's body language in Kenneth Werner's photograph of her performing *Cut Piece* as "stony and her neck tense as two men snip at her dress."[33] I read Moorman's expression as rapture, akin to the visage of Bernini's *Ecstasy of Saint Teresa* (1647–1652) pierced by an arrow, the expression of intense eroticism at the juncture of danger. (See page 168 for the performance image.)

By 1967, Moorman had become more closely aligned with the milieu of artists associated with destruction in art, ranging from Ono to Lil Picard, Raphael Montañez Ortiz, Jean Toche, Jon Hendricks, and Al Hansen, among others. Ortiz (like Ono, Hansen, and Toche) had participated in London DIAS, and then, with Hendricks, organized "Twelve Evenings of Manipulations" in October 1967 at the Judson Church in New York City. Moorman joined Paik in this series of events. Geoffrey Hendricks described the event this way: Moorman lay on her back to play the cello, while he "cut a fine line on his arm with a razor blade." Geoffrey Hendricks later asked, "Was this Nam June atoning for Charlotte's arrest?"[34]

Again with Jon Hendricks, Ortiz was responsible for organizing "DIAS / USA," which was to be the sequel to DIAS in London and was to take place in April and May

1968.[35] Eager to promote their upcoming symposium, they held "DIAS / USA: A Preview" on March 22. Its "most vivid moment" occurred, according to Geoffrey Hendricks, when Moorman performed Paik's *One for Violin Solo*:

> Saul Gottlieb, a political activist in the East Village and organizer of alternative programming, felt that Charlotte should not destroy the violin. From the back of the room, he got into a dialogue with Charlotte, explaining how the violin should be given to some poor child on the Lower East Side. . . . Charlotte said yes, things like that should be done, but this was music by a great composer and should be performed. . . . The suspense was great. Slowly she raised the violin high over her head. At that point Saul pushed his way through the crowd, slid over the long table, and stood in front of Charlotte just as she brought the violin down, smashing it on Saul's head. Everyone was stunned.[36]

A different version of this event by Jill Johnston of the *Village Voice* reports Moorman as "angry," demanding to know who Gottlieb thought he was (to interrupt her performance), slapping Gottlieb's face, accusing him of "being as bad as the New York police," and then when he "stretched himself out on the table in front of her . . . bash[ing] him on the head with the violin and the blood was spilled."[37] The violence of the event was debated in the counterculture newspaper *East Village Other*, with Gottlieb referring to Moorman as a "Mack truck" and insisting that "the DIAS people are two years behind the times—the time for purely SYMBOLIC destruction is over."[38] Moorman's action was anything but symbolic: it was a direct assault on Gottlieb's effort to alter her artistic performance. Geoffrey Hendricks "retrieved the neck of the violin [and] later . . . painted a bank of cumulus clouds on the fingerboard," titling it *In Memoriam: Saul Gottlieb*.[39] Within the year, Gottlieb died of cancer.

Another relic remained: the back of the violin, which Moorman signed and dedicated to the German American artist Picard: "To

Charlotte Moorman performs Nam June Paik's *One for Violin Solo*, "DIAS / USA: A Preview," New York City, March 22, 1968. © Julie Abeles. Courtesy of Charlotte Moorman Archive, Charles Deering McCormick Library of Special Collections, Northwestern University Library.

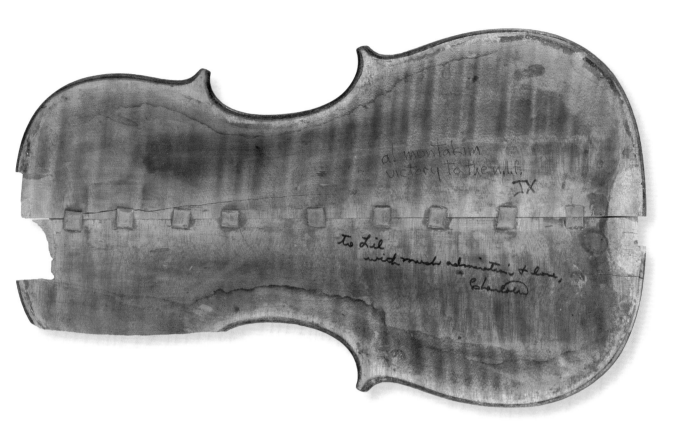

Lil with much admiration & love, Charlotte." Above her inscription, someone wrote:

al muntakim
victory to the n.l.f
JX

The words "al muntakim" refer to "Al Muntaqim," one of the ninety-nine names of Allah, and means "The Avenger" ("The Avenger, The One who victoriously prevails over His enemies and punishes them for their sins. It may mean the One who destroys them").[40] The initials "n.l.f" signify the National Liberation Front of the Viet Cong with which the United States was at war. It may be relevant to this inscription that the My Lai Massacre, in which U.S. troops slaughtered between 347 and 504 unarmed South Vietnamese civilians, had occurred only six days earlier, on March 16, 1968, possibly inspiring the unidentifiable author's allusion to vengeance. Upon close inspection, the phrases "al muntakim" and "victory to the n.l.f." are written with a sharp-pointed pen in the same hand. Whoever signed the initials "JX" wrote with the thick black-tipped pen

that Moorman used, but the initials are not in Moorman's handwriting.

At some point, the back of the violin passed into Ortiz's archive.[41] Although the handwriting of the mysterious inscriptions resembles his, Ortiz vehemently denies authorship.[42] Together, Ortiz, Toche, Schneemann, Jon Hendricks, and Moorman's good friend and collaborator Jim McWilliams all concede no knowledge of anyone with the initials JX.[43] Nor had any of them heard of a "JX Williams," who emerged as an elusive if not illusive person/persona in my search for the signatory. A clandestine figure variously cited as a pulp adult fiction writer and soft-porn filmmaker, JX Williams has also been identified as an "exploitation filmmaker with a storied past," and credited as "director of the 1965 documentary *Peep Show*—a kind of spiritual vortex of sub rosa Americana surrounding the Kennedy assassination."[44] JX Williams is also considered by some to be a hoax perpetrated by Noel Lawrence, the self-appointed "curator" or "director of the JX Williams Archive."[45] But, doubling the mystery of the signatory, the

Charlotte Moorman's and JX's inscriptions on the violin from "DIAS/USA: A Preview," New York City, 1968. Courtesy of Charlotte Moorman Archive, Charles Deering McCormick Library of Special Collections, Northwestern University Library.

Charlotte Moorman performs Otto Muehl's *Manopsychotic Ballet (Part 2)*, Happening & Fluxus, Cologne, West Germany, November 8, 1970. Photograph by Hanns Sohm. © Archiv Sohm, Staatsgalerie Stuttgart. Courtesy of Charlotte Moorman Archive, Charles Deering McCormick Library of Special Collections, Northwestern University Library.

unsolved identity of JX Williams becomes more challenging and provocative when one learns that Lawrence, in his "mid-30s" in 2005, had not been born when "JX" signed the violin.[46]

Sunday Orgy

What the inscription indicates is that the beauty queen of Little Rock was trafficking in dark waters. Moorman descended further into the domain of Eros and Thanatos in her nude cello performance two years later in Otto Muehl's *Manopsychotic Ballet (Part 2)*, performed on the Sunday afternoon of November 8, 1970, for the *Happening*

& Fluxus exhibition in Cologne. This was Muehl's last, and one of his most intentionally obscene, public events. By far the most outrageous of the Viennese Action artists, soon after this performance, Muehl abandoned the art world to devote himself to the formation of the AA Kommune, which he founded in Friedrichshof, Austria, in 1972.[47] *Manopsychotic Ballet (Part 2)* included two men (Muehl and Herbert Stumpfl) and two women (Romilla Doll and Mica Most) with Moorman playing the cello on the edge of their performance. All were naked, as were two cameramen and two sound engineers, who appeared as "both the observers and the observed, distanced witnesses and exposed performers."[48]

In addition to the public performance of cunnilingus, according to art historian Philip Ursprung, who based his description on photographs and films of the event, the performance began

> with a ritual dance of the performers, who caress each other's genitals and mimic sexual intercourse. Muehl then extracts a tampon from the vagina of one of the female performers, presents it to the audience and carries it triumphantly between his teeth. Later, he inserts a rolling pin into her vagina. He whips her with a belt before being whipped himself by her and the others. There is a scene where a cameraman pretends to rape a female performer by inserting the lens of a camera into the vagina. In another scene the two male performers urinate on the body of one of the females. Towards the end, a live chicken is introduced into the proceedings. It remains unclear if it is actually slaughtered on stage, but the performers tear the dead bird to pieces and act as if they are devouring it. In the closing scene, Muehl defecates towards the lens of the camera.[49]

Ursprung's description is as uncompromising as his analysis. Rather than an example of the rebellion of the counterculture against the mainstream, "the action can be read as persiflage of a happening, the performers aping performance art and mimicking the closed-circuit structure of ephemeral media by including a naked film team as part of the performance."[50]

Moorman's dissociation from the content of the behavior during Muehl's performance is vivid in her letter to her husband, Frank Pileggi, and exemplifies her denial of the meaning and implications of the action in which she consented to perform:

> Today (Sunday) Otto Muehl asked me to play in his happening naked since all his performers and cameramen were naked. So I sat there very serious and played one note over and over again (20 minute happening) while Otto and his performers did sensual things and cut up a live chicken and put blood all over themselves. It was quite good. You would have liked it too. Then Hermann Nitsch asked me to play in his orchestra to make noise.) They are all real good to me and carry my cello and insist I sit down.)[51]

Photographs of Moorman during the performance depict her as impassive, playing the one note on the sidelines of the action. Did she grasp Muehl's performative critique "of repressive structures of European post-war society [and] the authoritarian structure of the emerging art world"?[52] I do not think so, as she would not have shared that conviction. Was she able to grasp the content of what was occurring before her? Or, did she prefer to focus only on the generosity that the Viennese artists extended to her? Or, was Moorman's emotional distance from this confrontational and inflammatory performance the very sign of the provocateur at her most rebellious?

Thinking about the nature of a rebel, the French feminist philosopher and psychoanalyst Julia Kristeva once commented:

> People who rebel are malcontents with frustrated, but vigorous desires. The subversion they desire can even be a sign of the eroticization of

thought—a psychic vitality Thanatos can't negate. . . . Rebellion is a condition necessary for the life of the mind and society.[53]

Insofar as Moorman's vigorous life-in-art manifested as psychic vitality, it brought her through and to the other side of destruction. In this regard and to a degree, she fit aspects of Kristeva's description of the rebel. Moorman could be said to have been something of a malcontent as well. But most of all, Moorman was a provocateur, who would make such outlandish comments as that the cellophane covering she wore in *Variations on a Theme by Saint-Saëns* made her feel "totally clothed," like wearing "a snowsuit."[54] Moorman thrived on and deliberately provoked controversy and spectacle, prodded the public and incited the law to rebuke her, and relished being victim / crusader on Johnny Carson's *The Tonight Show* or the *Merv Griffin Show*.

"Strong as Death Is Love"

Moorman could be said to have united the "consubstantiality of rationality and affectivity"—namely, the harmony of reason and emotion, cited by the French philosopher Catherine Malabou in her theory of "plasticity."[55] For Malabou, plasticity merges science with psychology in the formation of identity, suturing biology and culture into a new philosophical and scientific paradigm. In her theory, Malabou draws especially on neuroscientist Joseph LeDoux's dictum, "You are your synapses," to propose a unified neurological theory of personality in which synaptic plasticity determines form, matter, and meaning, or "plastic ontology," consciousness, and "cerebral plasticity."[56] She further describes the capacity of the synapses to act for the good of the individual, as well as "to act as a 'plastic bomb' with the potential to unravel the self in profound ways."[57] Such observations place her theory of plasticity in line with Freud's discussion of Eros and Thanatos. Following Freud, Malabou writes that "ontological plasticity . . . is both positive," as in "the plasticity of the affects," and negative, exemplified by a "destructive plasticity" that can result in "the disorder of its directions."[58] The continuum between the vital forces of life and death brings Malabou to observe further, "Denegation is born in this strange place, where the concept of birth itself trembles," meaning denial always harbors genesis. This is also the site of what Malabou terms "necessity's other," a location that she describes as the place of interlocking positive and negative plastic capabilities of the synapses that not only form but also deform an individual.[59]

Such is the intersection at which Moorman's denial merged with her consent, granting herself permission to mine what she held to be the magnitude of visionary avant-garde art. By her own account, Moorman lived with "extreme passion, extreme beauty, extreme sex."[60] This description of her life evinces Moorman's high degree of fervor and exceptional excitement about which Rothfuss concludes that she "had

no regrets."[61] The closest Moorman seems to have come to unraveling as a person, the result of the "plastic bomb" of negativity, may have been in her flailing attempt to offer a counternarrative of her arrest. Otherwise, Moorman faced her life and untimely death with panache. If such a way of conducting oneself in the world demonstrates "plastic ontology," then Moorman exhibited a remarkable, even exquisite, capacity of mind to navigate the consequences of the extremes of her period. While the artists closest to Moorman (Paik, Ono, Schneemann, Lebel, Muehl, and others) theorized the content of their actions, Moorman did not. But could a theory of the content of Moorman's work reside in her negotiations with "necessity's other"? In her balance of Eros and Thanatos? In action itself in its resonant context? I think so.

Notes

Every page of this essay is indebted to Joan Rothfuss's painstaking, insightful biography, *Topless Cellist: The Improbable Life of Charlotte Moorman* (Cambridge, Mass.: MIT Press, 2014).

1. Faubion Bowers, "A Feast of Astonishments," *Nation* 199, no. 8 (September 28, 1964): 173, quoted in Rothfuss, *Topless Cellist*, 102. Rothfuss writes that there are no photographs of this moment and that the photographs of both Peter Moore and Fred McDarrah "show her hanging in front of the balcony fully clothed. Perhaps she was lifted up in gauze during one of the five performances that was *not* photographed, but there is no evidence to

support that." Joan Rothfuss comments emailed to the author (January 13, 2015); hereafter cited as Rothfuss, January 13, 2015. I submit that the "evidence" of this moment is Bowers's description of it.

2. Carolee Schneemann, interview by Joan Rothfuss, June 1, 2003, New Paltz, New York, quoted in Rothfuss, *Topless Cellist*, 102.

3. Rothfuss, *Topless Cellist*, 22–23.

4. Rothfuss, quoting a telephone conversation of July 27, 2009, with the artist Jim McWilliams, Moorman's close friend with whom she would collaborate in the 1970s: ibid., 110.

5. While there are no pictures of this event, McWilliams described the intervention in Moorman's performance in this way to Rothfuss; ibid., 110.

6. Ibid.

7. Rothfuss, *Topless Cellist*, 112.

8. Practice bombs were originally filled with water and sand and used by the U.S. Navy for target practice. Thanks to Kathy O'Dell for the research on these bombs (which are described in greater detail in her essay in this volume).

9. On the equipment for and sexing of objects, see Edward J. Geisweidt, "The Erotic Life of Objects: 'Venus and Adonis' in the Puppet Theater," *Hare* 1, no.

2 (2012), http://thehareonline.com/article/erotic-life-objects-venus-and-adonis-puppet-theater.

10. Mario Vrančić, *The Lacanian Thing: Psychoanalysis, Postmodern Culture, and Cinema* (Amherst, N.Y.: Cambria Press, 2011), 317.

11. Ibid.

12. Nam June Paik, "Charlotte Moorman: Chance and Necessity," undated typescript [1992], Emily Harvey Foundation Archives, New York, quoted in Rothfuss, *Topless Cellist*, 123.

13. Ibid.

14. Paul O'Neil, "Nudity," *Life*, October 13, 1967, 115.

15. Critical of *Love's Body*, Marcuse discussed the book in the influential journal *Commentary* in February 1967, to which Brown replied in the March issue. Brown and Marcuse had known each other since the mid-1940s when Brown "served [from 1943–46] in the Office of Strategic Services, the forerunner of the Central Intelligence Agency," where he met and befriended "Marcuse, another intelligence analyst." Douglas Martin "Norman O. Brown Dies; Playful Philosopher was 89," *New York Times*, October 4, 2002, http://www.nytimes.com/2002/10/04/arts/norman-o-brown-dies-playful-philosopher-was-89.html.

16. Todd Gitlin, *The Sixties: Years of Hope, Days of Rage* (Toronto: Bantam Books, 1987), 28. See also Abe Peck, *Uncovering the Sixties: The Life & Times of the Underground Press* (New York: Pantheon Books, 1985).

17. See Kristine Stiles, "'Beautiful, Jean-Jacques': Jean-Jacques Lebel's Affect and the Theories of Gilles Deleuze and Félix Guattari," in *Jean-Jacques Lebel* (Milan: Edizioni Gabriele Mazzotta, 1998), 7–30.

18. Laurel Jean Fredrickson, *Kate Millett and Jean-Jacques Lebel: Sexual Outlaws in the Intermedia Borderlands of Art and Politics* (Ann Arbor, Mich.: UMI, 2007), 307–8.

19. Günter Berghaus, "Happenings in Europe: Trends, Events, and Leading Figures," in *Happenings and Other Acts*, ed. Mariellen R. Sandford (New York: Routledge, 1995), 263–328.

20. Carolee Schneemann, email to the author, December 4, 2014. Schneemann added that "we had some talk together about what our bodies brought to our work—both from our personal lived experience and from the crazy range of reactions within masculine traditions . . . because in those days there wasn't a clearly defined feminist erotic concept."

21. Morris would also appear naked with the equally nude Yvonne Rainer, pressing their bodies together in *Waterman Switch* in March 1965.

22. See a photograph of Knowles performing in Amsterdam, in October 1962, in *Happening & Fluxus: Materialien zusammengestellt von Hanns Sohm* (Cologne: Kölnischer Kunstverein, 1970), n.p.

23. Paul Moor, "Musik, die immer mehr in die Nähe von Theater rückt," *Die Zeit*, July 22, 1966, quoted in Rothfuss, *Topless Cellist*, 153.

24. Ibid.

25. O'Neil, "Nudity," 116. Norman Lebrecht's 2014 review of Rothfuss's book *Topless Cellist* continues the portrayal of Moorman as innocent and gullible when he writes that Moorman was "altogether oblivious to her impact on puritanical spectators and society." Norman Lebricht, review of *Topless Cellist*, by Joan Rothfuss, *Wall Street Journal*, October 3, 2014, http://www.wsj.com/articles/book-review-topless-cellist-by-joan-rothfuss-1412367204.

26. This unpublished text may be found in the Charles Deering McCormick Library of Special Collections, Northwestern University. Thanks to Scott Krafft, curator, and his staff for providing me with a copy of the document. All subsequent quotations related to Moorman's arrest are from this document.

27. Rothfuss, *Topless Cellist*, 186.

28. Ibid., 203.

29. Rothfuss points out in an email to the author of January 13, 2015, that "'An Artist in the Courtroom' had three authors: Moorman, Paik, and Pileggi," and she interprets the text as a "collage of their words" in which "one can only guess at who actually wrote the words [which were] smoothed out in the final version," such that it appears "*as if* CM were its sole author." While a valid point, whoever used the language in the document, they agreed that it represented Moorman's point of view and the ways in which she expressed herself; and she signed off on the document.

30. See Yoko Ono, "Statement," *Village Voice,* October 7, 1971, 20. Quoted in Kristine Stiles, "Unbosoming Lennon: The Politics of Yoko Ono's Experience," *Art Criticism* 7, no. 2 (Spring 1992): 35.

31. Charlotte Moorman in conversation with Jud Yalkut, 1971, quoted in Rothfuss, *Topless Cellist*, 156.

32. Ibid.

33. Ibid.

34. Geoffrey Hendricks, "Geoffrey Hendricks," in *Remembering Judson House*, ed. Elly Dickason and Jerry G. Dickason (New York: Judson Memorial Church, 2000), 317.

35. Upon learning that Martin Luther King had been assassinated, Ortiz and Hendricks cancelled DIAS/USA, explaining that there had been too much destruction.

36. Hendricks, "Geoffrey Hendricks," 318.

37. Jill Johnston, "Over His Dead Body," *Village Voice*, March 28, 1968, quoted in Rothfuss, *Topless Cellist*, 216.

38. Saul Gottlieb, "Yesterday Whitehall, Tomorrow the Finch Museum," *East Village Other*, April 5–11, 1968, quoted in Rothfuss, *Topless Cellist*, 217.

39. Hendricks, "Geoffrey Hendricks," 317.

40. M. R. Bawa Muhaiyad-deen, *Asma'ul-Husna: The 99 Beautiful Names of Allah* (Philadelphia: Fellowship Press, 1976), no. 081.

41. In the late 1980s, Ortiz gave me his archive, along with this object, which I have now given as a gift to the Charlotte Moorman Archive in the Charles Deering McCormick Library of Special Collections, Northwestern University Library (hereafter cited as CMA).

42. When asked if he knew of or could identify the mysterious "JX," Ortiz researched the name on the Internet and came up with the same conflicting information that I describe. Such findings led Ortiz to respond to my question whether he had made the inscription as follows: "My art, political and religious work have never had anything what so ever to do with the vomit spewed by the person or organization you are researching. It is an insult to even imply there is such a relation to me what ever you divine from the hand writing." Raphael Montañez Ortiz email to the author, May 15, 2014.

43. I contacted each of these artists by email in an attempt to identify "JX."

44. Paul Cullum, "Wrapped in an Enigma, Hidden in a Film Archive," *New York Times*, October 2, 2005, http://www.nytimes.com/2005/10/02/movies/02cull.html?_r=0.

45. Ibid.

46. On J. X. Williams, see Noel Lawrence and Jean-Emmanuel Deluxe, *J. X. Williams: Les dossiers interdits*, with preface by Jean-Pierre Dionnet (Rosières-en-Haye, France: Camion Noir, 2010).

47. See Otto Muehl and Peter Noever Muehl, *Life/Art/Work: Performance, Utopia, Painting—1960–2004* (Cologne: Walther König and Museum Moderner Kunst Stiftung Ludwig Wien, 2004). See also William Levy, *Impossible: The Otto Muehl Story* (New York: Barany Artists, 2001).

48. Philip Ursprung, "More Than the Art World Can Tolerate: Otto Muehl's Manopsychotic Ballet," *Tate*, December 1, 2011, http://www.tate.org.uk/context-comment/articles/more-art-world-can-tolerate.

49. Ibid.

50. Ibid.

51. Charlotte Moorman to Frank Pileggi, November 8, 1970, CMA. The inaccurate punctuation in her letter is Moorman's own. Thanks to Rothfuss for sending me the contents of this letter, as it pertained to her participation in Muehl's happening. Rothfuss has also noted that Moorman performed as a passive participant in Nitsch's fortieth Action held at the Kitchen in New York City on December 2, 1972. Quoting from Moorman's appointment diary, Rothfuss writes that it reads: "Nitsch's 'Orgies Mysteries Theater'—MOORMAN NUDE SACRIFICE—sacrificed ME–blood under lamb." This description conforms to how Nitsch works with his passive participants, requiring them to perform nude and acquiesce to having lamb's blood dripped, and entrails applied to, their bodies. Rothfuss adds: "Geoff Hendricks, who also performed, told me that it was his impression that CM did not enjoy it and would not have consented to perform with Nitsch again." Rothfuss, January 13, 2015.

52. Rothfuss, January 13, 2015.

53. Julia Kristeva, *Revolt, She Said: An Interview by Philippe Petit*, trans. Brian O'Keeffe, ed. Sylvère Lotringer (Los Angeles: Semiotext(e) Foreign Agents Series, 2002), 84–85.

54. Charlotte Moorman in conversation with Andrew Gurian, Kit Fitzgerald, Elliot Caplan, Michael Lytle, Nam June Paik, Frank Pileggi, and others at the Whitney Museum of American Art, audiocassette, recorded August 1982, New York City; cited in Rothfuss, *Topless Cellist*, 124.

55. Catherine Malabou, *Ontology of the Accident: An Essay on Destructive Plasticity*, trans. Carolyn Shread (Cambridge: Polity, 2012), 22; originally published in 2009 as *Ontologie de l'accident* by Éditions Léo Scheer in Paris. Malabou uses this phrase near the beginning of chapter 2 as part of her argument for destructive plasticity, or the "ontology of the accident." There is much to admire in her theorization of the plastic integration of logic and biology, but Malabou's understanding of the etiology of trauma is deeply flawed, epitomized in her claim that the traumatized "become indifferent to their own survival and to the survival of others" (27). Nothing could be farther from the role of the dissociative function in trauma, whose affect she perceives as "indifference" but which is the very expression of the cognitive plasticity that enables the mind to protect the psyche in its ability to numb precisely in order to survive. The phrase that is the title of this section summons the oneness of Eros and Thanatos and comes from Robert Alter's book *Strong as Death Is Love* (New York: W. W. Norton, 2015).

56. Joseph LeDoux, *Synaptic Self: How Our Brains Become Who We Are* (London: Penguin, 2002), n.p., quoted in ibid., 38. For "plastic ontology," see Catherine Malabou, *Changer de différence, Le féminin et la question philosophique* (Paris: Galilée: 2009), 75. Malabou also ascribes to plasticity the ability to "take over" and "become the resistance of difference to its textual reduction" in a bid to overturn the primacy of writing and the text (as theorized by her dissertation adviser Jacques Derrida in *Of Grammatology* [1967]), with what Maïté Marciano and Anna Street, in their review of Malabou's book, call "the new paradigm of plasticity". Maïté Marciano and Anna Street, "Catherine Malabou and the Concept of Plasticity," in *Theater, Performance, Philosophy Conference: Crossings and Transfers in Contemporary Anglo-American Thought,* trans. Anna Street (University of Paris–Sorbonne, June 26–28, 2014), http://tpp2014.com/catherine-malabou-concept-plasticity/.

57. See Stacey Smith, review of *Ontology of the Accident* by Catherine Malabou, *Society and Space* (2012), http://societyandspace.com/reviews/reviews-archive/malabou_smith.

58. Malabou, *Ontology of the Accident*, 37. Freud wrote that "affirmation—as a substitute for unity—belongs to Eros; negation—the successor to expulsion—belongs to the instinct of destruction." Sigmund Freud, "Negation" (1925), in *Standard Edition of the Complete Psychological Works of Sigmund Freud*, vol. 19, trans. and ed. J. Strachey, in collaboration with A. Freud, assisted by A. Strachey and A. Tyson (London: Hogarth Press, 1957), 235–39. The critical synaptic locus of such changes conveys information and stimulates functions within the brain that shape an individual's experiences, giving rise to unique thoughts and feelings that permit "the constructive plastic formation of . . . identity, but also the identification of being as the possibility of its own neuronal destructive plasticity" (38).

59. Ibid.

60. Moorman in conversation with an unidentified astrologer, February 2, 1982, audiocassette in CMA, quoted in Rothfuss, *Topless Cellist*, 361.

61. Ibid.

"Don't Throw Anything Out": Charlotte Moorman's Archive

Scott Krafft

Charlotte Moorman is remembered for two strands of a dovetailing career. One is her colorful work as a musician and performance artist, and the other is her role as the entrepreneurial producer and promoter of the annual New York avant-garde festivals. But there is a third important Moorman accomplishment: the creation, or conscious accretion, of her vast archive, which documents not only her own life and two careers but the works and lives of contemporary artists and friends from the early 1960s until her death in 1991. The archive's importance to Moorman was evidenced during her life by the sacrifices she made in domestic comfort and money to house it, by her dogged spoils gathering while traveling, and by her cajoling of friends to contribute material to it. She had faith in her own worth and in the worth of those in her world, and there is evidence that she conceived of her archive as akin to a work of art in itself, or more certainly as the spent chrysalis of a life lived as performance.

In Peter Moore's fish-eye photograph we see Moorman in her studio apartment in the Hotel Paris in Manhattan's Upper West Side, where she lived from 1962 until 1971, the year this photograph was taken. The photograph aptly pictorializes Moorman as the gravitational vortex of her stuff, a voracious black hole. Hers is clearly a nature that abhors a vacuum, and, as would be the case in later apartments, the place is filled floor to ceiling, wall to wall, with her hoarded treasures and borderline trash. In a way radically more true than most who leave behind so-called archives, Charlotte Moorman lived inside of hers. She walked through it, slept in it, sat on it, ate in it. The Hotel Paris apartment was so full that Moorman had to store her cello in the bathtub and practice it on the building's roof.[1] There's another story about Moorman buried behind this photograph, and it's one about her chronic lateness. It was taken on the very day that Peter Moore and his wife, Barbara, had arrived at the Hotel Paris to help Moorman and her husband, Frank Pileggi, move to their next apartment on West 46th Street. The Moores had come to help lug boxes, but, as one can see, the apartment was far from packed and ready to go.[2] Patience with Moorman—who was routinely late for planes, trains, paying bills, her own performances and festivals, and even an event sponsored by New York City mayor David Dinkins to honor her cultural contributions to the city—was a quality required of her friends.[3]

OPPOSITE
Peter Moore. Charlotte Moorman in her room at the Hotel Paris, New York City, March 24, 1971. Photograph © Barbara Moore / Licensed by VAGA, NY.

185

Charlotte Moorman's apartment at the Hotel Paris, New York City, ca. 1970. Photographs by Frank Pileggi. Courtesy of Charlotte Moorman Archive, Charles Deering McCormick Library of Special Collections, Northwestern University Library.

Color snapshots of the Hotel Paris apartment give more evidence of the clutter and depict a few larger items that survived the years and remain part of the archive, such as Jörg Immendorff's hand-painted brown paper poster for a performance in Germany[4] seen hanging on the wall near the foot of Moorman's bed and the lettered white sheet "Welcome Cultural Leaders Moorman and Paik" hanging beneath a wire hanger cello sculpture (whereabouts now unknown) that foreshadows the cello sculptures Moorman would make in the last years of her life.

Not long after Moorman and Pileggi moved to 47 West 46th Street, a monthly stipend from Yoko Ono and John Lennon allowed them to fund the rental of a second apartment in that same building. It was used to house the overflowing archival material, and the two spaces together served as office and command center for the festivals.[5] Moorman and Pileggi (who was titled "Festival Chairman") worked from home, often with a bevy of volunteers. The fact that she was her own employer gave Moorman the freedom to determine her own schedule, and for almost all her adult life she was free from anything akin to a nine-to-five regime.

By temperament she was something of a night owl; she worked when she liked and could do so for huge stretches of time.[6] This elastic detachment from clock and calendar most likely enhanced her native tendency to be late. The fact that she worked where she lived meant that not only did she not have a regular routine, but her days were not spatially divided into a workplace and a domestic space. Her life was a continuous Möbius strip of work, home, and play, of life and performance. This fluidity in turn is represented by the diversity of the archive, the span of which includes things as different as the corporate records of the festivals, manuscript scores by such notable artists as Philip Corner and Ornette Coleman, and a scribbled note from Charlotte to Frank saying that she's off to the store to buy Preparation H and makeup. It contains both important cultural relics and snapshots of Moorman's life in progress. Like Moorman's own personality, it's an unusual and bemusing mix of the highbrow and the unashamedly down-to-earth.

In 1977 Moorman, Pileggi, and the archive made one more move together, to a two thousand-square-foot loft at 62 Pearl

Festival volunteers, West 46th Street, New York City, 1974. Juan Crovetto, who briefly lived in the supplemental apartment that helped house Charlotte Moorman's archive, is in the upper left image. Others are unidentified. Photographs by Frank Pileggi and Charlotte Moorman. Courtesy of Charlotte Moorman Archive, Charles Deering McCormick Library of Special Collections, Northwestern University Library.

Note from Charlotte Moorman to Frank Pileggi, August 26, 1981. Courtesy of Charlotte Moorman Archive, Charles Deering McCormick Library of Special Collections, Northwestern University Library.

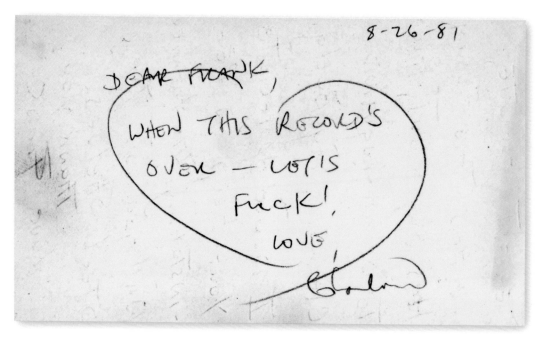

Street, near the southern tip of Manhattan. It would be Moorman's home until her death in 1991. Although a large space, especially for a Manhattan apartment, the loft also was almost immediately filled with Moorman's hoard of material.

Moorman never really recovered from her 1979 mastectomy. The last festival she staged was in 1980, and, as that decade progressed and her cancer returned, she became more and more homebound. As the quantity of morphine she used to ameliorate her pain increased, her ability to tame the shaggy beast of her belongings dwindled. The archive grew out of control in the loft like some external analogue of the cancer invading her body. In one Peter Moore photo, taken not long before her death, it resembles an avalanche about to bury her alive.

Of course not all the stuff we see in these photographs would be defined as being part of Moorman's archive, and after her death it became the task of a series of people to sift through the material and determine what ought to be kept. This was no easy task, as Charlotte would scribble on any scrap of paper—an airsickness bag, a paper plate, a Korvette's shopping receipt—but what she wrote on those trashlike things could be of importance.

Frank Pileggi was the first to try to dig things out, to separate the empty yogurt cups from the rainbow Ay-O prints. One comical discovery he made was that there was a clothes dryer in the loft. It had been buried under piles of papers and other things for years and forgotten.[7]

Money had always been tight for Moorman and Pileggi, and Frank enlisted the assistance of Barbara Moore, who with her husband, Peter, had remained a family friend and a part of Moorman's artistic circle, to help arrange an auction of some of the valuable art objects that Moorman had been given by her friends in the previous decades. It was hoped that the sale would give him money to live on for some of the forthcoming years. Barbara Moore, an art historian, was familiar with the ways of the marketplace due to her work as a dealer of artists' books and multiples. The auction of seventeen items took place at Sotheby's in London on June 24, 1993.[8]

Though most of the items sold, the auction was a disappointment. Some handling errors occurred on the part of some Sotheby's staff. Most ironically of those, the twine tied around the 1967 Christo–Nam June Paik collaborative sculpture *Wrapped Television* was cut by staff who mistook the wrapping—for wrapping.[9] More significantly, the authenticity of the Beuys piece, *Infiltration Homogen for Cello*, was challenged by the Beuys estate, and it was withdrawn from the sale.[10] This piece had been anticipated to be by far the high-ticket item of the auction, estimated to fetch between £200,000 and £250,000, and the loss of that money was a huge blow to Pileggi. Two days after the auction, he died of heart failure.[11]

In his will, Pileggi had declared Barbara Moore executor of his estate, and the enormous jobs of clearing out the Pearl Street loft, trying to define the contents of Moorman's archive, and finding an appropriate home for it were suddenly hers. Pileggi had provided some rough guidelines as to what should be included in Moorman's archive. For example, unlike what happened with Nam June Paik's huge collection of figurines and toys, Moorman's similar collection of dolls was defined as "household goods" akin to pots and pans rather than as part of her archive.[12]

Since the Pearl Street rent was draining money from the estate, Moore was under pressure to clear out all the stuff and make on-the-spot value decisions about what to keep and what to deal with in some other way.[13] What she finally retained would become the core contents of the Charlotte Moorman Archive and would remain in her possession and care for almost a decade.

My own introduction to Moorman and her archive occurred in 2001, when R. Russell Maylone, the former curator of the Charles Deering McCormick Library of Special Collections at Northwestern University Library, handed me a folder and asked me what I thought about the library trying to acquire the archive of Charlotte Moorman.

Peter Moore. Charlotte Moorman wearing Nam June Paik's *TV Bra* in her loft, 62 Pearl Street, New York City, October 16, 1991. Photograph © Barbara Moore/Licensed by VAGA, NY.

As would have been true for most people, my first thought was, "Who is Charlotte Moorman?" When I read the contents of the folder, which was Barbara Moore's description of Moorman and her collection, I saw what Maylone had seen, that the materials would be a natural augmentation to at least two major archives that already resided at Northwestern: the John Cage Collection, which Cage began donating to Northwestern's Music Library in 1973, and the Dick Higgins Archive, which had been donated in 1999 by Higgins's daughters, Hannah and Jessica. In varying ways, Cage, Higgins, and Moorman had positions within or connected to the Fluxus art movement, and likewise in varying ways, the three knew one another, sometimes worked together, and had overlapping friends, interests, and lives in the art worlds of New York City. The aggregate of these three archives would be a fantastic resource for scholars of that era. Maylone secured support and funding from others in the library,[14] an agreement was settled with Moore, and the archive was purchased.

The delivery on May 18, 2001, was a memorable event. Though I'd seen the inventory of the shipment, I was taken aback when the big cargo truck reared up to the dock. The truck was driven by Laurence McGilvery, an old friend of Barbara Moore's, who was also a dealer specializing in books by and about artists. We spent an exhausting afternoon unloading the truck, and when we were done, McGilvery shook my hand and said to me, "Take good care of all of that: you have an entire life."[15]

The shipment contained 178 bankers' boxes, 31 oversize boxes or flats, and 48 poster tubes, all filled to capacity. Many of the boxes were indexed on the inventory list by some kind of material category (films, books from Moorman's library, tape recordings) or by some kind of subject classification (avant-garde festivals, grant applications). The rest were more ominously labeled "Unsorted" or "Miscellaneous." The initial era of my work on the Moorman archive was spent sitting in a chair in the center of my office opening the boxes and

Charlotte Moorman's doll collection, 62 Pearl Street, New York City, 1990. Photograph courtesy of Christian Xatrec.

piece by piece distributing items into open boxes that covered the floor around me like a nest of open-mouthed baby birds. The table surfaces and the shelves that stretched the length of one wall were also demarcated into subject piles, so that at any given time there were perhaps thirty or so categories at play.

Since at that time I didn't know much about Moorman and there wasn't a lot written about her to help, I was immersed in a giant puzzle. What was one to make of a torn chit of paper upon which she wrote notes about sharks (*Great*, *Mako*, *Tiger* . . .) or a miniature log of events of the 1979 Iranian revolution as she watched it transpire on TV? Sometimes the meaning of such ambiguous things would be revealed by later encounters with other items in the archive. For example, fairly early on in the unpacking I came across a wad of taped-together fragments of cardboard packaging of Danish baby formula and Wasa bread upon which were written the pronunciation-keyed Danish instructions for how to use Tampax tampons. Later I noticed in her annotated score of Cage's *26'1.1499" for a String Player* that she had taped a piece of paper of Italian Tampax instructions onto a page, and I realized that reciting these instructions was sometimes part of her performances of the piece. The more I got to know Moorman, the more I became delighted by these idiosyncratic bits of ephemera, even if I couldn't make sense of them.

The archive includes (among other things): correspondence, manuscript music and performance scores, grant applications, medical records, financial records, souvenir objects, small art objects/sculptures, mail art, banners, paintings and prints, performance props and remnants, astrological charts, phone call logs, passports and other official documents, magazines, news clippings, legal documents, family heirlooms, and juvenilia.

Among the currently quantified parts of the collection are 2,100 printed books and pamphlets, several hundred periodical issues, 120 vinyl LPs, 500 printed music scores, 800 oversize posters, 31 motion picture films, 393 audiotape recordings

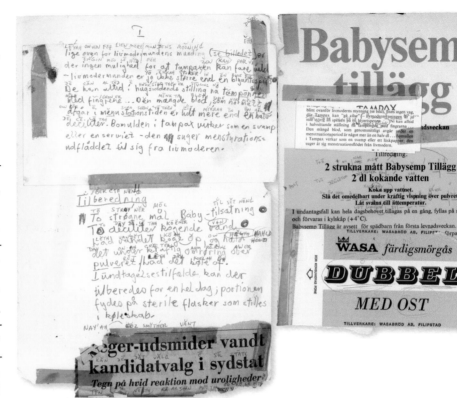

(including eleven years of Moorman's incoming answering machine messages), 90 videotape recordings (both original and commercial), 24,000 photographs, and printed documentation (flyers, handbills, etc.) for about 2,100 events (concerts, etc.).

It provides incredibly rich documentation of the fifteen annual avant-garde festivals, including artists' proposals and correspondence with Moorman about their works, as well as her own notes on those pieces and the space, equipment, and power requirements they demanded. It also documents Moorman's dogged courting of the civic and corporate sponsors of the festivals and her endearing charm when doing so.

When did Moorman start conceiving of her collection as an archive? In the 1979 letter shown here she provides her fullest written description of it. The letter to the Rockefeller Foundation was written after her mastectomy in an attempt to secure funds to process the archive. Among other things, she claims to have started the archive in 1963, the year of the first avant-garde festival; she claims it weighs twenty thousand pounds, and, interestingly, she says that

Charlotte Moorman's collage with instructions for tampon use (in Danish), undated. Courtesy of Charlotte Moorman Archive, Charles Deering McCormick Library of Special Collections, Northwestern University Library.

new address: 62 Pearl Street, 5th Floor
New York City, N.Y. 10004

September 9, 1979

Howard Klein
Director, Arts Program
Rockefeller Foundation
1133 Sixth Avenue
New York City, N.Y. 10036

Dear Howard,

Nam June Paik suggested I write you regarding the organization of the Avant Garde Archive that I started in 1963. He has titled it "Art as Information & Information as Art" which is most appropriate.

When the history of the art of the 1960's and the 70's is finally written, my Archive of thousands of brochures, newspaper clippings, letters, post cards, hundreds of books, articles, drawings, photos, proposals, and art works from over 1000 well-known and unknown artists will emerge as a most valuable source of information and research.

My recent mastectomy surgery at Memorial Sloan Kettering Hospital has made me realize the urgency to get things in order with my Archive. I know where most everything is, even Frank occasionally gets lost in the 20,000 pounds of paper weight. The Archive must be properly catalogued, alphabetized, cross referenced, etc. so that students, artists, librarians, critics, and historians can have efficient access to it. Eventually, I hope to donate the completed project to a University, Museum, or Library.

Such a project will take time. I would like to apply for a three-four year grant to cover our rent and real estate tax of $7,000. per year. We would pay our monthly food, telephone, electricity, gas, art expenses, and my cancer treatments through performances and lectures. Of course, we will present our Annual Avant Garde Festival of New York as soon as I gain the strength — but the Festival is a labor of love not a source of income.

Frank and I want you to have one of the thirty documented sets of posters of all 14 Festivals (our 46th Street apartment flood destroyed all others); we hope you will want them in your library.

We would be honored if you could come visit our loft to see first hand what organizing our "Information as Art & Art as Information" Archive will require and how important it will be once it is completed.

Our love to Pat.

Love,
Charlotte

Letter from Charlotte Moorman to the Rockefeller Foundation requesting support of the Avant Garde Festival Archive, September 9, 1979, on letterhead designed by Jim McWilliams. Courtesy of Charlotte Moorman Archive, Charles Deering McCormick Library of Special Collections, Northwestern University Library.

Nam June Paik has titled the archive "Art as Information & Information as Art," thereby defining its collective entity as a work of art. Moorman writes in the letter that the title is "most appropriate."

Unlike the collections of Jean Brown or Hanns Sohm,[16] who also collected performance documents and relics of Fluxus and contemporary artists, Moorman's archive has an exact center, and that is Charlotte Moorman. Almost everything within it was either created by her, given to her by friends and fellow artists, or laboriously gathered and saved by her. She has some personal connection with every piece of it. Unlike Moorman, neither Brown nor Sohm were artists, and their collections were obtained by purchase and solicitation. Neither of their collections documents their own lives. Moorman's archive, on the other hand, documents her own life in uncanny, even disturbing, spectrographic completeness.

Though she claims to have begun the archive in 1963, Moorman had been an assiduous saver of things since her childhood, and the archive contains, for example, many homework essays she wrote as a child in grade school. This is not a particularly odd thing, but the archive does contain many examples of Moorman going well beyond a normal horizon of self-documentation. For example, she made an audio recording of the wedding ceremony of her first brief marriage to Thomas Coleman. Today, videotaping one's wedding is commonplace, but in 1958 a recording like this was unusual. She also made crude drawings of some of the wedding gifts she received, a habit that recurred later in her life when she would make childlike sketches of her dolls and of jewelry she saw for sale on television's Home Shopping Network.

In her many years of event diaries she would record prosaic facts that most people would not bother to mention: that she washed her hair, that she ate fish sticks for dinner, that she watched TV from eleven to four o'clock, giving these trifles the same graphic weight as the fact that she was photographed by Andy Warhol for an *Esquire* magazine article. She lists every ride she rode on a 1976 visit to Disneyland. She lists the names of pornographic videos she watched with Frank, as well as the operas they saw at the Met. She doesn't seem to elevate or diminish the importance of what her life contained and encountered. High and low and life and art are as if they are all the same air she breathed. From another angle one sees this in the way she would often perform on the *TV Cello*, chatting casually with audience as if the real or invisible plinth she performed upon were nothing.

Not only did she rerecord and save over ten years of answering machine messages, but she would sometimes create written

indices to these noting where on a tape a particular person's message might be found. Part of this was practical. The logistics of running the festivals were complicated, and the telephone was a tool of central importance. But archiving the calls for years afterward is unusual.

In a moving valedictory letter that Nam June Paik sent to *New York Times* writer Grace Glueck on the day that Moorman died, he wrote that when he first met Moorman in 1964, she told him she did not think she would have a long life and that, as he put it in his letter, "Everything must be done presto, presto."[17] Did this supposed belief in her own brevity encourage Moorman's lupine hunger for intensity, activity, and self-documentation?

She certainly loved to be dramatic. Beyond the overt drama of her concert performances, she liked to amplify the theater of her daily life. The archive has multilevel documentation including photographs and an audio recording of a 1979 comic / heroic trip Moorman made to visit Frank, who had been hospitalized with an eye injury.[18] Moorman herself was in another hospital at the time for a more serious problem, having just undergone her mastectomy days

earlier. After repeatedly insisting to her doctor and the hospital's staff that she be unhooked from her tubes and allowed to visit Frank, they finally relented. Ono and Lennon arranged for a limousine to take Moorman and her party across town to Frank's hospital for the surprise visit. On the recording one can hear a hospital staff member cannily remarking on the fact that Charlotte had refused to switch out of her hospital gown into regular street clothes—it would have diminished the dramatic effect had she done so.

Several of the people who knew Moorman observed that Moorman could conquer her fear and distress if she knew (or believed) that what she was doing was a performance.[19] She could conquer her fear of heights while performing *Sky Kiss*. She helped deal with her fear of death and disease by having many of her operations filmed. She even had the euthanization of her and Frank's dog Victor photographed.[20] Performing helped her cope with life, and saving documentation of those performances of life and of art was of key importance to Moorman. In fact, the title of this essay is taken from Moorman's last, deathbed words to Frank: "Don't throw anything out."[21]

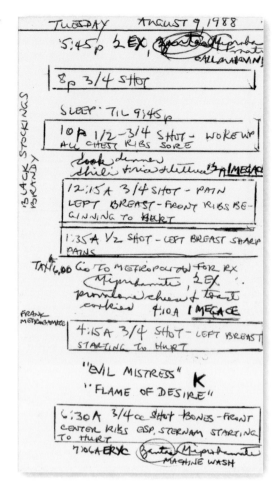

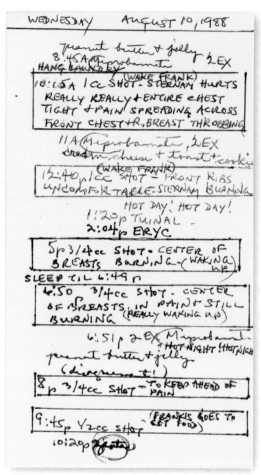

In 1986 a significant sea change occurred in Moorman's life. She stopped keeping event diaries and instead started keeping what I decided to call "pain diaries." Mostly written on the backs of envelopes, but sometimes paper towels and other scraps, they are chronological logs of the hours of her mostly homebound days, which for the most part lacked the appointments and events of her formerly active life. They note injection times of morphine and other drugs. They list particularly painful spots in her body and other immediate symptoms. They note what she watched on television and other small occasions. They record the five years until her death in 1991 in a way that's modest and disposable on the surface (writing on the backs of random, grubby envelopes) and epically poignant in their cumulative effect. Objectifying and documenting her disease was as crucial to Moorman as the documentation of her performances of Cage.

"Don't throw anything out" is not only applicable to Moorman's zealous archiving but indicative as well of her attitude toward her festivals, where she ignored the advice of friends such as Dick Higgins to reduce their scale and to allow only the "best" artists to perform. She did not edit down, she promoted. Her archive is a messy but transparent monument to her ebullient bounty.

Peter Moore. Charlotte Moorman and Frank Pileggi on the roof outside their loft, 62 Pearl Street, New York, July 15, 1984. Photograph © Barbara Moore/Licensed by VAGA, NY.

Notes

Many thanks to Joan Rothfuss, Barbara Moore, Andrew Gurian, and Christian Xatrec for their generous help with this essay. Thanks to my colleagues in the Charles Deering McCormick Library of Special Collections and to D.J. Hoek, for their support, and to the Northwestern University Library and the Alice Kaplan Institute for the Humanities for giving me research leave to work with Moorman's archive. Unpublished transcripts cited in the following notes are mostly from the Charlotte Moorman Archive, hereafter cited as CMA. The unpublished Rothfuss interview transcripts are in the Joan Rothfuss *Topless Cellist* Archive at the Charles Deering McCormick Library of Special Collections, Northwestern University Library, and will soon be available to the public.

1. Barbara Moore, conversation with author, New York City, November 14, 2013.

2. Ibid.

3. Evidence of Moorman's tardiness abounds throughout the archive. The story of her lateness to Mayor Dinkins's 1988 ceremony is told in an unpublished transcript of an interview between Joan Rothfuss and Christian Xatrec conducted in New York City on November 14, 2007, CMA.

4. The performance took place on July 28, 1966, at the Düsseldorf Art Academy. Along with Moorman and Nam June Paik, the performers included Joseph Beuys, then a faculty member of the school. Joan Rothfuss, *Topless Cellist: The Improbable Life of Charlotte Moorman* (Cambridge, Mass.: MIT Press, 2014), 158.

5. Rothfuss, *Topless Cellist*, 307.

6. Moorman's friend the filmmaker Andrew Gurian said, "She would work until she fell asleep, with a pen in her hand." Andrew Gurian, interview by Joan Rothfuss, New York City, November 18, 2007, unpublished transcript, CMA.

7. Barbara Moore and Andrew Gurian, interview by Joan Rothfuss, November 9, 2007, unpublished transcript, CMA.

8. *Contemporary Art, Including Property from the Charlotte Moorman Estate* [London: Sotheby's, 1993]. The sale included works by Ay-O, Joe Jones, Joseph Beuys, Nam June Paik, Yoko Ono, Geoffrey Hendricks, Takehisa Kosugi, Ben Vautier, a Christo/Paik collaboration, and by Moorman herself.

9. The twine was replaced under the supervision of Barbara Moore, and the piece was sold without notice of its altered state. This fact was discovered by the buyer, and a financial compensation took place. The story is told in the unpublished transcript of an interview between Andrew Gurian and Joan Rothfuss from May 2, 2005, CMA.

10. Rothfuss details the Beuys story in *Topless Cellist*, 418n3.

11. Pileggi suffered from very high blood pressure.

Barbara Moore believes the stress of the failed auction was a direct cause of Pileggi's death. Barbara Moore, telephone conversation with author, May 16, 2014.

12. Paik's figurines now are part of the Paik Archive at the Smithsonian Museum of American Art. Some of Moorman's dolls were kept by Pileggi relatives, but most were given away to thrift shops.

13. Moore hired a few assistants to help clear out the loft. Their task was worsened by the fact that it was a hot summer and the place had no air-conditioning or running water, but the chaos of Moorman's belongings was the worst part of the labor. For example, one of the jewels of the archive, Moorman's annotated score of John Cage's *26'1.1499" for a String Player*, was discovered buried at the bottom of a sloping corner heap that nearly reached the ceiling. Barbara Moore and Pileggi estate coadminstrator Andrew Gurian, conversation with the author, New York City, November 14, 2013.

14. Chief among these supporters were Don Roberts, former head of the Northwestern Music Library, and David Bishop, former university librarian.

15. Author's possibly flawed but in spirit correct memory.

16. The Jean Brown Archive is now located at the Getty Research Institute; the Hanns Sohm Archive now resides at the Staatsgalerie Stuttgart.

17. Nam June Paik to Grace Glueck, November 8, 1991, Nam June Paik Archives, Smithsonian Museum of American Art.

18. He poked his eye on the twig of a get-well bouquet that had been sent to Moorman by Yoko Ono and John Lennon. Unpublished interview between Joan Rothfuss and Andor Orand. Joan Rothfuss *Topless Cellist* Archive, Charles Deering McCormick Library of Special Collections, Northwestern University Library.

19. For some examples of this, see Rothfuss, *Topless Cellist*, 281, 337.

20. In fact, in a rather extreme example of attempted archiving, Moorman took Victor's body to a taxidermist to be stuffed, but, lacking the money to pay for the work, had to leave the body there.

21. Rothfuss, *Topless Cellist*, 355.

Index

Page numbers in **bold** refer to illustrations.

Adorno, Olga, **60**, 67
Andersen, Eric, 85
Annual New York Avant Garde Festival, 11–12, 13, 17n17, 63–89, 109, 114–15, 120, 135–36, 191; chronological chart, 72; posters, 92–93, **93–107**
  1st, 19, 63, 65–67, **94**
  2nd, 10, 23, 58n39, **60**, 63, 67–68, **95**, 115, 136, 169
  3rd, 49, 63, **68–71**, 69–72, **96**, 115, **117–18**, 141–42, 150n29
  4th, xi, **12**, 58n39, **72–74**, **92**, **97**, 115, **142**, 143, **144**, 145
  5th, **75**, **98**, **109**
  6th, 73, **76–78**, 79, **98**, 124, 161
  7th, 89, **98**, 147
  8th, 9, 12, 15, **79–80**, 92–93, **99**
  9th, **viii–ix**, **xii**, **81**, **100**
  10th, **82–83**, **101**, 119, **120**
  11th, **x**, **102**
  12th, **xiii**, **84**, 85, 93, **103**
  13th, 93, **104**
  14th, 93, **105**
  15th, 85, **106**, 188
Ashley, Robert, 19–21, 23
avant-garde revolution of 1950s, 19–20, 22, 23
Ay-O, **viii**, **x**, xi, 9, 67–68, 188; *Rainbow Environment no. 11*, **87**; *Statue in Rainbow*, **75**

Bach, Johann Sebastian, 131, 169–70
Bapat, Shridhar, **x**
Barab, Seymour, 23, 27n18
baroque art, 128–31
Bauer, Lissa, 150n38
Behrman, David, **60**, 63, 67
Berke, Joseph, 45
Bernini, Gian Lorenzo, 128–29, 175
Beuys, Joseph, vii, 10, 11, 77, 78, 135, **136**, 140, 143–47, **148**, 151nn50–51, 171, 195n4; *I Like America and America Likes Me*, 145, **147–48**; *Infiltration Homogen for Cello* (and/or *Grand Piano*), ix, 15, 143–47 (**144–46**), 189

Birnbaum, Dara, xi
Bishop, David, 195n14
Block, René, 139, 148, 149n19
Block, Ursula, 148
Blocker, Jane, 50
"bombshell" term, 157–58
Boston, Bernie: *Flower Power*, 17n20
Bourdon, David, 54
Bowers, Faubion, 10, 169
Brahms, Johannes, 3, 52, 57
Brecht, George, 63, 68, 88
Breer, Robert, **60**, 67
Britten, Benjamin, 21
Brock, Bazon, 135, **136**, 141, 171
Brook, Peter, 172
Brouwn, Stanley, 140
Brown, Earle, vii, 19, **20**, 23–24, 63; *Music for Cello and Piano*, **18**, 22–23; *November 1952*, **24–25**; *Synergy*, 23–24
Brown, Jean, 192
Brown, Norman O., 172, 181n15
Brown, Robert Delford, **60**, 67–68
Brown, Trisha: *Roof Piece*, 91n35
Buchanan, Mark, 87
Bussotti, Sylvano, 20–21
Byrd, Joseph, 154

Cage, John, vii, xi, 9–10, 19–20, 38n16, 42, 61–62, 65, 85, 90n13; Moorman and, 29, 33, 37, 39n21, 66, 173; Northwestern collection, 190; Paik and, 173
  WORKS: *59½" for a String Player*, 38n21; *Hymns and Variations*, 27n13; *Music for Carillon*, 30, 38n7; *Theater Piece*, 17n19, **69**; *34'46.776"*, 66; *26'1.1499" for a String Player*, viii–ix, 3, 5, 10, 13, 15, 22, **28**, 29–37 (**29–36**), 65–67, 121n14, 137, 139, **152**, 191, 195n13; *Work in Progress*, **82**; *0'00"*, 37
Carnap, Rudolf, 156
Carson, Johnny, 10, **32**, 179
Cavarero, Adriana, 25–26
Cédille qui sourit, 88
cello: history and qualities, 153–54, 155–56, 166n15; Moorman's cellolike objects, 156–60, 165, 170

Center for Advanced Visual Studies (CAVS), 161
Chiari, Giuseppe, vii, 24, 63; *Per Arco*, 5, **14**, 15, 23, 139
Chicago, Judy, 43–44, **44**
Christo: with Jeanne-Claude, *Valley Curtain*, 85; with Nam June Paik, *Wrapped Television*, 188, 195n9
Clarke, Shirley, vii; *Video Ferris Wheel*, 79, **80**
Coleman, Ornette, **20**, 65, 186
Coleman, Thomas, 192
collage, 115, 116, 119; *dé-collage*, 141–42; Moorman and, **191**
composer-audience relationship, xii
composer-performer relationship, 20–21, 23–26; Cage and, 29–30, 33, 37
Corner, Philip, vii, **71**, 114, 186; *Complements 1*, **8**; *New Piece* (aka *Message Prelude*), **75**
Correggio, Antonio da: *Assumption of the Virgin*, **128**, 133n24
Creti, Donato: *Moon*, **130**
Crovetto, Juan, **x**, **187**
Cunningham, Merce, 27n16, 33, 85

Dada, 54, 141, 143
Delgado, Alexis, 41
Descartes, René, 156
Doll, Romilla, 178
Douglas, Mike, 15
Duchamp, Marcel, 172
Dunn, Robert, 62
Düsseldorf Art Academy, 11, 143, 145, 147, 150n40, 195n4
Dworkin, Andrea, 48

Eastman, Julius, 37
Eisenhauer, Letty, 67
Eros and Thanatos, 170–71, 178, 179–80, 182n55, 183n58
Erró, **50**, 173
Experiments in Art and Technology (EAT), 78–79
extension concept, 155–56, 160, 163, 165

Feldman, Morton, vii, 19–26 (**20**), 27n11, 63; *Intersections* series, 22–23; *Ixion*, 27n16; *Piano Piece*, 26n6; *Projections* series, 21–23 (**22**)
feminism and women's movement, x, 42–48, 50, 55, 57n6, 113–14, 120, 153, 160
Ffarrabas, Nye (Bici Forbes Hendricks), 79
Filliou, Robert, 88–89, 91n42
fire drakes, **130**
First National Church of the Exquisite Panic, 67
Fluxus, 4, 9–10, 23, 37, 58n39, 63, 68, 73, 135, 141, 190; German festival, 136; sexism in, 39n27, 50
Forti, Simone, vii, 61, 62, 154; *Five Dance Constructions*, 63
Foss, Lucas, 25
Freud, Sigmund, 170, 172, 179, 183n58
Fried, Si, **x**
Friedan, Betty, 172

Gallina, Gino, 51, 54, 57
Gann, Kyle, 63
Garbo, Greta, 171
Gerhard, Jane E., 44
Gibbard, Les, **31**
Ginsberg, Allen, **60**, 67–68
Gitlin, Todd, 172
Godard, Jean-Luc, 172
Goldring, Elizabeth, 163, 167n91
Goldstein, Malcolm, 110, 115
Goodman, Paul, 172
Gosewitz, Ludwig, 141, 150n38
Gottlieb, Saul, 176
Grabill, Vin, 162–63, 167n46
Graves, Gloria, **60**, 67
Green, Leslie, 160
Grey, Camille, **44**
Grier, James, 31
Gronemeyer, Gisela, 41, 48
Gruen, John, 54
Gurian, Andrew, 41, 195n6

Haar, Thomas, **4**
Hales, Peter, 87
Halprin, Anna, 91n35
Hansen, Al, 77, 90n13, 150n24, 175; *Pigeons Eating Art*, **ix**
Happening & Fluxus exhibition, 11, 179
Happenings, Fluxus, Pop Art, Nouveau Réalisme (Becker and Vostell), 140
Harlow, Jean, 157
Harris, Gary, **71**
Heckman, Don, **109**
Hendricks, Geoffrey, vii, 89, 175–76; *Flux Divorce*, 79; *Ring Piece*, 9, **79**, 85

Hendricks, Jon, 175–77
Higgins, Dick, vii, 9–10, 61, 67–68, **71**, 85, 90n13, 150n28, 194; Northwestern archive, 190
Higgins, Hannah and Jessica, 190
Höch, Hannah, 143
Huddleston, Robert S., 130
Hudson, James R., 62
Huelsenbeck, Richard, 141, 150n24

Ichiyanagi, Toshi, vii, 62, 63, 90n9, 154
Immendorff, Jörg, 11, 143, 147–48, 186; and Chris Reinecke, 144, 147

Järling, Rolf, **136**, 139
Jarman, Joseph, 38n16
Jennings, Terry, 63, 90n9
Johnson, Ray, 89; *Disco Duck for Shelley Duvall Fan Club*, **88**
Johnston, Jill, 176
Jones, Amelia, 50
Jones, Joe, 78
Judson Dance Theater, 62, 63, 113, 119

Kabalevsky, Dmitry, 154
Kaprow, Allan, vii, 19, 49, **60**, 67–68, 89, 91n45; *Barreling*, 77; *Push and Pull*, 49, 58n31, 69, 71, 109; *Towers*, 11
Keith, Shirley, 148
Kennedy, John F., 140
Kennedy, Robert F., 79
Kesey, Ken, 87
King, Kenneth, **71**
King, Martin Luther, Jr., 79, 181n35
Kinnell, Galway: "The Cellist," 153–56, 158, 160, 165
Kirby, Michael, 67
Klophaus, Ute, 149n1
Klüver, Billy, 67
Knowles, Alison, vii, xi, 9–10, 48, 61, 91n45; *Bean Garden*, 85; *Identical Lunch*, 11; *Serenade for Alison*, 173
Knowlton, Ken: and A. Michael Noll, 78
Kobayashi, Kenji, 62, 90n9, 154
Kohlhöfer, Christof, 144
Kostelanetz, Richard, 61
Kosugi, Takehisa, vii, **71**, **144**, 145; *Chamber Music* ("Anima 2"), ix, 5, **6**; *Piano '66*, **74**
Kramer, Lawrence, 37
Kristeva, Julia, 179
Kroll, Jack, 54–55
Kubera, Joseph, 27n16
Kuemmerle, Judith, **71**
Kurchin, Al, **71**

LaBelle, Brandon, 37
Lacan, Jacques, 170
LaFaro, Scott, 90n9
Lawrence, Noel, 177–78
Leavitt, Leon, 79
Lebel, Jean-Jacques, 109, 172–73
Lebrecht, Norman, 181n25
Leibniz, Gottfried Wilhelm, 156
Lennon, John, 17n24, 89, 103, 186, 193, 195n18; *Baby Grand Guitar*, 79, **80**
Levine, Les: *Photon Two*, **77**
Lewis, Jerry, 32
Lindsay, John, 58n20, 89, 115
Lippard, Lucy, 50
Lucier, Alvin, 67

Maciunas, George, 39n27, 63, 90n13, 139; opposition to Moorman's festivals, 9, 50, 58n39, 68, 85
Mac Low, Jackson, 19, **60**, 62, 67, 90n13; *The Pronouns*, **68**
Mahmood, Saba, 55, 57
mail art, 89, 91n43, 147
Malabou, Catherine, 179–80, 182–83nn55–56
Mandillo, Michael, 51
Man Ray, 172
Marcuse, Herbert, 172, 181n15
Marzorati, Gerald, 49
Massenet, Jules, 51
Mathews, Max, 52, 59n53, 78
Maxfield, Richard, **62**, 62–64, 90n9, 154
Mayazumi, Toshiro, 62
Maylone, R. Russell, 189–90
McDarrah, Fred, 12, 180n1
McGilvery, Laurence, 190
McPherson, Bruce, 48, 58n42
McWilliams, Jim, vii, **x**, 10, 132n6, 177; *American Picnic*, **12**; *A Balloon Dance for Children*, 123; *Body Color Kiss*, 124, 132n8; *Candy*, 124; *Ice Music*, 124, 159–60, **161**, 166n30; *The Intravenous Feeding of Charlotte Moorman*, **7**; Moorman's letterhead, **192**; posters, **56**, 92–93, **97–107**; *Sky Kiss*, ix, xiii, 11, **78**, **122**, 123–31 (**124**, **126–27**, **131**), 161–62, **163**; *Street Kiss*, 124, 132n8
Medium Is the Message (documentary), 132n12, 132n14, 161
Monk, Meredith, **68**, **71**, 110
Moore, Barbara, 41, 185; as executor, 188–90, 195n13
Moore, Carman, 54, 57

Moore, Peter, xi, xiii, 10, 12–13, 180n1, 185, 188; *Doubletakes*, 67; photographs, **viii–xiii, 5–7, 9–10, 13, 40, 47, 49, 60, 66, 68–75, 77, 79–84, 86, 108–9, 111, 144, 152, 184, 189, 195**

Moore, Robin and Rebecca, **81**

Moorman, Charlotte: apartments, **184**, 185–89 (**186–87, 189**); archive, vii–x, 12, 185–94 (**186–87, 191–92**); background and training, ix, 3, 4–5, 9, 15, 41, 53, 137, 139, 154; bomb cellos, 3, 13, 15, 16n2, 17n19, 156–58 (**157**), **170**; cultural critiques, 13, 15, 46, 139–40, 148; doll collection, 189, **190**, 192, 195n12; "electric bikini," 51, **52**, 57, 59n49; femininity and sexuality, x, 12, 33, 41–42, 44, 46, 48–49, 51–55, 113, 137, 144, 147, 157–58, 169–80; festival planning, viii, x–xiii, 11–12, 15, 20, 50, 63–68, 71–73, **77**, 78–79, 85, 87–89, 92–93, 110, 135–36, 141, 154–55, 186, 191, 193, 194; Germany and, **134**, 135–48, 150n40; health problems and death, 5, 9, 41, 79, 85, 126, 160, 162–63, 166n36, 167n48, 188, 193–94; ice cello, 159–60, **161**; indecency arrest and trial, 4, 10, 26, 45–46, 51–57, 57n6, 174–75, 180; marginalization, x, xiii, 4, 48, 50, 55, 113; "pain diaries," **194**; paper cellos, **159**, 159–60; performance style, 115, 125, 126, 130–31, 139, 142–43, 155–56, 171; self-image, viii, 45–46, 173–75, 180; stage setups, **29**, 31–32, 38n13; tardiness, 115, 125, 185, 186, 195n3; television appearances, 10, 15, 32, 156, 179; "topless cellist" nickname, 4 , 10, 15, 41, 45; *TV Glasses*, **vi, 9**; work habits, 186, 195n6

ILLUSTRATIONS: **ii, vi, x–xiii, 4–11, 13–14, 20, 28, 30–32, 36, 40–42, 46–47, 49, 52–53, 56, 60, 71, 78, 83, 109, 122, 124, 126–27, 131, 136, 142, 144, 148, 152, 155, 157–58, 161–64, 168, 170–71, 174, 178, 185, 189, 193, 195**

PERFORMANCES: *Bag Piece*, 144; *Candy*, 124; *Cello Sonata*, 161–62, **162**; *Chamber Music*, ix, 5, **6**; *Chinatown*, 142; *Complements 1*, **8**; *Concerto for TV*

Cello and Videotapes, **vi**, viii, ix, 4, **9**, 161, 192; *Cut Piece*, ix, 5, **10**, 11, 15, 17n11, **168**, 175; *Guadalcanal Requiem (aka Peace Sonata)*, **13**, 13–14, 146; *Ice Music*, 124, 159–60, **161**; *Infiltration Homogen for Cello*, ix, 15, 143, **144–46**, 151n48; *Lullaby for Karl May*, 148; *Manopsychotic Ballet (Part 2)*, **178**, 178–79; *Morning Glory*, **142**, 143, 145; *Music Is a Mass Transit Too—So Is the Bra*, **83**; *One for Violin Solo*, **176–77**; *Opera Sextronique*, 4, **5**, 10, 15, 26, **42**, 45–46, **46–47**, 50–57 (**52–53, 56**), 59n73, 147, 156–57, **170**, 174; *Originale*, 10–11, 48, **49, 60**, 67, 136, 169–72, 173, 180n1; *Per Arco*, 5, **14**, 15, 23, 139; *Projection 1*, 21–23, 25; *Robot Opera*, 140, 149n21; *Sky Kiss*, ix, xiii, 11, **78, 122**, 123–31 (**124, 126–27, 131**), 161–62, **163**, 193; *Sonata No. 1 for Adults Only (aka Pop Sonata)*, **40**, 169–70, 172; *Synergy*, 23, 25, 27n21; *Tele Paik Tele Moorman*, **158**; *TV Bed*, 11; *TV Bra for Living Sculpture*, ix, 4, 15, 42, 162–63, **164**, **189**; *26'1.1499" for a String Player*, viii–ix, 3, 5, 10, 13, 15, 28–37 (**28–32**), 38n11, 39n21, 65–67, 121n14, 137, 139, 142, **152**, 156, 191; *Variations on a Theme by Saint-Saëns*, 48, **171**, 173, 179; *Vexations*, 143, 173, **174**

WRITINGS AND ARTWORKS: *An Artist in the Courtroom* (with Nam June Paik and Frank Pileggi), 57, 174–75, 181n26, 181n29; *Bomb Cellos*, **157**; *Neon Cello*, **vi**; *Two Bomb Cellos*, **2**; wire hanger cello, 186

Morris, Robert, 61, 63, 151n51; *Site*, 173; *Waterman Switch*, 181n21

Moses, Robert, 90n2

Most, Mica, 178

Muehl, Otto: *Manopsychotic Ballet (Part 2)*, **178**, 178–79

Mumma, Gordon, 19, 21, 22–23

Museum of Contemporary Art (MCA), 3, 4

naked female in art, 50–51, 54–55

Native Americans: German fascination with, 147–48

Neel, Alice: *Woman Playing Cello*, **8**

network theory, 87–89

Neuhaus, Max, vii, xi, **60**, 67, 115

Neumann, Peter, 78

Neville, Phoebe, **71**

Niese, Henry, **124**

9 Evenings: Theater and Engineering, 79

Nitsch, Hermann, 179, 182n51

Nussbaum, Martha, 160

Oldenburg, Claes, 58n20

O'Neil, Paul, 172, 174

Ono, Yoko, xi, 9–10, 17n24, 19, 37, 79, 110, 154, 195n18; deportation threat, 89; financial support for Moorman, 85, 91n36, 186, 193; SoHo loft, 61–63 (**62**)
WORKS: *Bag Piece*, 144; *Cut Piece*, ix, 5, **10**, 11, 15, 17n11, **168**, 175; *Shadow Painting*, 11

Ordover, Jerald, 45

Ortiz, Raphael Montañez, 175–77, 182nn41–42

Paik, Nam June, vii, 17n19, 20, **60**, 67, **69, 71, 109**, 193; collaborations with Moorman, viii, ix, 3, 4, 9–11, 13, 15, 29–30, **30**, 31, 33, **36**, 37, 48, 113, 123, **146, 152**, 159, 171–73; eroticism and violence in, 173; figurines collection, 189, 195n12; in Germany, 135–37 (**136**), 140–41, 143–44, 173; Guggenheim retrospective, 162–63; robot, **66**, 136, **138**, 140; Rosler on, 42
WORKS: *Etude for Piano*, 173; *Guadalcanal Requiem*, **13**, 13–14, 146–47; *Music Is a Mass Transit Too*, **83**; *One for Violin Solo*, 173, **176**; *Opera Sextronique*, 4, **5**, 10, 15, 26, 45, 51–53, 147, 156–57, **170**, 173–74; *Robot Opera*, **66**, **138**, 140, 149n21; *A Room for Charlotte Moorman*, 41, **43**; *Serenade for Allison*, 173; *Sonata No. 1 for Adults Only*, **40**, 169–70, 172; *Tele Paik Tele Moorman*, **158**; *A Tribute to John Cage*, **156**; *TV Bed*, 11; *TV Bra*, ix, 4, 15, 42, 162–63, **164, 189**; *TV Cello*, viii, ix, 4, **9**, 161; *Variations on a Theme by Saint-Saëns*, 48, 171–72; *Violin to Be Dragged on the Street*, **84**, 85; *Wrapped Television* (with Christo), 188

Peters, Susan, 125

Pfisterer, Verena, 144
Phillips, Liz: *Tuned Electric Spaghetti*, **81**
Picard, Lil, **x**, 175, 176
Piekut, Benjamin, viii, 19, 33, 156
Piene, Otto, vii, 10, 125–26, **126**, 128, 130, 131, 161–62; Sky Art, 125–26, 128, 162 WORKS: *Berlin Star*, 161–62, 165; *Flying Girl Sculpture*, 125, 132nn14–15, 161; *Grand Rapids Carousel*, xi; *Red Rapid Growth*, 79
Pierce, John, 78
Pietkiewicz, Veronika, **75**
Pileggi, Frank, 109, 160, 162, 163, 179, 185–86, 188–89, 192–93, **193**, 195n11, 195n18, **195**
Planck, Max, 156, 160
Polke, Sigmar, 140
Pollock, Jackson, 113
pop art, 116, 136–37, 139, 142–43
Pound, Ezra, 115
Presley, Elvis, 116
Proust, Marcel, 115

Rahn, Eckart, **136**, 171
Rainer, Yvonne, 63, 110; *Three Satie Spoons*, **70**; *Waterman Switch*, 181
realization (of compositions), 20–21, 27n10, 30
Reich, Wilhelm, 172
Reilly, Maura, 113
Reisman, Marty, **x**
Richter, Gerhard, 140
Riley, Terry, 90n9
Roberts, Don, 195n14
Robinson, Julia, 63
Rosenberg, Karin, 3
Rosenberger, Ernst, 52–54
Rosler, Martha, 42
Roth, Dieter, 123; *Lullaby for Karl May*, 148
Rothfuss, Joan, ix, 4, 16, 42, 45, 50, 57n6, 58n26, 71, 154, 173, 174–75, 180, 181n29, 182n51
Roth v. United States, 51, 52
Rühm, Gerhard, 150n38
Rzewski, Frederic, **20**, 63

Sargeant, Winthrop, 66
Satie, Erik: *Vexations*, 143, 173, **174**
Schapiro, Miriam, 44
Schmit, Tomas, 58n20, 135, **136**, 171
Schneemann, Carolee, vii, 10, 12, 37, 39n27, 44–46, 48–50, **50**, 58n29, 58n42, **109**, 169, 177, 181n20; interview, x, 114–20 WORKS: *Eye Body*, 50, 54, 113, 116, 173; *Fur Wheel*, 112, **113**, 118; *Fuses*, 116; *Meat Joy*, 113, 173; *Nightcrawlers II*, 109; *Noise Bodies*, 12, 69, **108**, 109, **110–12**, 113, **114**, 115–20 (**117–18**), 121n7; *Rainbow Blaze*, 109, 121n3; *Site*, 173; *Trackings (Up to and Including Her Limits)*, 12, 109–10, 119, **120**
Schneider, Rebecca, 50
Schwitters, Kurt, 141
Seaman, Norman, 71, 154
Servais, Adrien-François, 153
Seuss, Dr., 77
Shalleck, Milton, 51, 53, 55, 58n45
Shiomi, Mieko, 161, **162**
Sohm, Hanns, 192
SoHo (TriBeCa), 61–63, 85, 87, 90nn1–2, 90n13, 91n35
Soyer, David, 23
Spinoza, Benedict, 156
Stein, Gertrude, and Alice B. Toklas, 25–26
Steiner, Rochelle: *Autumn Piece*, **81**
Stern, Fred, 125
Stiles, Kristine, 50
Stockhausen, Karlheinz, 65; *Originale*, 10–11, 48–49, **60**, 67–68, 115, 136, 169–71
Strider, Marjorie, 67
Stumpfl, Herbert, 178
Stüttge, Johannes, 143
Summers, Elaine, 61, 110
Sun Ra, 77

Tenney, James, vii, 63, 67, **71**, 110, **114**, 114–19 (**117–18**)
Toche, Jean, 175, 177; *Carcan*, 78
Topless Cellist (Weinberg and Paik), 37
Torelli, Giacomo, **129**
Tudor, David, 19, 20–21, 26n6, 27n16, 62, 154; Cage and, 30, 33, 38n9, 63, 66–67
Turetzky, Bertram, 38n21
24 Hours (24 Stunden), 11, 15, 135, **136–37**, 139–40, 149n1, 150n40, 171

Ursprung, Philip, 178–79

Varble, Stephen, 85
Varèse, Edgard, vii, ix, 19, 41
Vautier, Ben, vii
Vietnam War, 13, 15, 57n6, 119–20, 139, 146–47, 177
Viola, Bill, xi
Vostell, Wolf, vii, 11, 135, **136**, 137, 139–43, 147, 150n24, 150n28, 171; *Chinatown*, **141**, 142; *Cityrama*, 150n27; *Kleenex*, 141; *Morning Glory*, **142**, 143, 145, 150n35

Vrančić, Mario, 170

Wada, Yoshi, 119
Walther, Franz Erhard, 144
Warhol, Andy, 192
Waring, James, 63
Watts, Robert: *Oraculum*, **73**
Werner, Kenneth, **168**, 175
Williams, Emmett, 78, 91n45
Williams, JX, 177–78
Wolff, Christian, 19–20
Wolpe, Stefan, 19
Wood, Bob, **x**
Wood, Marilyn (and Celebration Group), **x**, 91n35, 125; *SoHo Fire Escape Dance*, 91n35; *Sun Struck*, 85, **86**
Woodstock (film), 87

Yalkut, Jud, 32–33, 53, **109**
Young, La Monte, vii, 26n2, **62**, 62–63, 90n9, 90n13, 154; *Two Sounds*, 63

Zazeela, Marian, 62
ZERO, 79, 125, 161

Mary and Leigh Block Museum of Art
Northwestern University

This catalogue is published to accompany the exhibition *A Feast of Astonishments: Charlotte Moorman and the Avant-Garde, 1960s–1980s,* Block Museum of Art, January 16–July 17, 2016.

The exhibition is organized by the Mary and Leigh Block Museum of Art, Northwestern University, in partnershp with Northwestern University Libraries.

Supporters

The exhibition is supported by major grants from the Terra Foundation for American Art, the Andy Warhol Foundation for the Visual Arts, and the National Endowment for the Arts. Additional generous support is provided by the Elizabeth F. Cheney Foundation; the Alumnae of Northwestern University; the Colonel Eugene E. Myers Foundations; the Illinois Arts Council Agency; Dean of Libraries Discretionary Fund; the Charles Deering McCormick Fund for Special Collections; the Florence Walton Taylor Fund; and the Block Museum Science and Technology Endowment.

Northwestern
MARY AND LEIGH
BLOCK MUSEUM OF ART

Northwestern University Libraries

Northwestern
UNIVERSITY LIBRARIES

Grey Art Gallery, New York University

The exhibition will be presented at the Grey Art Gallery from September 8 to December 10, 2016.

Director: Lynn Gumpert

Associate Director | Head of Collections and Exhibitions: Michèle Wong

Head of Administration: Jodi Hanel

Head of Education and Programs: Lucy Oakley

Exhibitions and Publications Coordinator: Laurie Duke

Chief Preparator: Richard Wager

Preparator: Noah Landfield

Assistant to the Director | Press Officer: Ally Mintz

Administrative Assistant: Amber Lynn

Registrarial Assistant: Saskia Verlaan

The Grey Art Gallery is New York University's fine arts museum. The presentation at the Grey Art Gallery is supported in part by the Abby Weed Grey Trust, the Grey's Director's Circle, Inter/National Council, and Friends.

Museum der Moderne Salzburg

Museum der Moderne
Salzburg

The exhibition will be presented at the Museum der Moderne Salzburg from March 4 to June 18, 2017.

Director: Sabine Breitwieser
Assistants to the Director: Birgit Berger, Anna Rechberger

Director's Office

Marketing and Communication: Susanne Susanka (Head), Hannah Zundel; Library: Jürgen Dehm (Curator Generali Foundation Study Center), Cattrin Ramesmayer; Museum Security: Kai Kuss and team; Technicians: Gerald Horn (Head), Friedrich Rücker (Audiovisual Media), Christian Hauer, Alija Salihovic

Exhibitions and Collections

Curators: Beatrice von Bormann (Modern Art, Head of Collection), Petra Reichensperger (Generali Foundation Collection Curator), Tina Teufel (Contemporary Art); Registrar: Susanne Greimel; Curatorial Assistants: Barbara Herzog (Digitalization and Picture Archive), Andrea Lehner (Photography and New Media), Christina Penetsdorfer (Exhibition Office), Marijana Schneider (Director); Art Education: Martina Pohn (Head), Lena Hofer, Elisabeth Ihrenberger

Administration

Assistant to the Administration and Finance Officer: Daniela Eibl; Head of Accounting: Jürgen Kinschel; Head of Museum Store: Brigitte Fortner and team

Supervisory Board

Heinrich Schellhorn (Chairman); Gertrud Frauenberger; Heideswinth Kurz; Brigitta Pallauf

The Museum der Moderne Salzburg is sponsored with funds provided by the Province of Salzburg.